Hidden Agender

# Hidden Agender

## Transgenderism's Struggle against Reality

Gerard Casey

**SOCIETAS**
essays in political
& cultural criticism

imprint-academic.com/societas

Copyright © Gerard Casey, 2021

The moral rights of the author have been asserted.
No part of this publication may be reproduced in any form
without permission, except for the quotation of brief passages
In criticism or discussion

Published in the UK by
Imprint Academic Ltd, PO Box 200 Exeter EX5 5YX, UK

Distributed in the USA by
Ingram Book Company
One Ingram Blvd., La Vergne, TN 37086, USA

ISBN 97817883650586

A CIP catalogue record for this book is available from the
British Library and US Library of Congress

A promise given ...
A promise kept .....

*Patrem tuum in pace et caritate nunc dimittis*

*There is one sin: to call a green leaf gray.*
*Whereat the sun in heaven shuddereth.*
—G. K. Chesterton (1914)

*My father said that a Parliament could do any thing*
*but make a man a woman, and a woman a man.*
—Lord Pembroke & Montgomery (1648)

# Contents

| | |
|---|---|
| *Foreword* | ix |
| *Note* | xiii |
| *Introduction* | 1 |
| *1. Sex & Gender* | 17 |
| The sex & gender two-step | 18 |
| Straight from the horse's mouth | 25 |
| Once more with feeling | 26 |
| What about sex? | 32 |
| Intersex in brief | 34 |
| *And now for something completely different* | 41 |
| *2. Transgender Issues* | 43 |
| Gender dysphoria | 45 |
| I'm in the wrong body! | 56 |
| Detransitioning | 66 |
| Conversion therapy | 72 |
| *3. Transgenderism in Practice* | 77 |
| Feminism | 77 |
| Education | 92 |
| Sport | 98 |
| Medical services | 104 |

| | |
|---|---|
| **4. Transgenderism and the Law (1)** | 111 |
| Gender Recognition Acts | 111 |
| Validation | 115 |
| Self-identification and the UK's Gender Recognition Act | 117 |
| Official forgery | 120 |
| Transracialism | 125 |
| Equality Act, USA | 134 |
| | |
| **5. Transgenderism and the Law (2)** | 141 |
| Not worthy of respect in a democratic society | 143 |
| Legal incoherence | 150 |
| A *Grimm* reality | 152 |
| *Bostock* | 158 |
| | |
| **6. A Struggle against Reality** | 163 |
| The sexual revolution | 163 |
| Absolute freedom | 171 |
| *The shadow of that hyddeous strength ...* | 180 |
| | |
| *References* | 183 |

# Foreword

*H*idden Agender is the third and final part of a research project that I began in 2017 in response to a challenge I felt obliged to meet. The first book to be published was *ZAP*, a defence of free speech and toleration, and an attack on the currently sacrosanct dogmas of diversity, inclusion and equality; the second was *After #MeToo*, a critique of radical feminism, focusing primarily, but not exclusively, on the latent misandry of the #MeToo movement, and its implications, both social and legal, for relations between the sexes. All three books are, in their own ways, a defence of freedom against prejudice, social intolerance and legal intimidation.

*Hidden Agender* is not a book I ever enthusiastically desired to write. Having carried out extensive research and done some preliminary writing on the topic throughout 2018 and 2019, I spent the months of December 2019 through February 2020 in a more or less constant state of 'Will I?, Won't I?" The advice of those I took into my confidence was, for the most part, a set of variations on—'Don't do it!', 'Are you crazy?', 'Do you want to draw the wrath of the transactivist establishment on you?', 'It's not worth the grief you're sure to get.' Many times I was inclined to take this advice, more especially as it coincided with my own not unreasonable fears, combined with my deep-seated inclination to avoid work if at all possible. My courage wasn't exactly bolstered by witnessing the barrage of abuse that landed on the head of the normally PC-friendly J. K. Rowling in June 2020 for having the temerity to support a woman who was fired from her job for expressing 'gender critical' views on Twitter ('gender critical' meaning simply that she didn't believe people can change their biological sex), and for Rowling's objecting, humorously, to the bizarre expression *people who menstruate* instead of just *women*. No sooner had I overcome my innate pusillanimity and the depression of winter than the politically-induced panic surrounding the Covid-19 virus broke out in March 2020. I was so depressed (again) and angered by the political establishment's rush to impose quasi-totalitarian restrictions on basic freedoms, and by its politically inept but economically effective destructive interference with people's means of making a living, that I found it difficult to concentrate on anything as seemingly trivial and foolish as transgender ideology. Since you are reading these words, it is obvious that, despite the serried ranks of discouragement, cowardice, depression and laziness, I have persevered in my efforts. Whether my expenditure of time and energy was worth it, only time will tell.

There really shouldn't be any reason for this book to exist. That there is, says something—and not a good something—about the deep intellectual, moral and legal confusion of the times in which we live. If this book were to be redundant when or soon after it is published, then I should be a very happy, but also a very surprised, man. If, as I suspect, it is not redundant, then I should welcome its rapidly becoming an historical curiosity, to serve as a memorial to a cultural moment of madness, and perhaps to help hinder (vain hope!) similar mad moments in the future.

Of the three books that this research project has produced, *Hidden Agender* has been by far the most difficult to write. In part, this is because I feel like an idiot having to argue for what is blatantly obvious to anyone who is not in the blinkered grip of transgender ideology: *Males cannot become female; females cannot become male.* How difficult is it to grasp this truth, a truth so blatant that no one until the last microsecond of human existence has ever thought to deny, a denial that, to adapt the words of Jane Austen in *Sense and Sensibility*, scarcely deserves 'the compliment of rational opposition'. It is absurd to pretend that such changes can take place, and it is tyrannical to force people by law to pretend that they can, and to punish them if they persist in speaking the truth. In addition to this intellectual equivalent of stepping on a stair that isn't there, a practical difficulty I encountered in writing this book was that the various topics tended to bleed into each other, so much so that it was far from obvious which topic should be dealt with before which and in what way and in how much depth. In the end, I made the decisions I have made in the ordering and exposition of the text, with the result that there is perhaps more anticipation, overlap and repetition than would normally be desirable or acceptable.

Much good material has been published already in relation to this topic and, where it is suitable, I have made use of such material in this book. A look at the bibliography will give some idea of what is available, and this is only a representative sample. From this material, however, some books must be singled out for special mention: Ryan Anderson's *When Harry Became Sally*, and Gabriele Kuby's *The Global Sexual Revolution: Destruction of Freedom in the Name of Freedom*, and the brilliantly written, intellectually incisive, and eminently quotable book by Theodore Dalrymple, *Our Culture, What's Left of It*. The final chapter, inasmuch as it has any claim to intellectual respectability, relies heavily on the ground-breaking work of Pitirim Sorokin in his *Social and Cultural Dynamics*. As I was putting the finishing touches to my manuscript in July/August 2020, Joanna Williams's *The Corrosive Impact of Transgenderism* appeared, just in time for me to incorporate some of its findings in *Hidden Agender*. To be sure, there are some differences between Williams's approach and mine, but our conclusions are for the most part convergent which, if what we say is true, is to be expected. Debra Soh's *The End of Gender* was published just as the manuscript of this book was being typeset, too late for me to make use of it in chapters 1 & 2.

The book falls into two distinct sections. What little competence I have in philosophical analysis I employ in chapter 1, 2 & 3, which treat of sex and gender, gender dysphoria, and transgender ideology; what little competence I have in legal analysis I employ in chapters 4 & 5 which treat of transgenderism in a legal context. These two substantive sections are sandwiched between a brief introduction that disposes of some preliminary issues, and a brief conclusion (chapter 6) that sketches the broader social context in which transgenderism is, I believe, to be located.

When asked what the most difficult aspect of his job as Prime Minister was, Harold Macmillan is reputed to have responded, 'Events, dear boy, events!' It is the inevitable fate of books such as this to be overtaken by events. Just as I was finishing the writing up of my material on the US Equality Act in chapter 4, I was blind-sided, as were many commentators, by the US Supreme Court's bizarre and baffling decision in *Bostock*. When I first began to write up, it looked as if the UK Government was going to permit self-identification in its proposed reform of the Gender Recognition Act, so that some passages in the book reflect that expectation. However, as I began to conclude the writing up, it became apparent that the Government wasn't going to allow self-identification after all, but what other changes it would permit were not immediately evident. By the time *Hidden Agender* is actually published, who knows what else will have happened or been done, where, when, by or to whom? However, sufficient unto any book is the evil thereof, and the future must take care of itself.

I believe that all the statements made in this book about named or identifiable individuals are substantially true. In every such case, these statements are a re-publication, either verbatim or in paraphrase, of reports already available in the public domain. In any event, the statements made in this book are my honest opinions and are made in the public interest.

When this book is published and I hold a copy in my hand, I know, with an unshakeable certainty, that as I glance through it, my eye will inevitably fall upon a typographical error. Typographical errors ('typos' to their friends) are the cockroaches of the literary world—they are omnipresent and virtually ineliminable.

Thanks to all those who helped me in the writing of *Hidden Agender*.

The writing of this book was completed on 1 September 2020.

# Note

Given the current legal environments in the UK and Ireland with their respective Gender Recognition Acts and their various forms of equality and anti-discrimination legislation, I have, when referring to identifiable transgender people in the third person, adopted the practice of using the compound pronouns, he/she, him/her, his/her, s/he, her/him, her/his. This practice of using compound pronouns may also have the ancillary and welcome effect of decreasing the risk of giving gratuitous offence to some readers' sensitivities.

I am a libertarian for whom the most fundamental politico-legal principle is the zero-aggression principle—*no one may initiate or threaten to initiate physical violence against the person or property of another*. From a libertarian perspective, no laws should be made that impede freedom of thought, or opinion, or speech, or that would prevent the free association or dissociation of competent adults, whether in the workplace or in their social friendships, or that would prevent competent adults from engaging in any activity, whatever anyone else may think of it, provided that it does not infringe the zero-aggression principle.

Emancipated individuals should be free to believe that there is an incongruence between their biological sex and their gender, and should be free to act in any way they wish to reconcile that incongruence, whether socially, hormonally or surgically. Others should be equally free to believe that those individuals are mistaken in their beliefs, but may not act to prevent them giving expression to their beliefs, or prevent those individuals from acting in accordance with those beliefs, provided the expression of their beliefs or their acting upon them does not violate the zero-aggression principle. No one should be legally obliged to accede to the truth of another's beliefs, nor should he be prevented from disputing their truth—again, within the bounds of the zero-aggression principle.

*Hidden Agender* is a book that opposes ideas, not individuals. My objection to transgenderism is not primarily with what any person may think or say or do, but with people being forced, on pain of legal or social sanctions, to believe (or to pretend to believe) what to them is patently false, namely, that a man can become a woman or a woman a man, and to be legally obliged to treat those who claim to have transitioned from one sex to another as if they really had managed to do so.

# Introduction

*Anything could be true. The so-called laws of Nature were nonsense.*
*The law of gravity was nonsense.*
—George Orwell

*Think for yourself;*
*and let others enjoy the privilege of doing so too.*
— Voltaire

In 2017, weight-lifter Laurel Hubbard won the women's 90kg+ division at the Australian International in Melbourne, setting four unofficial national records in the process. Nothing to wonder at there, except that Laurel used to be called Gavin, and had set junior male records before transitioning from male to female at the age of 35. Laurel was allowed to compete in a competition supervised by the Commonwealth Games Federation on the grounds that they support fairness, non-discrimination and inclusion.

Rachel McKinnon came first in a women's cycling championship at the UCI Masters Track Cycling Championship in Los Angeles in October 2018. Well done, you might think, but why is news of this achievement of interest to anyone other than cycling enthusiasts? The answer: because Rachel used to be Rhys.

BBC News reported in March 2017 that Jessica Winfield had been relocated to Her Majesty's Prison Bronzefield. Bronzefield is a women-only prison. Nothing particularly newsworthy in that, surely? Well, yes, there is, because Jessica Winfield was formerly known as Martin Ponting. In the UK, prisoners are assigned to prisons according to their gender as recognised by UK law, usually stated on a birth certificate. But if prisoners have gender recognition certificates, then the Prison Service is legally required to move them to the prison corresponding to their new gender.

Also in the UK, a teacher who was accused of 'misgendering' a child was told by police that she had committed a hate crime. [Turner 2018] According to the *Telegraph's* report, the teacher 'who claimed they were a "grammatical purist", refused to acknowledge that the pupil self-identified as a boy and failed to use the pupil's preferred pronouns of "he" or "him". Susie Green, the CEO of Mermaids, an organisation that supports transgender children and their families, said 'We spoke to a member of the police force, who contacted the CPS [Crown Prosecution Service] and clarified the position. The CPS said it was a hate crime". [Turner 2018] It's not a little amusing that the report, in relaying the information about the grammatical purism of the teacher, refers to her as 'they' rather than 'she'.

A report appeared in the *Mirror* with the following attention-grabbing headline: 'Transgender man gives birth to non-binary partner's baby with female sperm donor.' [Whitehouse 2019] You've got to admit that this is firmly in the class of 'Man bites dog!' However, shorn of all its double-speak, what the story actually amounts to is that two women, one of whom believes s/he is a man but still has her/his womb and ovaries, and the other woman who believes s/he is neither a man nor a woman, have a baby together, using the sperm of a transwoman, that is, of a man who believes he/she is a woman. This is described by the author of the piece as 'a remarkable journey' and indeed it is remarkable—remarkably mundane, except for the remarkably wilful and obscurantist confusion of sex and gender. A more accurate headline might have been, 'Woman has a baby by means of IVF'—but then, that would have been more a case of 'Dog Bites Man!' than 'Man Bites Dog!'. Reuben, who gave birth to the child said, 'I don't think pregnancy is the ultimate female experience, therefore it didn't challenge me as a man.' I am sure we can all be glad for Reuben.

On 17 February 2020, the Labour Party MP Dawn Butler said on the national television programme *Good Morning Britain*, without any evidence of her tongue in her cheek, that 'a child is born without sex, a child is formed without sex in the beginning', before she went on to say that 'transwomen are women'. [Butler 2020] The claim about the amazing sexless babies would appear to be, as Brendan O'Neill irenically put it, 'as loopy and anti-scientific as saying the Earth isn't a sphere,' while the second claim about transwomen being women, while scarcely less loopy and anti-scientific, is a dogma of the Labour Campaign for Trans Rights, a dogma to which a significant number of Labour politicians (and others) have subscribed. [see Labour Campaign for Trans Rights, pledge 4; see also O'Neill 2020]

In the UK, a transgender woman (that is, a man—remember that; it's easy to get confused!) sued the Government to pay five years of state pension that he/she said that he/she had unfairly missed out on because of the Government's failure to recognise his/her transgendered status. The man won his/her case in 2018, after the European Court of Justice ruled in his/her favour. (In the UK, the women's pension age was 60, the men's 65, and if *that* wasn't discriminatory, I don't know what was!) The European Court of Justice, which didn't appear to be too concerned about the patent anti-male discrimination in the UK's general policy, ruled that it was discriminatory in this case as it 'treats less favourably a person who has changed gender after marrying than it treats a person who has retained his or her birth gender and is married.'

The *Telegraph* reported in August 2020 that the mother of a dead transgender girl was to launch a legal bid 'to preserve her sperm so that she [the mother of the dead transgender girl] can have grandchild.' [Johnson 2020] *Her* sperm?

Before I get to the main topic of my book, the phenomenon of transgenderism and its legal implications, there are a number of preliminary circumstantial issues I feel that I must address. If you're anxious to get into specifics, then skip immediately to the first chapter and return here if and when you think it might be helpful. Also, some of the points I make in this introduction are anticipations of points that are articulated and defended in greater detail in the body of the book.

Common to all the strange occurrences just mentioned is the apparent ability of some human beings to change their sex, although, as some of the examples also illustrate, not everyone is persuaded of the existence or cogency of this ability. Transgenderism— the idea that we all have a gendered essence that is distinct from our biologically male or female bodies and that it is possible to change one's sex—is a dogma that has moved from weirdness to orthodoxy with a speed that is breath-taking. [see William 2020, 14] Whereas just a few years ago, no one would have questioned that there are two and only two sexes in human beings, and that one's sex is a matter of biological fact, today, one's sex is presented as a matter of more or less arbitrary assignment made by disinterested observers at one's birth, an assignment that can be reconsidered and re-evaluated as circumstances warrant. Moreover, this revolution in our thinking, for it is nothing less than a revolution, has happened and is happening without any credible scientific evidence to support it. As Joanna Williams remarks, 'That transgenderism has moved from niche to mainstream tells us more about the rest of society than it does about transgender individuals. People in positions of power within the realms of media, education, academia, police, social work, medicine, law, and local and national government have been prepared to coalesce behind the demands of a tiny transgender community.' [Williams 2020, vii; also 64-5] Even the *Telegraph*, that supposedly most reactionary of daily newspapers, has been running Diana Thomas's 'Transgender Diary' throughout 2020.

Apart from the warp-speed at which this shift from weirdness to orthodoxy has taken place, one other feature of the change is also remarkable, namely, that it has taken place with little or no public debate; either that, or the great debate must have happened on a night when I wasn't watching TV. To be sure, there has been a significant amount of media reportage, almost uniformly positive, and a plethora of enthusiastic opinion pieces, but you're going to have to search really hard to find any serious and considered public discussion on the issues. Given the abnormally aggressive attitude of transgender ideologists and their hostility to any criticism of their ideology, it would appear that there is little or no prospect of any such discussion taking place in the immediate future. Those who do attempt a rational consideration of the issues, such as some radical feminists, have been subjected to name-calling and, occasionally, violence. The deprecation by transgender activists of public discussion on this issue would appear to be part of a deliberate policy if the advice contained in a report entitled *Only Adults?* is anything to go by. This report, produced by the law firm Dentons and the Thomson Reuters Foundation, advocates the avoidance of what it calls 'excessive press coverage and exposure' on the grounds that 'much of the general public is not well informed about trans issues, and therefore misinterpretation can arise'—all the more reason, one might have thought, for *more* press coverage and exposure rather than less. [Dentons, 20 § 8; see also Turner 2019, Kirkup 2019]

The liberal media and the majority of our politicians are solidly on board with the new orthodoxy, and those of us who find it difficult to believe that men can become women or women men had better mind our language or we'll find ourselves caught in the vice-like grip of the new laws mandating what we can, what we cannot and, most alarming of all, what we must say. As I already mentioned, if you would like to peruse the grave and serious deliberations that attended this momentous change in public policy, good luck to you! You will have difficulty finding any such discussions. Sometimes, however, the issue manages to ooze out under the cone of silence. In late 2019, potential voters in the UK were treated to the rare spectacle of a politician forced to discuss the issue of gender self-identity, but only because it had become the official policy of the Liberal Democrats. Several members of the Party came under media scrutiny on this issue, including the then Party Leader, Jo Swinson. She was asked on the BBC's Radio 4 *Today* programme if she accepted that biological sex existed; she responded with admirable linguistic clarity and not-so-admirable intellectual muddle, 'Not on a binary.' [Kirkup 2019a]

We have had ideologies aplenty before and we will have them again, but surely few with as little grounding in fact as the transgenderist ideology have ever triumphed so completely and at such an incredible speed. Other ideologies have had to hack away at the coalface for some considerable time before capturing the high ground, and even then, they have often required the police power of

# Introduction

the state to make them stick. In contrast, transgender ideology has triumphed in the Western world without a shot being fired in anger, and with only truth and common sense as casualties.

I mentioned in the *Foreword* that there is some excellent material available on this topic, in particular, the books by Kuby and Anderson. If the Anderson and Kuby books are so good, what, then, is the added value of *Hidden Agender*? My purpose in writing *Hidden Agender* is not to cover exhaustively every possible aspect of this subject, assuming that that were possible, but is limited primarily to two particular perspectives. First, as a philosopher, I have an interest in all areas of philosophical thought, not least in metaphysics, which is the philosophical approach to what is fundamentally real, and in philosophical anthropology, a philosophical investigation of the nature of the human person. Transgender ideology presents fundamental challenges in both of these philosophical areas. That said, *Hidden Agender* is not a treatise in metaphysics or the philosophy of mind or philosophical anthropology, and so what is presented later in the book is simple and suggestive, rather than complete and comprehensive. [see chapter 2, § 'I'm in the wrong body!'] Second, as a libertarian, I am concerned about anything that might gratuitously limit or restrict our liberty. I am especially concerned about the implications of transgender legislation, in association with equality legislation, as it determines what one may not do or say, and what one must do and say. Many other aspects of the transgender phenomenon, especially the morality and legality of transgenderism in relation to children, are more adequately dealt with elsewhere, as, for example, in the Anderson, Kuby and Williams books.

Let me state unequivocally that in this book I am opposing ideas, not persons. I have no desire to offend anyone gratuitously, whatever their sex or gender, although I have little doubt that some will be offended by what I write. That's unfortunate, but it cannot be helped. To pre-empt possible misunderstandings, let me make it clear where I stand on transgenderism. If Claud wants to call himself Claudette and walk around in a dress, that's not an issue of major concern to me. I'll call him Claudette if that's what he really wants me to do. Similarly, if Claudette wants to call herself Claud, that's not an issue of major concern to me either. I'll call her 'Claud', if that's what she really wants me to do. Furthermore, if competent adults want to have radical alterations made to their bodies by means of surgery or hormones, I have no rooted objection to their so doing. I might consider the surgery or hormone treatment to be unnecessary or bizarre or even unethical, but it's not my body, and provided that the activities of such adults do not violate the zero-aggression principle (*No one may initiate physical violence against the person or property of another*), no objection can be offered to their actions on libertarian grounds. Judith Butler writes, 'Those who claim that transsexuality is, and should be, a matter of choice, an exercise of freedom, are surely right, and they are right as well to point out that the various obstacles posed by the psychological and psychiatric professions are paternalistic forms of power by which a basic human freedom is being suppressed.' [Butler 2004, 88] It might surprise some readers to find that I am in (partial) agreement with Butler in this matter, but I am, provided some conditions are met. First, the exercise of such freedom is a matter for the fully mature, not for the young and the legally incompetent. Second, people should not be obliged, as a matter of law, to participate in, support, provide services for, or contribute financially towards the processes of sex/gender alteration, nor should they be obliged to recognise, adapt to, or conform their speech or behaviour to match the putative outcome of such alterations.

The hackneyed phrase used to end personal relationships—'It's not you, it's me'—is an apt expression of my attitude to transgenderism. My objection to transgenderism is not with what *you* (and others) think or say or do, but with *my* (and others) being forced, on pain of legal or social sanctions, to believe (or to pretend to believe) what is patently false, namely, that a man can become a woman or a woman a man, and to be legally obliged to treat those who claim to have transitioned from one sex to another as if they really had managed to do so. My objection is not that a man can't behave as if he were a woman or a woman as if she were a man, assuming always, of course, that there are characteristic ways that men behave and women behave. What I am objecting to is my (and others) being legally coerced into recognising and affirming someone as something other than what they really are. To the extent that gender recognition laws are promulgated, then they, in conjunction with anti-discrimination laws, constitute a form of legal intolerance of my (and others) right to free thought, free speech and action. Joanna Williams points out that transgender activists demand the freedom to call themselves what they choose. In so doing, they are exercising their right to speak freely. However, that is not all they demand. They also demand that others use prescribed language when talking to or about them. That is a use of free speech to demand that the right to free speech of others be restricted. 'Dictating the language use of others not only restricts their free speech but, more significantly, in compelling speech it imposes a demand upon them that calls into question their freedom of conscience. The right to determine the language use of others becomes significant to the transgender community as a means of compelling others to confirm the "truth" of their identity.' [Williams 2020, 48]

When it comes right down to it, what's my issue with transgenderism? In some ways, nothing at all. The target of my criticism isn't gender dysphoric individuals, people who experience a disconnect between their biological sex and their perceived gender. For these individuals, I have nothing but sympathy, as I do

*Introduction* 7

for anyone who suffers from any form of dysphoria, such as body dysmorphic disorder or anorexia nervosa. The object of my critique is rather transgender ideologists or trans activists who campaign for changes to the law so that others can be coerced, on pain of legal sanctions, into doing or saying what they do not wish to do or say, or not doing or not saying what they do wish to do or say. As I do, Joanna Williams makes a distinction between the ideological movement that is transgenderism, and those people who are or who want to be transgender. The political agenda of transgenderism, she says, 'has been embraced by activists and campaigning organisations. As a movement, it has proven to be far more influential than a numerical count of transgender individuals may suggest.' [Williams 2020, 1]

Not all gender dysphoric individuals are transgender ideologists, nor are all transgender ideologists necessarily gender dysphoric individuals. Gender dysphoric individuals are people who experience a mismatch between their biological sex and what they believe to be their real gender. Transgender ideologists, on the other hand, are those who push for enforcement of transgender ideology by legal means, such as gender recognition laws, or who use methods of non-legal intimidation to inhibit rational discussion of all aspects of transgenderism. Jeff Shafer writes, 'There is therefore a vital difference between our charitable concern and compassion for the exceptional individual who suffers from dysphoria, and the revolution of making that person's confusion a reason to overthrow the universe in order that dysphoria itself cannot endure as a sensible category. While individuals suffering from transgender confusion desire a different body, the gender ideologues exploiting the condition of those individuals desire a different cosmos.' [Shafer 2017] You can be a transgender ideologist without being a gender dysphoric individual; and you can be a gender dysphoric individual without being a transgender ideologist. You can, of course, be both a transgender ideologist *and* a gender dysphoric individual, and you can also, of course, be neither a gender dysphoric individual nor a transgender ideologist, as I suspect most of us are.

Some gender dysphoric individuals are, in fact, not transgender ideologists, and they reject the transgender ideologists' claims. These gender dysphoric individuals know that they aren't really members of the opposite sex and don't believe that their gender dysphoria is constitutive of reality. But transgender ideologists do. And that's the rub. One such gender dysphoric individual, Debbie Hayton, writes, 'I transitioned at the age of 44, having always struggled with my gender .... I am worried by the direction things are going. Transsexuals never used to try to control or compel language. We transitioned and got on with it .... Every time an activist demands compliance or uncovers screaming evidence of a thought crime, sympathy for trans people is replaced with exasperation, suspicion and exclusion.' [Hayton 2019] In a delightfully ironic twist, Hayton was accused of hate speech for wearing a T-shirt that had blazoned on it, 'Trans women are men. Get over it!' [Lyons 2019c] It appears that members of the Trade Union Congress (TUC) LGBT committee wrote to the General Secretary of the TUC to complain that in wearing the T-shirt, Hayton had, as they put it, 'gone beyond discourse, and the expression of alternative viewpoints, and is now propagating hate speech against the trans community'. As Nicola Williams, founder of Fair Play for Women, remarked, 'Accusations of transphobia are thrown at women so often for so little that the word has lost all meaning. When even trans people can get called transphobes, I hope people now understand how ludicrous and far-fetched these attacks have always been. The trans movement has been hijacked by gender extremists.' [Lyons 2019c] And that brings me neatly to my next point.

Certain views are so bad they must not be granted the courtesy of rational rebuttal, but must be pre-emptively dismissed by being described as irrational. Welcome to the land of the 'phobias'! As Brendan O'Neill pointed out in a speech given (*mirabile dictu*) at Oxford in 2018, 'The word "transphobia" is used to demonise the belief that men cannot become women. Fighting transphobia isn't about ending discrimination against trans people—it is about silencing moral views that are now considered unacceptable; it is about turning certain beliefs into heresies. "Transphobia" is really a new word for blasphemy. To accuse someone of "transphobia" is to accuse them of having sinned or libelled against the new orthodoxy that says gender is fluid, some men have female brains, binaries are a myth, and so on. Make no mistake: transphobic means heretic.' [O'Neill 2018] To be accused of any of the new phobias—for example, homophobia or Islamophobia—is to have your views characterised not only as irrational, and thus not worthy of serious consideration or rational rebuttal, but rather as dangerous, corrupt and corrupting. Such is the rhetorical force of 'You're a _____phobe' accusations in contemporary discourse that, like a rugby player of old, I feel the need to get my anticipatory rebuttal in first!

Are the judgements and arguments that I present in this book transphobic? It depends on what one means by *transphobia*, and that depends on what a phobia is. Let's see what the *Oxford English Dictionary* gives as the meaning of *phobia*: 'A fear, horror, strong dislike, or aversion; *esp.* an extreme or irrational fear or dread aroused by a particular object or circumstance.' Let me move away from the emotionally fraught issues surrounding transgender ideology for a moment

## Introduction                                                                  9

to consider the dynamics of intellectual disagreement, and its connection to our emotions or to our psychological attitudes.

There are people who believe that reality consists exclusively of matter and its modifications. Such people are usually described as materialists. I believe that they are wrong about this and so I reject their claims. I do not hate materialists; I do not fear them; still less do I harbour an irrational fear, dread or hatred of them. I do not wish them any harm, in fact, I wish them well. I am not, then, a materialistophobe, nor are my beliefs materialistophobic.

There are people, transgender ideologists, who believe that human beings can change their sex. I believe that they are wrong in holding this belief and I reject their claims. I do not hate them. I do not fear them. Still less do I harbour an irrational fear, dread or hatred of them. I do not wish them any harm, in fact, I wish them well. I am not, then, a transphobe, nor are my arguments and judgements transphobic. If transgender ideologists were to limit their claims to asserting the possibility of a change of gender but not sex, then that might be another matter, but that would depend on how one understood the related concepts of sex and gender. [see chapter 1, passim]

There are people, gender dysphoric individuals, who believe that there is a mismatch between their sex and their gender. If gender and sex are the same thing, there can, of course, be no mismatch, and the source of their psychological distress must be located elsewhere. However that may be, I do not hate gender dysphoric individuals; I do not fear them; still less do I harbour an irrational fear or hatred of them. I do not wish them any harm, in fact, I wish them well. If I do have a dominant affective attitude towards them, it is one of compassion, a compassion I feel for anyone in psychological distress. I am not, then, a transphobe, nor are my beliefs transphobic. Even though I do not have a phobia of either transgender ideologists or gender dysphoric individuals, there *are* phobias that I will freely admit to having, such as didaskaleinophobia (look it up!).

Of course, people may use '_____phobe' terms to characterise those who reject their arguments and claims but, if so, this is to use the term *phobia* and its derivatives in a linguistically non-standard way, more or less as a content-free but rhetorically effective term of abuse. More seriously, it is to commit a category mistake by conflating intellectual disagreement with affective attitudes. If you hold that a proposition is true, then, of necessity, you must deny truth to the propositions that are contrary to it or contradictory of it. This is *intellectual intolerance*. It doesn't follow, however, from the mutual intellectual intolerance of contrary or contradictory beliefs that one is thereby committed to persecuting or prosecuting those who hold opposing beliefs and who act on them, or fearing them, or hating them. Being prepared to live with others who hold beliefs that are inconsistent with ours, or who engage in practices that we locate on a spectrum from the mildly objectionable to the disgusting, is a matter of *practical tolerance*. Intellectual intolerance doesn't necessarily carry with it any particular emotional or affective charge. We are not obliged to hate or fear or despise those who hold beliefs that are contrary or contradictory to ours. We may in fact do so, but we do not have to do so. We may simply be indifferent to those others, or perhaps even pity their intellectual benightedness. But whatever one's emotional or affective attitude to those others, one cannot, in the name of practical tolerance, hold their beliefs and yours, where those beliefs are mutually exclusive, to be simultaneously true. To do so is simply incoherent. Writing in the context of a twitter attack on J. K. Rowling for her support of a woman who was fired from her job for tweeting gender critical views, that is, for saying that she does not believe people can change their biological sex, Theodore Dalrymple makes what one might think is the obvious and ungainsayable point that 'Users of the term [*transphobic*] make no proper distinction between two questions: the nature of transsexuals and how people should behave toward them. A question of truth—whether a transsexual woman is in no respect inherently different from a biological female—is transformed into a question of loyalty to a new doctrine, nonacceptance of which in its totality being taken by the right-thinking as a mark of bad or evil character and intent, such that he or she who fails to accept it should be excommunicated by all decent people, discriminated against, and denied employment.' [Dalrymple 2019]

Here are some examples that demonstrate the restrictions that exponents of the new orthodoxy are willing to inflict on those of us who are not willing to sign up to the articles of the new faith and who are thereby to be forced to say what we do not believe to be true, to deny what we believe to be true and to do things that are against our conscience. In the USA, Peter Vlaming was fired by a Virginia School Board when he declined to use a female student's preferred masculine pronouns. [see Burke 2018; Associated Press 2019] Mr Vlaming was willing to use the student's new name and was prepared to refrain from using all pronouns in connection with the student, saying, 'I'm happy to avoid female pronouns not to offend because I'm not here to provoke, but I can't refer to a female as a male, and a male as a female in good conscience and faith.' However, this wasn't enough to satisfy the student's family or the Board of Education and so Mr Vlaming lost his job.

In 2020, the *Denver Post* fired one of its opinion columnists, Jon Caldara, for committing the heinous crime of saying there are only two sexes, identified by an XX or XY chromosome. [see Jones 2020] Caldara may have been the *Post*'s most read columnist, but that did not dispense him from the requirement to use the approved transgender terminology. Having fired him, the *Post* published

Introduction

an advertisement for two opinion columnists. The job description said that the paper was 'looking for writers with strong voices, strong opinions' and for both conservative and liberal writers. 'We do not,' said the *Denver Post* virtuously, 'have any type of political litmus test for our columnists.' Of course they don't.

The Vlaming and Caldara cases are not earth-shattering but they form part of a larger trend towards compelling certain forms of speech and action. If the Equality Act passed by the House of Representatives in the USA becomes law, it will make gender identity into a protected class under Title VII of the Civil Rights Act of 1964. The manager of the ACLU's Trans Justice Campaign, LaLa Zannell, believes the Equality Act to be important because it would protect Americans who identify as transgender from harassment, and that includes misgendering. [see below, chapter 4, § 'Equality Act, USA']

On the other hand, maybe this is all just a storm in a teacup. Why can't we all just get along? Isn't the fuss over male and female pronouns really only a matter of respecting, or failing to respect, other people's legitimate choices? What's the big deal? That would seem to be the view of Fred McConnell. 'Choosing to use someone's preferred pronoun,' McConnell tells us, 'is about respect. The only way you can be wrong is to ignore that person's preference, and this can change with time.' 'Each of us, McConnell says, 'can choose to disrespect another person, but let's not hide behind arguments about it being confusing or illogical.' If you should object that calling a man 'she' or a woman 'he' is illogical, McConnell puts your doubts at rest. Language, we are told breezily, 'is simply a way of communicating how we feel and feelings often aren't logical.' [McConnell 2015]

What would happen if you weren't respectful? Then, McConnell solemnly warns us, the consequences could be dire: ' ... if you choose to ignore what someone is saying about who they are ... then I believe you're choosing disrespect. It is a choice that may seem inconsequential, but at a societal level results in statistics like trans people being at a 40% risk of suicide or seven trans women of colour being murdered in the first seven weeks of 2015 alone.' Goodness gracious me! And what if a trans person decides to change pronouns and then change them again? What then? Well, according to McConnell, we just have to get on with it. 'Many of us have spent periods switching between pronouns (I know I certainly did) for practical or personal reasons. Many of us have also cycled through different names. And plenty of us take years just to figure out whether or not we're trans and then whether or not to transition.'

McConnell has this advice for those of us who might be a little lost when set adrift on the sea of the new sexual norms. 'I've met straight trans men, gay trans men and pansexual trans men. I've also met bisexual and asexual trans men. If that's confusing, just take out the trans and it will become clear. I've met women

12                                          *Hidden Agender*

whose sexualities are equally diverse. I've met trans men who identify as lesbians and now, thanks to Jenner, I know of a female-identified trans person who is attracted to women but doesn't identify as a lesbian. That is quite a mouthful, but it would never occur to me to be annoyed by it. If anything, it makes me marvel at what human beings are capable of feeling and thinking. And sometimes, how our language fails to capture it neatly because the reality is more complex than the words we have to describe it.' [McConnell 2015] Indeed, Fred McConnell, now that my head has stopped spinning, what you have just written makes *me* marvel at what human beings, some human beings anyway, are capable of feeling and thinking! It is easy, perhaps all too easy, to be amused by such flagrant nonsense, but sometimes the issues are rather more serious. Feminists who are sceptical of the transgender agenda are routinely accused of criminal action. Sheila Jeffreys wrote as early as 2012 that she and other feminists, in criticising transgender activism, are deemed to be guilty of hate speech.

> For several years there has been a concerted campaign via the internet and on the ground, to ensure that I, and any other persons who have criticised transgenderism, from any academic discipline, are not given opportunities to speak in public .... Whatever the topic of my presentation, and whether in Australia, the UK or the US, transgender activists bombard the organising group and the venue with emails accusing me of transhate, transphobia, hate speech, and seek to have me banned. On blogs, Facebook and Twitter they accuse me of wanting to "eliminate" transgendered persons, and they wish me dead. One activist has created an image of a pesticide can bearing a photo of me and the slogan "kills rad fems instantly". These activists threaten demonstrations and placards against me at any venue where I speak. [Jeffreys 2012]

Together with the charge of transphobia, the related charge of employing hate speech is a particularly effective strategy used to restrict free speech, often inducing speakers and writers to self-censor for fear of attracting this criticism. Let's take a moment to consider what hate speech might be.

Hate is an affective attitude and not a particularly attractive one. It is, and should be, the object of moral and spiritual evaluation but hate just by itself has never been, until now, a matter for the law. If I sit in my study hating all sorts of people and objects and groups and actions with an all-encompassing and virulent hatred, I may thereby cause some moral or spiritual damage to myself but, as long as I sit in my room and do not act on my hatreds, no one else is harmed. Hate that expresses itself in speech also does no harm to others unless it is a credible threat to their persons or property. Hate, then, just by itself isn't and shouldn't be a crime. You can hate just about anyone or anything you like and the law should not be able to touch you. Hateful thoughts are not crimes; neither is hate speech. [see Casey 2019, 27-50]

Moreover, what is hate speech to you may be someone else's genuine moral conviction. In April 2019, the Australian rugby player Israel Folau said in a social media post that gay people would go to hell if they didn't repent. Folau might be correct in his theological opinions or he might not, but, whether or which, he seems to have fallen victim to the 'You can't say that!' culture. Rugby Australia, with which Folau had signed a multi-million dollar contract in February, said that Folau would be sacked if there weren't what they termed 'compelling mitigating factors' that would justify the post. Australia's opposition leader remarked, 'There is no freedom to perpetuate hateful speech,' and New Zealand's prime minister commented, somewhat more vaguely, '[Folau is] a person in a position of influence and I think that with that comes responsibility ... I'm particularly mindful of young people who are members of our rainbow community, there is a lot of vulnerability there.'

It seems to have been assumed by the congregation of the perpetually outraged that what Folau wrote was, in fact, an example of *hate* speech, but why should that assumption be made? Perhaps what Folau wrote could be taken as an example of *love* speech, a friendly and charitable warning addressed to those in moral or spiritual danger, much as one might warn those with a propensity for walking on cliff edges of the perils to life and limb that such an activity entails. The journalist Crispin Hull points out that there is, in fact, nothing necessarily hateful about Folau's tweet, remarking that 'Folau—however misguided—had the interests of homosexuals and atheists and others at heart. In his Christian world, he was trying to help them avoid the horrors of the eternal hellfire.' [Hull 2019] When Folau was finally fired in May 2019, the chief executive of Rugby Australia, Raelene Castle, commented, apparently without any sense of irony, 'Rugby Australia fully supports [players'] right to their own beliefs ... When we say rugby is a game for all, we mean it. People need to feel safe and welcomed in our game regardless of their gender, race, background, religion, or sexuality.' Ms Castle's 'all' doesn't seem to include fundamentalist Christians who express their beliefs publicly. I wonder just how safe and welcomed by Rugby Australia Israel Folau feels?

This book is written from a libertarian perspective. Libertarianism is the philosophical and political position that takes as its grounding the fundamental importance of freedom in inter-human relations—the clue is in the name! The final chapter considers the issues raised in earlier chapters from a culturally conservative (that is, small 'c' conservative) position, but always within the boundaries of libertarianism. From the libertarian perspective, individual freedom forms the necessary and ineliminable context for all mature and responsible social relations. For libertarians, the basic operative principle that governs human interactions without the requirement for consent is the zero-aggression principle I mentioned earlier: *No one may initiate, or threaten to initiate, aggression (coercive physical violence) against the person or property of another.*

What if you are not minded to accept this principle as constituting the proper parameter for freedom in general, and for freedom of speech in particular? If you reject the zero-aggression principle you must be prepared to accept the legitimacy of using physical violence against the person or property of another or to have others do so on your behalf in circumstances other than that of resisting aggression. Perhaps more significantly, you must also be prepared to accept the legitimacy of having others use physical violence *against you* or *your property* when *you* are not engaged in aggression!

It is possible to reject the zero-aggression principle without lapsing into intellectual incoherence, but to do so is to play a zero-sum power game of winner-takes-all. Lose this game and the winners may treat you as they wish, and you will have no principled grounds for complaint. I think it is true to say that the laws that currently govern our right to speak freely in most Western democracies are largely a hodgepodge of made-on-the-fly measures, erected upon no coherent principled foundation. If you reject the zero-aggression principle, you must either accept this legal goulash, or propose some other *principled* ground upon which freedom and freedom of speech might be erected. And what would *that* look like?

Two particular aspects of libertarianism are particularly relevant to this book— freedom of speech, and freedom of association and dissociation. From the libertarian perspective, there should be no legal restraints on either—not, please note, no restraints of any kind, but no *legal* restraints. I have dealt at length with the topic of freedom of speech, and tolerance, and the unholy trinity of diversity, inclusion and equality in my 2019 book, *ZAP*. I shall have more to say on and off throughout *Hidden Agender* about freedom of speech, but, given the fraught and highly emotive nature of the subject of this book, permit me to raise a few preliminary points here for your consideration in respect of tolerance.

Shouldn't we be tolerant of others' beliefs and practices? Yes, of course, but tolerance is not at all the same thing as endorsement or validation. Given that the zero-aggression principle tells us that we are entitled to use force or have others use force on our behalf only to defend ourselves against aggression, that means that if others have beliefs that we think are false, or if they engage in actions that

## Introduction 15

we find mildly distasteful or reprehensible or even repulsive, we are not entitled to use force to prevent them believing or acting as they do, unless their beliefs or actions constitute aggression. As is the case with speech, methods of limitation or control that do not violate the zero-aggression principle may be used as people consider appropriate.

However, the justifiable demand for the practical tolerance of the beliefs or actions of others has a tendency to slide towards an entirely unjustifiable demand for some other attitude, such as respect, where respect requires one to esteem or honour or otherwise validate another's beliefs or actions. Toleration, of course, requires no such validation and, indeed, is functionally inconsistent with it, for we do not tolerate that which we agree with or like or respect, but rather that which we believe to be false or misguided or even repulsive. Because tolerance necessarily implies a negative judgement by A in respect of B's beliefs or practices, it has increasingly come to be seen as objectionable; tolerance, it seems, has become intolerable! For our ideologues, tolerance of difference is not enough. We must defer to others and celebrate their differences, but of course, not *all* differences, only the privileged ones.

Are there any limitations to what one can tolerate? Can others do anything at all that they like, say anything at all that they wish, in any and all circumstances? Clearly not! What, then, are the constraints that should operate to limit a person's actions? Here, there are different approaches. Some people would grant society at large through the State (regarded as society's organ of administration) the power to determine what should and what shouldn't be tolerated. This is problematic, not least because there is no guarantee that those who control the levers of power will make their policies on the basis of any morally defensible principle. If the state adopts this role, then various parties in the state will engage in contestation to control the process, and to the victor will go the spoils. Much of the controversy surrounding free speech, for example, derives from the dispute over who may and who may not use what are deemed to be public spaces, and who gets to set the rules for their use.

The libertarian approach to this problem is principled, especially when compared to the hodge-podge of pragmatic rules commonly employed, and it is, as one might expect, maximally liberal. A person may believe whatever he wishes to believe and give practical effect to those beliefs in speech or action provided that in so doing he does not violate the zero-aggression principle, that is, provided he does not aggress or threaten to aggress against the person or property of another. This, while throwing up some inevitable, but not insuperable, boundary problems is less prone to grant legitimacy to unacceptable limitations on an individual's actions and speech. Another's actions, including the expression of his beliefs, are however also subject to the rubric of 'my house, my rules'—what may be said or done on a person's property is a matter for the owner of that property and only the owner of that property to determine. This means that while there are no limitations other than the zero-aggression principle to what a person may believe or do on his own property or on the property of others with the permission of the property owner, he has no right to use the property of others without their consent. This has consequences for our ability to speak freely.

But, in the new normative environment, tolerance appears to be no longer tolerable—what is now required is, at a minimum, acceptance and, more often than not, enthusiastic validation. Justice no longer means giving to each his own—*suum cuique*—but the granting of special privileges to special groups. Equality too, has been re-purposed in much the same way, being used primarily to propose and advocate substantive, rather than formal, equality, at a minimum, but more often, as with justice, the treatment of different groups unequally. 'All animals are equal, but some are more equal than others.' And, to come to the point: the combination of gender recognition laws with anti-discrimination or equality laws legally constrains the freedom of those who cannot sign up to the new normative transgender environment.

I would like to make it clear, once again, that my purpose in this book is not to recommend limitations on the freedom of others to engage in actions that I (and others) might consider strange or bizarre or even harmful to themselves, but rather to reject attempts, legal and otherwise, to limit the freedom of those who find themselves unable to conform to the new normative environment for reasons of conscience or truth.

And that, I think, is quite enough by way of preliminaries.

# 1. Sex & Gender

*At the heart of liberty is the right to define one's own concept of existence,
of meaning, of the universe, and of the mystery of human life*
— US Supreme Court Justice Anthony Kennedy

*If I had a world of my own, everything would be nonsense.
Nothing would be what it is, because everything would be what it isn't.
And contrary wise, what is, it wouldn't be.
And what it wouldn't be, it would. You see*
—Lewis Carroll

Once upon a time, we used to have sex (no sniggering at the back of the class!) Those of a certain age will remember the innocent fun that could be had by writing 'Yes, please!' in the space on official forms that inquired, peremptorily, 'Sex'. Happy days! That was then. Now, we still have sex and, in addition, we also have gender so, where once we had one term, now we have two, *sex* and *gender*, that either refer to the same thing or not. If they refer to the same entity or thing or character or reality, then one or other of the terms is functionally redundant; if they *don't* refer to the same thing, then either the terms *sex* and *gender* are simply diverse and essentially unrelated, or they are different but related in some way or other.

Let's see if our linguistic usages can give us some help here. In English, we have contrasting terms of the following kind: (1) male and female; (2) man and woman; (3) masculine and feminine; (4) manly and womanly; (5) mannish and womanish; (6) boyish and girlish, and there may well be other pairs of contrasting terms. I would suggest that it is not completely crazy to believe that the contrasting terms (1), male and female, are primarily *descriptive*, terms that refer to matters of biological fact, whereas the contrasting terms (3), (4), (5) and (6) are primarily *typical* or *normative*, referring to modes of appearance, forms of behaviour, or psychological or physiological properties which are taken to be distinctive of those who are male or female, and which males and females either usually do manifest (hence typical), or ought to manifest, socially or morally (hence normative). The contrasting terms (2), man and woman, hover somewhere between the descriptive and the normative. *Man* is a term that is normally descriptive, meaning 'belonging to the male sex', but when a man is told to 'Be a man!', or to 'Man up!', that is a normative demand that he behave in a way that is taken to be characteristic of a male, that is, to act in what is deemed to be a masculine way. It's not an adequate response to such injunctions to reply, indignantly, 'But I *am* a man!' It is interesting to note that there doesn't seem to be a corresponding way to speak to women. Can a woman be told, 'Be a woman!' or 'Woman up!'?

### The sex and gender two-step

Sex and gender: are they the same, or are they different? If sex and gender are the same thing, then, since there are only two sexes, there can only be two genders; or, since, as we shall see, there appear to be many genders, there would have to be equally many sexes. Two entities that are identical must have exactly the same properties so, if sex and gender are identical, there could be multiple genders only if there were multiple sexes. If, however, sex and gender are *not* the same thing, then what exactly *is* gender, as distinct from sex?

John Money, the sexologist and psychologist, introduced the contemporary distinction between sex and gender in 1955. Before that time, the term *gender* was used more or less exclusively to refer to the grammatical category of nouns and pronouns. If it was used otherwise, it was as a kind of twee Victorian genteelism for sex. Henry Watson Fowler, author of *The King's English*, wrote, 'Gender ... is a grammatical term only. To talk of persons ... of the masculine or feminine g[ender], meaning of the male or female sex, is either a jocularity (permissible or not according to context) or a blunder.' [Fowler 1994, 211] I'm of a generation which, given the classical education I received (an education that has enabled me to despise the wealth it has prevented me from acquiring), when presented with the gender option on a form, is inclined to answer 'neuter'! A point perhaps worth making in passing is that, as the renowned linguist David Crystal remarks, 'There is no necessary correlation between grammatical gender and sex'. The linkage of sex and gender in the minds of native English speakers is an instance of linguistic parochialism. Insofar as there is a close relationship between grammar and sex, it is, as Frank Palmer notes, 'largely restricted to languages with which scholars are most familiar, those of the Indo-European and Semitic groups. In other languages, especially in Africa, gender in a strict grammatical sense has nothing particular to do with sex but is concerned with the distinction between living and non-living creatures and even between big and small.' [Palmer 1971, 38] In a later work, Palmer remarks 'If masculine, feminine and neuter are defined in terms of male, female and sex-less creatures we have no explanation at all for the use of the

*Sex and Gender* 19

feminine *la sentinelle* in French to refer to the very male guardsman, while a young lady in German is referred to by the most inappropriate neuter nouns *Fräulein* and *Mädchen*. Clearly, then, the categories of number and gender are formal categories—based upon the form and in particular, the syntax of the language ... ' [Palmer 1975, 30] It is worth noting that our classical languages, Greek and Latin, with their mere three genders are rank amateurs when compared to the sixteen genders of Fula, a West African language. [see McWhorter 2003, 186ff]

Money's sex/gender distinction didn't become widespread until the 1970s, when it was enthusiastically adopted by second-wave feminists. However, a rigid or even clear distinction between *sex* and *gender* is not always observed, and sometimes *gender* is used simply as a synonym for *sex*, or *sex* as a synonym for *gender*, which, as one might expect, is a major contributor to intellectual obfuscation. As we shall see, from the perspective of feminist and transgender activists, such obfuscation is not necessarily always a disadvantage

*Gender*, if it is not simply synonymous with *sex*, would appear to be a term used to signify some set of socially-manifested characteristics that are, or have been, taken to be typical of one or other of the sexes. These characteristics are often regarded by gender theorists as being substantially or entirely a matter of social construction, relatively independent of biological factors and, as such, it is concluded that they are completely malleable. 'The distinction between sex and gender,' writes Scott Yenor, 'was intended to capture the difference between what belongs to individuals biologically and, to a lesser extent, psychologically, and what was attributed to them socially and politically. The former was sex, the latter was gender.' The relationship between sex and gender was, he tells us, 'conceived to be either contingent or underdetermined. One's gender was primarily the outcome of social forces which, if adjusted, could produce different results.' [Yenor 2017] In general, insofar as the distinction bears on reality, *sex* is used to refer to whichever side of the sexual binary one belongs to, male or female, whereas gender can be used to refer to a person's self-presentation as masculine or feminine, the set of psychosocial characteristics that are often associated with one or other sex, though not exclusively so, or the manner in which a person is treated by various social institutions. In the case of *J.E.B. v. Alabama ex rel. T.B.*, US Supreme Court Justice Antonin Scalia wrote: 'The word "gender" has acquired the new and useful connotation of cultural or attitudinal characteristics (as opposed to physical characteristics) distinctive to the sexes. That is to say, gender is to sex as feminine is to female and masculine is to male.'

So far so good. Here we seem to have a rational principle of division between sex and gender. Sex is biological or, understood a little more widely, biopsychological. It is simply given and, apart from those individuals who may be described as intersex (about which, more later) consists of two classes, male and female. Gender, on the other hand, seems to be sociopolitical, a matter of social construction and so potentially infinitely variable. If this preliminary account of sex and gender is broadly correct, then one salient difference between the two is that sex is binary and discontinuous (male/female), whereas gender lies on a continuum extending from the hyper-masculine at one end, to the hyper-feminine at the other. Any two immediately adjacent points on the gender spectrum may be phenomenologically indistinguishable from one another, just as are any two adjacent shades on the colour spectrum. However, separate the points sufficiently and a gender difference becomes perceptible, just as we can perceive the traditional, if somewhat arbitrary, colour divisions ranging from red at one end, through orange, yellow, green, blue, indigo to violet. Sex on the other hand, cannot be represented as a continuous spectrum. Males and females are readily distinguishable from one another while being indistinguishable from other males and females in respect of their essential maleness or femaleness. There are human individuals who, because of developmental problems in gestation, cannot clearly be determined to be either male or female and are said to be intersex, but this is a statistically insignificant group. The existence of intersex individuals doesn't problematise the essential sexual binariness of human beings.

So, then, the distinction between sex and gender appears to be relatively clear: *sex* refers to a biological (or biopsychological) reality, and is binary, whereas *gender* refers to a sociopolitical reality, and is multivalent. Sometimes, the psychological component shifts its allegiance from sex to gender so that the distinction then becomes one between the biological and the psychosociopolitical. But perhaps we have arrived at a clear distinction between sex and gender a little prematurely, for, as it happens, the terms *sex* and *gender* are regularly conflated. Is gender after all the same thing as sex? Yes—and no. It depends on who is speaking, and in what context. Very often, the two terms are engaged in a conceptual two-step.

Let's see the conflation in action. Lorraine Courtney, writing in the *Irish Independent*, tells us that 'We've only recently begun to recognise gender diversity and understand that what a doctor sees between a baby's legs doesn't always determine a person's true gender.' [Courtney 2015] This is a particularly clear expression of the usual conflation. Ms Courtney is partly right. What a doctor sees between a baby's legs doesn't determine that baby's true gender, and that's because it doesn't determine that baby's gender at all. What it will do, in the vast majority of cases, is determine the baby's sex. Alice Thomson, writing in *The Times*, advises us to halt the tyranny of what she terms the 'gender brigade.' [Thomson 2016] However well-intentioned in other respects her piece might be, she too is apparently unable to distinguish between sex and gender. She tells us that

*Sex and Gender*                                                           21

Brighton and Hove City Council 'has told parents to help their four-year olds decide on their sex before they start primary school.' What the Council actually told parents was to 'support your child to choose the *gender* they most identify with,' which is a peculiar enough piece of advice to give to children but, to be fair to the Council, nothing like as peculiar as telling them to choose their sex. [emphasis added]

The Charity, Action Aid, which campaign's for women's rights all around the world also seems to have some difficulty with *sex* and *gender*. The Charity wrote to its supporters in July 2020 urging them to campaign for gender equality. One person who received the Charity's appeal responded by asking the Charity to change the word *gender* to *sex*, since it appeared that the two words were being regularly conflated and that this was causing some issues. 'Women and girls,' wrote the respondent, 'are being discriminated against and abused on the basis of their sex. Words are important and it needs to be crystal clear who is being subjected to the violence so we can help those most in need.' The Charity responded by saying that 'Action Aid UK defines women and girls as anyone who self-identifies as a woman or a girl .... Action Aid UK understands that there is no such thing as a "biologically female/male body", and that a person's genitalia doesn't determine their gender.' This short passage contains *four* points worth noticing: first, its uncritical endorsement of self-identification ('Action Aid UK defines women and girls as anyone who self-identifies as a woman or a girl'); second, its grammatical confusion of singular and plural ('a person's genitalia doesn't determine *their* gender'); third, its radical disconnect of sex and gender ('a person's genitalia [sex] doesn't determine their gender'); and fourth, its startlingly casual rejection of the facts of biology ('Action Aid UK understands that there is no such thing as a "biologically female/male body".) [see Ward 2020]

Here's a particularly delightful illustration of the sex/gender two-step where all the parties appear to be in the grip of a fundamental confusion. Watch how the terms *sex* and *gender* slither around the intellectual dance floor, now together, now apart. To help you follow the contours of the dance, I've italicised the terms 'gender' and sex' throughout.

The *Telegraph* reported that a doctor who worked for the NHS for over twenty five years was told that he couldn't be employed as a disability assessor for the Department of Work and Pensions (DWP) if he refused to identify patients as being of a sex other than their biological one. [see Bird 2018] Or maybe that should be gender? Let's see.

Dr David Mackereth actually appears to believe that sex is genetic and biological and established at birth. His role in the DWP would have entailed interviewing and then writing independent reports about the health of those claiming disability

22  *Hidden Agender*

benefits. 'However, when his instructor stated that reports must only refer to the patient—or "client"—by the *sex* that person identified themselves as, a discussion took place among the medics about the "fluid" nature of *gender*.' Dr Mackereth said that he believed '*gender* is defined by biology and genetics.' Dr Mackereth said he feared that many other professional people could also be dismissed from their jobs simply for holding opinions about *gender* that are centuries old. The DWP consulted lawyers and was adamant that any report or contact with clients should refer to them by their chosen *sex* otherwise it 'could be considered to be harassment as defined by the 2010 Equality Act'. Dr Mackereth could not conscientiously agree to this condition and so his contract with the DWP was terminated.

He protested that the termination of his contract was a denial of free speech and even of free thought. 'Firstly,' he said, 'we are not allowed to say what we believe. Secondly, as my case shows, we are not allowed to think what we believe. Finally, we are not allowed to defend what we believe.' He went on, 'By stating what has been believed by mankind for centuries—namely that *gender* and *sex* are determined at birth—you can come under ferocious attack. If we are no longer allowed to say that you believe *sex* and *gender* are the same and are determined at birth, everyone who holds my views can be sacked on the spot under this Act. I'm not an isolated case.' A DWP spokeswoman said that the Equality Act makes it unlawful to discriminate directly or indirectly against a person on grounds of a 'protected characteristic', such as *gender* reassignment, adding, 'Dr Mackereth made it clear during his training that he would refuse to use pronouns which did not match his own view of a person's biological *gender*.' [Bird 2018]

In this sad story, are we talking about sex? Or gender? Or sex *and* gender? Or even, as the DWP's spokeswoman's enigmatic comment suggests, about a hybrid entity called 'biological gender'? Who can tell? Certainly, not any of the characters in this little morality play.

A delightfully egregious example of the sex/gender slip 'n slide is to be found in the *Guardian* where, in a piece that appears to be a re-presentation of a report in the *New York Times*, Alex Myers tells us that the Trump administration is considering 'defining gender as biological and immutable—based on genitalia at birth'. [Myers 2018] Apparently ready to display what can only be described as supernatural or quasi-supernatural powers, the US President's administration is about to define transgender people out of existence! A whole segment of the population could disappear, just like that, as the comically inept magician Tommy Cooper used to say.

Well, no. Whatever other consummate evils the Trump Administration may be guilty of, attempting to define gender as biological and immutable doesn't happen to be one of them. The proposal from the Department of Health and

Human Services [DHSS] is to define *sex*, not *gender*. It is true that the Administration's action is intended to abjure the Obama administration's generous, if somewhat reckless, expansion of the term *sex* as used in Title IX of the 1972 Federal Education Amendments to include gender and gender identity, but nonetheless, while textual glosses are one thing, and perhaps irresistible, the primary training of any scholar is not to tamper with the text, and the text, as we shall see, says *sex*.

The report in the *New York Times* on which the Myers piece seems to depend was written by Erica Green and others, and had the attention-grabbing headline, '"Transgender" Could Be Defined Out of Existence Under Trump Administration'. The story opens with the following sentence: 'The Trump administration is considering narrowly defining gender as a biological, immutable condition determined by genitalia at birth, the most drastic move yet in a government-wide effort to roll back recognition and protections of transgender people under federal civil rights law.' [Greene et al. 2018] Fairly forthright, I think you would agree? Clear and unambiguous, isn't it? There is just one small problem with this sentence, however, and that is with the word *gender*. Here we have a flagrant example of the familiar gender/sex two-step that we see danced so regularly by so-called progressive thinkers. We can see this clearly when we read on. The DHHS, we are told, 'is spearheading an effort to establish a legal definition of sex under Title IX, the federal civil rights law that bans gender discrimination in education programs that receive government financial assistance ... '

Hold it right there! As it is actually phrased, Title IX doesn't ban *gender* discrimination in education programmes in receipt of government assistance. The actual wording of Title IX is: 'No person in the United States shall, on the basis of *sex*, be excluded from participation in, be denied the benefits of, or be subjected to discrimination under any education program or activity receiving Federal financial assistance ... ' [emphasis added] I defy you to find the word 'gender' anywhere in this passage. So, Title IX doesn't then, despite what Green, Benner and Pear write, prohibit *anything* on the basis of gender.

It becomes clearer as we read through this story that whatever the Department is proposing to do pertains to *sex* as the term of art is used in Title IX. Our trio report that 'The agency's proposed definition would define sex as either male or female, unchangeable, and determined by the genitals that a person is born with, according to a draft reviewed by *The Times*. Any dispute about one's sex would have to be clarified using genetic testing.' Perhaps the writers of this story are finally getting clearer on whether what the DHHS is proposing relates to sex or gender. Alas, no. The passage just cited comes immediately after the following: 'The department argued in its memo that key government agencies needed to adopt an explicit and uniform definition of *gender* as determined "on a biological basis that is clear, grounded in science, objective and administrable". [emphasis added]

There is no need to gild the lily here. The confusion of sex and gender, accidental or deliberate, runs through the entire piece. When our authors come to discuss what they no doubt see as the reforms that took place under the Obama administration, they write, 'A series of decisions by the Obama administration loosened the legal concept of *gender* in Federal programs, including in education and health care, recognizing *gender* largely as an individual's choice and not determined by the *sex* assigned at birth. The policy prompted fights over bathrooms, dormitories, single-sex programs and other arenas where *gender* was once seen as a simple concept.' [emphasis added] To render the obscure doubly obscure, our trio add something called 'gender identity' to the mix. 'The move [by the Department] would be the most significant of a series of maneuvers, large and small, to exclude the population from civil rights protections and roll back the Obama administration's more fluid recognition of *gender identity*.' [emphasis added]

One of those who is unhappy about the DHHS's intention is Catherine E. Lhamon who was in charge of the Education Department's Office for Civil Rights under President Obama. She thinks that the DHSS's proposal implies that 'what the medical community understands about their patients—what people understand about themselves—is irrelevant because the government disagrees.' She also thinks, apparently, though on the basis of what evidence it's not entirely clear, that the proposed definition 'quite simply negates the humanity of people.' Yet another unhappy camper is Eric Klinenberg, a New York University sociologist, who described the proposed policy as 'an act of violence.' Am I being unsympathetic in thinking that Lhamon's and Klinenberg's comments, while no doubt heartfelt, are just ever so slightly hyperbolic.

The DHHS's definition doesn't, despite the fevered and breathless protestations of those who have been rendered distraught by this proposal, set out to eliminate anyone or to dehumanise them. Jennifer Finney Boylan expressed her surprise in the Opinion Pages of the *New York Times* to discover that she no longer existed, and Evan Urquhart took the DHSS's proposals to be tantamount to denying the humanity of transgender individuals. [Boylan 2018; Urquhart 2018] The protests of Lhamon and Klinenberg and Boylan and Urquhart remind me of the story of the Calendar riots that were supposed to have taken place in 1752 when Britain changed from the Julian to the Gregorian Calendar, the protesters outraged that they were losing eleven days of their lives. The outrage of the Calendar Rioters is very likely apocryphal; that of the DHHS protesters is, alas, not. But no one's humanity, still less their existence, is called into question by the DHSS's proposal, and to suggest otherwise is to engage in rhetoric in the pejorative sense of that

*Sex and Gender*　　25

term—an effort to persuade by an appeal to emotion and nothing else. To hold that men are men and women are women is not to deny any person's humanity or their existence; it's simply to reject an unarticulated and rhetorically (pejorative sense) enforced *assertion* about reality and the nature of personal identity. In effect, all that is proposed by the Trump administration is the rollback of the adventurous hermeneutical expansion of Title IX by the Obama administration. What the DHSS proposes to do is to restore the original meaning of Title IX by proposing a definition of *sex* that is boringly obvious, and also has the merit of being the one espoused, if they thought about it at all, by those who drafted and passed Title IX. To repeat, the administration proposes to define *sex* as 'a person's status as male or female based on immutable biological traits identifiable by or before birth.' This is what sex has been understood to be for thousands of years and, to be frank, it's a little difficult to see why Green, Benner and Pear et al. would consider it drastic. (See, however, the discussion of *Bostock* in chapter 5.)

### Straight from the horse's mouth

To see if we can get any help in this matter of sex and gender, let's consult a book that is tantalisingly entitled, *How to Understand Your Gender*. [Iantaffi & Barker] Surely, here, if anywhere, we can expect to find the answer to our questions. The authors, Alex Iantaffi and Meg-John Barker, begin by asking, not unreasonably in a book devoted to understanding your gender, 'when we talk about gender, what are we really talking about? [Iantaffi & Barker, 39] They make the usual pious comment about sex being assigned at birth. 'Sex,' they say, 'is often assigned at birth by medical professional and parents, usually on the basis of the genitals a baby happens to be born with.' [Iantaffi & Barker, 40] Their justification for using the term *assigned* is that they believe sex to be more complicated than genital appearance. In thinking that, they are correct. There *is* more to sex than genital appearance—there are also chromosomes, gonads, hormones, etc.—and so it is true to say that sex is complicated, but it's not *that* complicated. In only a tiny number of cases, is there a disparity between the evidence of external genitalia and the other biological markers of sex. Iantaffi and Barker's attempted undermining of the sexual binary continues more overtly and bizarrely when they comment, 'the ways in which our bodies are structured externally and internally are not inherently male or female. For example, penises and vaginas are not inherently male or female.' [Iantaffi & Barker, 40] Well, yes, and no, but mainly no! It is only in a statistically insignificant number of cases that the external genitalia may mismatch other sexual markers, so that it is false, and even worse, foolish to claim, because of this statistically remote possibility that penises and vaginas are not inherently male or female.

26                                     *Hidden Agender*

A little later on in their book, our authors tell us that there is 'diversity in our chromosomal make-up, our levels of circulating hormones, the size and shape of our genitals, our secondary sex characteristics like hairiness or chest size, our physiques, and our brain structures and chemistry.' [Iantaffi & Barker, 51] Once again, there is an element of truth in this, but it doesn't have quite the significance Iantaffi and Barker think it does in fuzzing the essentially binary nature of sex which, as their next sentence makes clear, is precisely what they think. 'None of these things can be divided into simple "male" and "female" boxes. A lot of people are somewhere between the two extremes on a spectrum ....' [Iantaffi & Barker, 51] To channel Michael Caine, not a lot of people are between the two extremes on a spectrum when it comes to sex. Chromosomes are, with the miniscule exception of people who are intersex, clearly distinct; so too with genitals and with all the other sex markers. [see later in this chapter § 'Intersex in brief']

Iantaffi & Barker remark that the term *sex* is used in a most confusing way in the English language and in some other languages. A cynic might remark that much of the confusion is generated by the literary productions of such as Iantaffi & Barker, but let that pass. How do they differentiate sex and gender? Sex, they tell us, is based on a complex set of inner and outer physical characteristics', whereas 'gender is a broad term that might indicate our identity, expressions, roles, or even larger sets of sociocultural expectations.' [Iantaffi & Barker, 41] Apart from the surprisingly reticent *might*, this account seems reasonably clear and uncontroversial. But hold everything! On the very next page, they tell us that 'Although the distinction between sex and gender is often made as sex being about physical attributes, and gender being about social expectations, you'll see that matters are much more complicated than this.' [Iantaffi & Barker, 42] A reader of their book will find that the terms *complicated* and *complex* occur in gay profusion. Gender, they tell us, is biopsychosocial because 'for all of us, gender experience is a complex mix of our biology, our psychology, and the social world around us .... the biological, the psychological, and the social: all feed back into each other in ... complex ways.' [Iantaffi & Barker, 46; 47] They tell us, as if we needed to be told, that 'We know we're using the word "complex" a lot here ...' [Iantaffi & Barker, 46]

**Once more with feeling**
Thank you for your efforts, Iantaffi & Barker, but I think we might honestly say that you perhaps haven't been as much help to us as we thought you might be. Let's try once more to get clear on what sex and gender are by stating what would seem to be a fairly ungainsayable principle:

## Sex and Gender

### *Principle SG*
*Either sex and gender are the same thing (A)*
*or sex and gender are not the same thing (B).*

This is an exclusive disjunction, which means that it's not possible for both disjuncts A and B to be simultaneously true. Now, there are only two sexes: male and female. The existence of a number of people who, because of developmental problems *in utero* cannot be easily assigned to one sex or the other no more compromises the sexual binary of the human race than shades of grey erase the distinction between pure black with pure white. If sex and gender are the same thing, then there are only two genders. However, if sex and gender are *not* the same thing, if gender signifies the manifestation in behaviour or appearance of what are normally considered to be masculine or feminine traits, then gender can range across an entire spectrum.

This is where the fun starts, because the sex/gender two step, as it is expertly danced by our progressive friends on the political Left and their fellow-travellers in academia, the media and the morally sound entertainment industry, denies in practice the principle SG so that, for them, sex and gender are sometimes the same thing, and sometimes not the same thing. This, of course, is logically incoherent but is, admittedly, rhetorically effective, keeping discussants permanently on the wrong foot and enabling our progressive friends to use whichever of the disjuncts (A or B) is best suited to make their points.

As we have just seen, the sex/gender two-step was used particularly effectively in the creative re-interpretation of Title IX by the Obama Administration. So, where the Title prohibits discrimination by educational establishments in receipt of Federal money on the grounds of sex, using the two-step, this was taken to prohibit discrimination also on grounds of gender. Clever, eh? So, if a man who self-identifies as a woman (gender) is denied permission to participate in women's sports, this would now be taken to contravene Title IX (sex). [see, for example, Associated Press 2020]

The Gender Recognition Acts of various jurisdictions are another example of where it appears to be expedient to equate sex and gender. The UK Parliament passed its Gender Recognition Act in 2004. The Act states that 'Where a full gender recognition certificate is issued to a person, the person's gender becomes for all purposes the acquired gender (so that, if the acquired gender is the male gender, the person's sex becomes that of a man and, if it is the female gender, the person's sex becomes that of a woman'. [UK Parliament 2004, s. 9.1] Note the-quickness-of-the-hand-deceives-the-eye shuffle between the terms *gender* and *sex* in this piece of lambent prose: 'if the acquired *gender* is the male *gender*, the

28         *Hidden Agender*

person's **sex** becomes that of a *man* and, if it is the female *gender*, the person's **sex** becomes that of a *woman*). [Bolding and italics added; see chapter 4, § 'Gender Recognition Acts']

So, then, sex and gender *are*, after all, the same thing? In appearing to conflate sex and gender, our legislators don't seem to have got the latest memo on the burgeoning number of genders. To bring them up to date, here is a representative sample of what's on offer on the gender menu today, taken from my list of almost four hundred—yes, that's right, almost four hundred—genders. My up-to-date list contains three hundred and seventy four types of gender. There would appear to be some duplicates among them, but then, who can tell for sure? I would list them all because they are almost as much fun to read as a Terry Pratchett novel except that I can't afford to waste the fifteen to twenty pages that would be required. You may think that not all of these genders are meant to be taken seriously but, then, again, why should we take any of them seriously? What incontestable criterion would you employ to distinguish the serious from the non-serious?

If gender is not binary, just how many genders are there? Writing in 2004, Judith Butler noted, 'One tendency with gender studies has been to assume that the alternative to the binary system of gender is a multiplication of genders. Such an approach invariably provokes the question: how many genders can there be, and what will they be called? But the disruption of the binary system need not lead us to an equally problematic quantification of gender'. [Butler 2004, 43] But that was back in the innocent early years of the new millennium, Ms Butler, this is now! Some gender theorists see a future in which a thousand genders will bloom, and in thinking that, they are surely on the right track. New York City recognises something in the region of 31 genders, including bi-gendered, crossdresser, drag king, drag queen, femme queen, female-to-male, gender-bender, genderqueer, male-to-female, non-op, hijra, pangender, transsexual, trans person, woman, man, butch, twospirit, trans, agender, third sex, gender fluid, non-binary transgender, androgyne, gender gifted, gender blender, person of transgender experience, androgynous. Facebook comes in with 72 genders, and there may be more yet to come.

Here are some of the more interesting, even exotic, gender options that one may choose from the gender menu. You can select the plain and somewhat boring option of being *agender*, which consists of having no gender or gender identity at all. Being agender shouldn't be confused with *quoigengender*, a condition in which one feels as if the concept of gender is inapplicable or nonsensical to one's self. For the perpetually and terminally confused, a reliable option is *alexigender* where one's gender identity is fluid between multiple genders, but one is unable to tell what those genders are. Then we have the logically ambitious (some fuddy

*Sex and Gender*

duddies might say contradictory) option of *ambonec*, in which one identifies as both a man and a woman and, at the same time, neither a man nor a woman. Along similar lines to ambonec, but perhaps more in keeping with today's fast-paced world, we have the Heraclitean option of *brevigender*, a species of gender fluidity in which one's gender is constantly changing, never stable. For someone who wants something more exciting, we have the Cartesian *cogitogender* option, in which your gender exists only when you think about it. Then, there is the popular option of the *cryptogender* in which one has a gender that one can't quite put one's finger on, describe clearly, still less define, and which puzzles not only innocent bystanders but principally oneself. Sometimes it is difficult to know if one is really cryptogender or is rather *genderwitched*, a gender option in which one is intrigued or entranced by the idea of a particular gender, but isn't certain that one is actually experiencing it. For the terminally boring there is always a bourgeois option, and so we find on our menu the *gender-neutral* option (not to be confused with agender) in which one simply does not identify with male or female genders. The list of possible genders is long and getting ever longer. For anyone who might be interested in following up this fascinating subject, here is a short list of the names of some other genders that might interest you: angenital, apconsugender, apollogender, aporagender, cendgender, cosmicgender, dulcigender, egogender, exgender, femfluid, genderflux, horogender, illusogender, levigender, necrogender, nesciogender, neurogender, neutrois, nobifluid, offgender, preterbinary, sychnogender, vapogender. [see also Iantaffi & Barker, 35-6]

Some feminists, such as Ann Oakley and Lynda Birke, admit the constancy and unchangeability of sex and the variability of gender; others, however, such as Judith Butler, believe that not only is gender a construction, but so too is sex, there being 'as many sexes as there are individuals'. If that is so, it lends a certain piquancy to the phrase 'the other sex'—*which* other sex? [Butler 1990, 118; see Oakley 1972, and Birke 2001; and, just for fun, Crews 2002, passim] She remarks, 'perhaps this construct called "sex" is as culturally constructed as gender; indeed, perhaps it was always already gender, with the consequence that the distinction between sex and gender turns out to be no distinction at all.' If that is so, and sex is itself a genderised category then, as Butler freely concedes, it would make little or no sense to define gender as the cultural expression of sex, and sex becomes 'no longer as a bodily given on which the construct of gender is artificially imposed, but as a cultural norm which governs the materialization of bodies.' A little later, Butler writes, 'the critique of male-to-female (MTF) transsexuality has centered on the "appropriation" of femininity, as if it belongs properly to a given sex, as if sex is discretely given, as if gender identity could and should be derived unequivocally from presumed anatomy. To understand gender as a historical category,

30 *Hidden Agender*

however, is to accept that gender, understood as one way of culturally configuring a body, is open to a continual remaking, and that "anatomy" and "sex" are not without cultural framing (as the intersex movement has clearly shown).' [Butler 2004, 9-10] I'm not sure what the intersex movement is, or what Butler thinks it is, but whatever it may be, it remains to be seen what the implications of intersex are for the sex/gender distinction.

Typical sex differences between men and women certainly do exist, but the extent and significance of these differences is sometimes controversial, sometimes not. Human sexual dimorphism—that men tend in the aggregate to be taller, heavier and have greater upper body strength than women and to have rather different body-fat-to-muscle ratios than women—is plainly evident and uncontroversial. However, the nature and extent of psychological differences between men and women in the aggregate, if any, is a much more controversial matter. Of course, there's a lot of psychological variation within both sexes. Does that imply that sex is a spectrum, rather than a binary?

No. Masculinity and femininity may lie along a spectrum, but sex does not. Did anyone ever think that all men are equally masculine or that all women are equally feminine? It's common knowledge that men and women vary in terms of how masculine and feminine they are. It's strange that people now want to say that this variation implies that actually only the most stereotypically masculine men are fully men and only the most stereotypically feminine women are fully women, and that everyone else lies somewhere in between in a sexual no-man's or no-woman's land. It seems much more sensible to say, as we have always done, that there are two sexes in our species, that the vast majority of people are easily categorised as male or female, and that people belonging to each sex vary in terms of their masculinity and femininity.

Human beings are sexually dimorphic, physiologically without a doubt, psychologically more controversially; they are also sexually binary. As applied to animal species, binariness and dimorphicism are distinct concepts. You can have a species that is sexually binary with little or no dimorphism; and a species, such as the mandrill, which is sexually binary and in which the dimorphism is extreme, a male weighing on average three times the weight of the average female. In human beings, sexual dimorphism is real and significant without being extreme. Men and women, then, are clearly biologically distinct, but what it means to be a man or woman in society would appear not to be determined, or, at least, not to be fully determined, by one's sex. As time has gone on, more and more of what is now called gender, the manner in which individuals act according to some idea of suitability of sex roles, has come to be perceived to be a matter of cultural conditioning and socialisation, and less and less linked directly to biology. If sex

*Sex and Gender* 31

and gender are not the same, then there would appear to be no reason why gender should be regarded as essentially binary.

So, then, one way of distinguishing between sex and gender is as follows. One's sex is determined by physiological characteristics such as chromosomes, hormones, internal and external genitalia and reproductive organs. One's gender, on the other hand, would seem to be a function of the complex relationship between one's physiological traits and one's sense of self as positioned on the masculine/feminine spectrum, as well as one's appearance and behaviours related to that sense. Thus conceived, sex and gender are different and one's gender is not related to one's sex in any simple one-to-one way. Gender, if it is to have any meaning at all other than a neo-Victorian genteelism for sex, is properly used to signify some set of socially-manifested characteristics that are, or have been taken to be, typical or normative of one or other of the sexes. These characteristics are usually taken by gender theorists to be entirely a matter of social construction, independent of biological factors. As such, it is concluded that they are completely malleable. On the other hand, it might be that sex and gender, while not identical, are also not completely independent of each other, so that there is a range of genders that is, as a matter of fact, associated more with one sex than another.

The distinction between sex and gender, however useful it might have been in its early stages to feminists and their fellow travellers, is not without its critics. The second-wave feminists, Millett and others, were, for some, such as Judith Butler, insufficiently radical. Even when gender is separated from sex, gender was still thought to be more or less binary, to be either masculine or feminine. Feminists were inadvertently complicit in the normalisation of the male gender and in tacitly encouraging women to move towards that model. But for Butler, gender identity is fluid, and so too is sexual identity. Neither gender nor sex is in any way natural; both are performances. Gender needs to be transcended, and the way to this transcendence is the employment of transgression, in particular, the idea of transgender. It's fairly clear that what Butler is up to is an undermining of any idea of normality when it comes to sex and gender. There is, for her, no reality here, no given, just the ersatz-Nietzschean raw exercise of power.

If this Butlerian subversion weren't bad enough, just when we thought we had sorted out the distinction between sex and gender—sex being biological and necessary, gender, being sociological and contingent—along come the transgender ideologists for whom the distinction between one's biological sex and one's experienced gender is sometimes presented in such a way that one's gender is *not* a contingent, socially-constructed matter but rather an aspect of one's identity that is deeply rooted, perhaps even *more* deeply rooted than one's sex. Instead of its being our sex that determines (at least in part) our gender, now, it seems, as if it's our gender that determines our sex, not the obvious anatomical sexual features, of course, that do not change as the result of behaviour, unless that behaviour is self-mutilating, but rather our brain structures. As our experience is gendered, so too are our brains. It is, then, not our gross anatomical features that determine whether we are really men or women but rather our brains. And our brains have the character they have because of our actions and our social environments. So instead of sex being fixed and gender more or less arbitrary, now it's the case that gender is more or less fixed and sex is arbitrary! Such a way of thinking about gender makes it to be more or less a natural kind, and essentialises what are often taken to be gender stereotypes.

On some accounts, gender appears to be socially constructed and thus essentially malleable; but on other accounts, it would seem that 'gender identity' is 'an inherent fact in the individual, which is to say that it sounds a lot more like what we used to call the individual's sex. Is it the case, then, that gender isn't a matter of choice after all, but a given? Wouldn't Caitlyn Jenner, for example, insist that he/she has always been a woman and has no choice but to be a woman? It's just that he/she simply took some time to realise that that's what he/she really was.

For your regular gender theorist, many of whom are feminists, gender is accidental, variable, and adjectival. For transgender ideologists, on the other hand, gender would seem to be essential, invariable, and substantive. If this is so—and it seems to be so—it might give us an insight into the tension that subsists between radical feminists and transgender ideologists. [see chapter 3, § 'Feminism']

**What about sex?**
We don't seem to be having much luck with gender. Let's try our hand at sex. A basic fact to grasp about sex is that it is *essentially* linked to reproduction. The sex of any organism is a matter of how that organism is constructed for purposes of reproduction. The part one plays in reproduction determines one's sex—and that's it. There shouldn't be anything controversial about this claim—it's so blindingly obvious that it's embarrassing to put it down on paper—but in today's progressive world, such a claim has all the hallmarks of stepping into a bar and challenging all comers to a fight!

Our sex is a biological fact and it is identified by the way in which we are organised for sexual reproduction. This is how it is understood in all species that reproduce sexually. We have bulls and cows, rams and ewes, roosters and hens, dogs and bitches, all distinguished from one another by their reproductive roles. How we fundamentally distinguish male and female then is based upon the two biological roles in reproduction. A human individual that has the basic capacity to reproduce with the female is biologically and truly a male; a human individual

*Sex and Gender* 33

that has the basic capacity to reproduce with a male is biologically and truly a female. Male and female are defined in reference to each other and are correlative procreative entities.

Whatever else human beings may be, it is undeniable that we are animals, and our being animals is the ground of our natural existence. Our sex is about as fundamental a characteristic of our being as one can get. Every human being is either male or female, and our maleness and femaleness resides in our root capacity for contributing to the reproduction of the human species. We can do many things alone—eat, drink, play solitaire, but human reproduction is a tango—it takes two to dance, despite Tallulah Bankhead's notorious quip, 'I'll come and make love to you at five o'clock. If I'm late, start without me.'

The primary sexual differentiation of human beings begins at conception and is unrolled developmentally in the womb. The sexual differentiation that begins in the womb continues after birth. It is at this point that a human being's sexual dimorphism becomes readily apparent. Our sexual nature that begins in the womb is realised in our bodily systems and organs, indeed, all the way down to and up from the molecular level. The way in which we are organised sexually for the purposes of reproduction affects us in every dimension of our bodily being from the very beginning of our lives. The sex of a child at birth is recognised (recognised, not assigned) by observing their external genitalia and, if required, their internal reproductive anatomies, their sex hormones, their gonads and their chromosomes. The sex of all humans is fixed by the time they are born and it is unchangeable. The sex of every individual is not merely some external alterable adornment but is present in the chromosomes of every cell in the individual's body.

Given that human beings reproduce sexually, they are biologically either only male or female. Men are men, and women are women. True hermaphrodites with fully functioning dual sexual organs do not exist in the human species. There is no *tertium quid*. It is sometimes said that one's sex is 'assigned' at birth, rather like your name. To the question, 'Is it a boy or a girl?', the answer might now be given, 'Well, we haven't assigned a sex yet, we'll let you know when we've made the assignment.' But, except in the distressing but statistically insignificant cases of intersex, sex isn't assigned and, as Ryan Anderson writes, 'People who undergo sex reassignment procedures do not become the opposite sex. They merely masculinize or feminize their outward appearance.' [Anderson 2018a, xii] One's sex is not assigned at birth and not being assigned, it cannot be reassigned. 'The concept of changing one's biological sex is, of course, nonsense,' Jane Robbins notes, 'as sex is determined by unalterable chromosomes. An individual can change his hormone levels and undergo surgery to better imitate the opposite sex, but a male on the day of his conception will remain a male on the day of his death ... the idea that there

34 *Hidden Agender*

is a real personal trait called "gender" that challenges or invalidates the identity significance of biological sex is ... fallacious.' [Robbins 2019]

It is important to realise that one's sex is not primarily a matter of structure alone, but of structure and *function*. For a human male to be a male, it is not enough to have a bodily feature that looks like a penis—it must also, deviations from the norm notwithstanding, be able to function like one. One cannot therefore make a vagina, say, simply by creating an orifice in a particular place. Unless the orifice relates functionally to the vagina's biological structure, it is not a vagina. Nor is a penis merely an organic structure that enlarges upon stimulation. It too must connect to the larger sexual context of which it is a part..

> But what those organs are—a penis or a vagina—can only be identified by reference to the role those organs typically play in the overall biological economy of a sexed human being. The penis typically penetrates the vagina but then also deposits sperm, which is in turn capable of procession towards and penetration of the female oocyte; the vagina is typically a receptacle and conduit of sperm to the oocyte, and so on. And both organs' identities are linked not only *forward* in these ways to the functions they might eventually perform, but are also linked *backward* to previous events and functions. For example, the origin of male gametes is to be found in the production of primordial germ cells that occurs many years before sexual intercourse is even possible, but this production occurs *in order that* sperm will eventually be produced which the penis will eventually deposit. An organ lacking this historical role in the biological economy is not a penis. [Tollefsen 2015a]

One's sexuality, then, male or female, is directed from the very beginning towards reproduction, and whatever may happen to us, or whatever we may do to ourselves, nothing can change that fundamental teleological orientation.

**Intersex in brief**

Sex, then, is binary; gender, whatever it may eventually turn out to be, appears to lie on a continuum. Of course, some of those who are fuzzy about the distinction between sex and gender are not slow to suggest that sex too lies on a continuum. This claim is usually based on the existence of intersex individuals. Judith Butler writes, 'The intersex movement has sought to question why society maintains the ideal of gender dimorphism when a significant percentage of children are chromosomally various, and a continuum exists between male and female that suggests the arbitrariness and falsity of the gender dimorphism as a prerequisite of human development.' [Butler 2004, 65] Once again, gender and sex are conflated, for it is clear from the context that what Butler refers to as the gender dimorphism is, in fact, the sexual binary but, putting to one side her sex/gender conflation, she

*Sex and Gender* 35

seems to be arguing that sex lies on a continuum. She is just one gender theorist who leans on the phenomenon of intersex to substantiate the claim that the simple binary of male and female doesn't accurately reflect the true number of sexes that there are. Of course, if there are more (even many more) than two sexes, then the possibility of changing one's sex becomes antecedently more plausible.

If you were to ask medical experts how often a child is born so noticeably sexually atypical that a specialist in sex differentiation has to be consulted, the figure usually cited is between 1 in 1500 and 1 in 2000. The figure may be much lower. Critiquing the work of Anne Fausto-Sterling, Leonard Sax argues that if we subtract the categories of LOCAH, vaginal agenesis, Turner's syndrome, Klinefelter's syndrome, and other non-XX and non-XY aneuploidies [cells with abnormal numbers of chromosomes], 'the incidence of intersex drops to 0.018%, almost 100 times lower than the estimate provided by Fausto-Sterling.' [Sax 2002, 177; see also Fausto-Sterling 2018] He concludes, 'The available data support the conclusion that human sexuality is a dichotomy, not a continuum. More than 99.98% of humans are either male or female. If the term intersex is to retain any clinical meaning, the use of this term should be restricted to those conditions in which chromosomal sex is inconsistent with phenotypic sex, or in which the phenotype is not classifiable as either male or female. The birth of an intersex child, far from being "a fairly common phenomenon," is actually a rare event, occurring in fewer than 2 out of every 10,000 births.' [Sax 2002, 177] Arguments about exact numbers must be treated with some caution inasmuch as some argue that intersex conditions are not always accurately diagnosed, and even experts in the field, as we have just seen, sometimes disagree on exactly what qualifies as an intersex condition. Still, even with this caveat taken into account, we can be reasonably confident that children born with ambiguous sexuality form significantly less than 1% of the total, and that is to put it at its highest estimate.

There is quite a number of different forms that intersexuality can take. It can sometimes be difficult to classify the newborn child's genitalia as either unambiguously male or unambiguously female. On the other hand, it's possible to have a child with incompletely or atypically developed internal reproductive organs. Again, a child's external and internal sex organs may fail to match perfectly. And then there are cases where there are chromosomal abnormalities or where the production of sex hormones is under- or over-stimulated. It is telling that among some experts, the term *intersex*, though medical in origin, has been succeeded by the phenomenologically more adequate term, *disorders of sex development* (DSD). But even when all this is taken into account, the existence of these intersex (or DSD) cases doesn't take away from the fact that determining the sex of the majority of newborns is almost entirely unproblematic. As I wrote elsewhere a few years ago, there may occasionally be boundary problems between any two categories. So, for example, while there are trees that are unambiguously trees and bushes that are unashamedly bushes, there may be bushes that are suspiciously arboreal, not to mention trees that appear to have a hankering to transgenerate into bushes. But this confused and confusing boundary area between trees and bushes does not prevent us from being clear about most trees and most bushes most of the time. The classical argument form known as the *sorites* uses the phenomenon of borderline cases between bushes and trees (or any other two pertinent entities) to conclude that, in the end, there's really no difference between bushes and trees at all and that it's all a matter of convention. Thomas Sowell uses the term 'precisional fallacy' to describe the use of fuzzy boundary issues to collapse distinctions that are, in fact, quite clear. 'The precisional fallacy is often used polemically,' he says. 'For example, an apologist for slavery raised the question as to where precisely one draws the line between freedom and involuntary servitude,' but, Sowell notes, 'Wherever you draw the line in regard to freedom, to any rational person slavery is going to be on the other side of the line. On a spectrum where one color gradually blends into another, you cannot draw a line at all—but that in no way prevents us from telling red from blue (in the center of their respective regions). To argue that decisive distinctions necessarily require precision is to commit the precisional fallacy.' [Sowell 1996, 292]

In some areas of inquiry, the discovery of the existence of an exception would be sufficient to upset an entire system of categorisation. So, if one were to discover a natural number that was neither odd nor even, this would cause seismic reverberations in the austere world of mathematics. But the realms of biology and human behaviour are not like mathematics. Here, we have norms or paradigms, from which there may occasionally be deviations. Such deviations do not call the norms into question. The bright-line clarity that attaches to the conceptual world of mathematics and classical logic cannot be applied to the real world of nature and man. Intersex (or DSD) conditions are not the only deviations from the human developmental norm. Abby and Brittany Hensel are dicephalic parapugus (two heads side by side on one torso) conjoined twins who share the same body but have their own internal organs. Each controls one arm and one leg but can eat simultaneously and separately. Deviations from the norm, then, occur in nature (and in human affairs), but such deviations not only do not compromise the norm but rather are constituted as deviations only by the very existence of the norm in the first place.

The account of sex and gender that I have been sketching so far, where sex is biological and necessary, and gender sociological and contingent, has come under attack not only from gender theorists such as Judith Butler, but even from some

## Sex and Gender

medical practitioners. Some physicians are prepared to declare on oath that there is no physical basis for determining whether a human being is male or female. Dr Deanna Adkins, a professor at Duke University's School of Medicine and the director of the Duke-affiliated gender clinic, testified in a North Carolina court that 'From a medical perspective, the appropriate determinant of sex is gender identity ... It is counter to medical science to use chromosomes, hormones, internal reproductive organs, external genitalia, or secondary sex characteristics to override gender identity for purposes of classifying someone as male or female.' [Adkins, no date] Counter to medical science, please note, not counter to the effusions of the denizens of your local gender studies department. This astonishingly bizarre and counter-intuitive claim would come as a surprise to the millions of doctors and billions of other normal people who, since the beginning of time, have been classifying individuals in precisely the way that Dr Adkins so breezily dismisses. As Ryan Anderson notes, 'This is a remarkable claim, not least because the argument recently was that gender is only a social construct, while sex is a biological reality. Now, activists claim that gender identity is destiny, while biological sex is the social construct.' [Anderson 2018b] He goes on to note that, 'Adkins doesn't say whether she would apply this rule to all mammalian species' and he asks, ' But why should sex be determined differently in humans than in other mammals?' [Anderson 2018b] In a spectacular example of what can only be described as chronological snobbery, Dr Adkins characterises the standard account of sex— an organism's sexual organisation—as 'an extremely outdated view of biological sex.' Styles of dress, or furniture, or modes of speech may become outdated, but it is a categorical mistake to try to apply the concept of outdatedness to biology. Biological concepts and theories may be false or true, more adequate or less adequate, fruitful or sterile, but it can never make sense, except perhaps as a feeble joke, to say 'Thinking that male and female is a matter of biology is *so* last year!' [see Soh 2020a, passim]

Oh well, you might think, you can find strange people in all walks of life, but Dr Adkins is not alone in having a Humpty-Dumptyish attitude to the relation between gender identity and sex. '"When I use a word," Humpty Dumpty said in rather a scornful tone, "it means just what I choose it to mean—neither more nor less." "The question is," said Alice, "whether you can make words mean so many different things." "The question is," said Humpty Dumpty, "which is to be master—that's all."' [Lewis Carroll, *Through the Looking Glass*]

A headline in the *New York Times* in October 2018 read, 'Anatomy Does Not Determine Gender, Experts Say.' [Grady 2018] One of the these experts, Dr Joshua D. Safer, is quoted as saying, 'The idea that a person's sex is determined by their anatomy at birth is not true, and we've known that it's not true for decades.' At the time he made this remarkable claim, Dr Safer was the executive director of the Center for Transgender Medicine and Surgery at Mount Sinai Health System in New York, and President of the United States Professional Association of Transgender Health. Just ten years ago, not to mention at any previous time in recorded history, that statement would have been regarded as so absurd that only a satirist or an opponent of rationality would have written it. When a practising physician tells us that someone who has two X chromosomes, a vagina, breasts, ovaries, a uterus, and a menstrual cycle might not be a woman, your society is in deep trouble. Making the most of the intersex phenomenon, yet another American physician, Dr. Eugene Gu, rejects the position that there are only two sexes. 'It is both a scientific and medical fact,' he tweeted, 'that intersex individuals do exist and gender is not as binary as mainstream society is set to believe. There have been documented cases of patients born with genetically male 46 XY karyotype who have gotten pregnant and gave [*sic*] birth.' Dr Gu uses the term *gender* but it is clear from that context that he is talking about sex.

The phenomenon of intersex individuals *does* mean that not everyone fits tidily into the male or female categories, which is true but hardly news. This doesn't change the fact, though, that there are only two sexes in our species; intersex isn't a third sex, because intersex people don't produce a third type of gamete. Biological human sex is binary—there is no sexual spectrum. The claims of Adkins, Safer and Gu are simply intellectually perverse and contrary to what is plainly evident to anyone whose perceptual and conceptual capacities have not been distorted by the latest intellectual fashions to blow in from Paris. From a human being's earliest moment, sex differences make themselves manifest and continue to do so as the organism develops from embryo to baby to child to teenager to mature adult. Surgical and hormonal interventions can modify one's appearance and, in extreme cases, interfere radically with one's reproductive capacities, but they cannot change one's sex. According to Dr Colin Wright, an evolutionary biologist at the University of California, Santa Barbara, 'The claim that classifying people's sex upon anatomy and genetics "has no basis in science" has itself no basis in reality, as any method exhibiting a predictive accuracy of over 99.98 percent would place it among the most precise methods in all the life sciences.' [Wright 2019a]

So, to sum up. Either sex and gender are the same, or sex and gender are not the same. If sex and gender are not the same, they are either related or unrelated. On this reading, what we might think of as the normal reading, sex is biological whereas gender is social. But, as we've noted already, there is a more radical take on the sex/gender distinction, and that is that sex and gender are not the same, may or may not be related but, in any event, that gender is the more fundamental of the two and sex is derivative [see Adkins et al.] Joanna Williams notes that

*Sex and Gender* 39

'A new orthodoxy that gender identity is brain-based and innate, something we need to discover for ourselves and then reveal to a readily accepting world, has rapidly gained ground.' [Williams 2020, 1]

Gender dysphoria does not appear, on first glance at least, to be necessarily connected to the condition of intersex (or DSD). The detransitioner, Walt Heyer writes, 'Don't be duped when trans activists conflate the unrelated condition of intersexuality with transgenderism to gain sympathy for a trans agenda. People with intersex conditions are not the same as self-identified transgender people. Being intersex is verifiable in the physical body; being transgender is not. People who identify as transgender usually have typical male or female anatomies.' [Heyer 2017a] Most of the individuals who desire to transition because of gender dysphoria, then, are not intersex, but people whose sex indicators—gonads (testicles or ovaries), sex chromosomes, sex hormones, reproductive anatomy and external genitalia—are clearly and unambiguously male or female.

People with intersex conditions are born with physically mixed or atypical bodies with respect to their sexual characteristics. However, these incongruent characteristics may not always be visible and individuals may not be aware of their condition. Because of that, it could be, and has been, argued that gender dysphoric individuals *do* in fact have some intersex markers, it's just that they're not obvious and may, for example, be in the brain. Joanna Williams notes that recently, 'there has been a shift in thinking about gender that heralds a renewed focus on biology. This is not a return to the idea that sex is inscribed in chromosomes, hormones and genitalia but a shift towards understanding gender identity, an internal sense of being male or female, as being 'hardwired into the brain at birth .... One theory is that this process of "hardwiring" occurs through prenatal exposure to abnormal levels of sex hormones or endocrine influences linked with the developing brain's sensitivity to androgen and testosterone secretions in utero. However, there is little scientific evidence to support this proposition.' [Williams 2020, 8, referencing Taylor et al. 2018, 13]

Jennifer Gruenke, professor of biology and director of the Hammons Center for Scientific Studies at Union University, is one who thinks that gender seems to depend strongly, but not exclusively, on the brain, and she says, 'Analysis of the brain can allow an outside observer to make a reasonable, albeit imperfect, guess about a person's gender.' [Gruenke 2015] Really? What analysis would that be? What features of the brain, specifically, would support a reasonably imperfect guess, still more a reasonably perfect guess, about a person's gender? Gruenke writes, 'Consider a case study of a genetic male with normal male genitalia who, since childhood, has had the first-person perception of a female identity. It's possible that this is a case of confusion about identity rooted in psychological

# 40                           *Hidden Agender*

trauma. But it's also possible that this person has some mutation that prevented the masculinization of the brain.' Isn't it likely, she asks, 'that this individual has some intersex condition, one in which the brain does not match genetic sex, in a way that is—currently—only discernible through introspection?' [Gruenke 2015] It may be possible—pretty much anything is possible—but the evidence to date does nothing to suggest it is likely or probable. Gruenke's claim is of a piece with the assumption of bio-psychiatrists that what they conceive of as mental illness is caused by some aberrant piece of brain biology, an assumption for which there is no direct evidence. [see Breggin 1993; Szasz 1974]

Let's look at how the argument is supposed to run. Sarah has a subjective feeling of being male. Gruenke's claim is that this is likely to be a matter of brain mutation. What's the direct evidence for this claim? Why, it's the subjective feeling! Why do I have the distinct feeling that in arguing in this fashion, we're taking a trip on the argumentation roundabout! [see Hornstein 2009, 149-51; Davies 2013, 117, 217-18, 222-25]

Gruenke herself frames an objection to the 'gender-is-a-matter-of-the-brain' claim. I give it in her own words.

> Now, it is worth considering a more principled objection from the conservative front. Some might contend that, if we accept first-person accounts with respect to gender identity, we will have no principled reason to reject them in other cases. For instance, the first-person report is unreliable in the case of anorexia. An anorexic person is convinced that she is overweight, even when she is already underweight. This, it might be claimed, is analogous to the case of a transgender person. A transgender person might sincerely believe that he is female, but that does not mean that he is not mistaken. Indeed, the objector might press that brain chemistry cannot solve this problem. For suppose that an anorexic person *does* have the brain chemistry of an overweight person, and this similarity is accountable in terms of genetic factors; in such a case, we would not say that the girl really is overweight, despite appearances. We'd say that she is really underweight, personal conviction notwithstanding. Anorexia just is a condition characterized in terms of a desire to be thin in spite of already being thin; her brain chemistry and emphatic beliefs don't defeat this. Moreover, the anorexic person is not *correct* merely because her reports match her brain and indeed her brain (if not the rest of her body) developed along pathways characteristic of overweight people. Why, our objector continues, can't a transgender person be similarly mistaken? The fact that a transgender person is making reports in line with her neurological development does not establish that she cannot be incorrect. [Gruenke]

This argument seems to me to be unanswerable, and it is one that I will myself rehearse in the next chapter. If we are prepared to accept the authority of first-

*Sex and Gender* 41

person reports of gender dysphoric individuals, and permit or recommend surgery or hormone treatment to bring their bodies into line with their minds, why do we not do so with anorexics or with those who exhibit body image integrity disorder?

Gruenke rejects the analogy between anorexics and transgender persons because, as she puts it, 'in anorexia, subjective perception is clearly at odds with the proper function of the human body. On the other hand, the part of the brain that contributes to the perception of gender doesn't regulate anything, but exists just for psychological identity. One can survive, and even reproduce, without having any gender identity at all.' I'm not entirely sure I understand Gruenke's response to the objection she so eloquently stated. If I do, it seems to be insufficient to undermine the relevance of the analogy, for it seems obvious to suggest that false beliefs do not, in general, contribute to the flourishing of the human being, whether to the body of the human being or to the mind of a human being and so, on that count, there is no difference in kind between anorexia and gender dysphoria. Without wishing to be unkind, I think it might be said that in the case of gender dysphoria, subjective perception *is* at odds with the proper function of the human body. In any event, it must be said that the claims for 'gender identity is brain based' are exceeding tentative, and Jane Robbins asserts roundly, '"gender identity" is a psychological phenomenon, not an immutable characteristic, and not found anywhere in the body, brain, or DNA. There is no medical test that can detect it. Because twin studies show the infrequency of both genetically identical twins' suffering gender dysphoria, the condition clearly is not genetic. Nor is there any evidence to support the common claim that a patient has a "girl's brain in a boy's body," or vice versa, as repeated in media sensations such as *I Am Jazz*. To the contrary, every cell of a male's brain has a Y chromosome and every cell of a female's brain has two X chromosomes, which is true regardless of whether the individual "feels like" the opposite sex.' [Robbins 2019]

### And now for something completely different

The UK's Office for National Statistics (ONS) suggested in 2017 that it may no longer require census respondents to say if they are male or female. The ONS carried out some research on this matter which revealed that the question was found to be 'irrelevant, unacceptable and intrusive, particularly to trans participants, due to asking about sex rather than gender'. Is the question about one's sex *more* irrelevant, *more* unacceptable and *more* intrusive than the questions relating to one's age, place of birth, occupation, level of academic certification or ethnicity? If so, perhaps the ONS might explain why it is so; if not, then perhaps the census should stop asking these other questions as well. I can't be the only person who finds quite a lot of the questions on the census to be irrelevant, unacceptable and intrusive. If the question about sex can be legitimately jettisoned because some small, ultra-sensitive group gets upset by it, why not jettison those other questions as well? As my friend and colleague Tim Crowley commented, satirically,

> I identify as non-numerical, so I'm offended at being counted as one person on the census. Indeed I, and others in my community, feel oppressed by the very existence of the census, as it is wedded to the patriarchal practice of calculation, the western scientific method of reduction of persons to numbers, and the assimilation of disparate communities to a unified 'population', which undermines self-determination of identity, imposes a blanket unity on diversity, and forces a sense of relationship with other members of a society that is heteronormative, homophobic, transphobic, misogynist and Islamophobic. The census also promotes the myth of nationhood, which is inherently fascist; and therefore endorses the notion of borders, which is, of course, racist. The census is utterly patriarchal and capitalist, the very symbol of the father figure counting and controlling his offspring, forcing all non-White, non-male bodies to be categorised and classified. All the questions are, not merely irrelevant, but violent. The census is rape.

If the census jettisoned all the questions that any group found irrelevant, unacceptable and intrusive, there wouldn't be much of a census left, it's true, but that's the price you pay for being ultra-woke.

Perhaps the idea of jettisoning the 'Sex' question could be more widely applied to the gathering of sex/gender statistics not just for the purpose of the census but in all situations, as all such questions are surely irrelevant, unacceptable and intrusive. This might create some difficulty when it comes to figuring out so-called gender pay gaps, or the numbers of men and women on company boards, or in university jobs, or male vs female rape and domestic violence statistics, but you can't make an omelette without breaking some *ova*.

# 2. Transgender Issues

*Come, you spirits that tend on mortal thoughts, unsex me here.*
—Shakespeare

*Breathes there a man with hide so tough*
*Who says two sexes aren't enough?*
—Samuel Hoffenstein

The scene: an amphitheatre, somewhere in Judea. The time: AD 30. The occasion: a mass meeting of the People's Front of Judea (PFJ), a revolutionary organisation not to be confused with those splitters, the Judean People's Front or, even worse, the Judean Popular People's Front! *All* the members of the PFJ have turned up: Judith, Reg, Francis (Francis!) and Stan. A discussion is in progress.

'I do feel, Reg,' Judith says, 'that any Anti-Imperialist group like ours must reflect such a divergence of interests within its power-base.' Francis, the Fred Kite [YouTube 1959] of the group, grants that Judith's point is valid, provided, he adds, that 'the Movement never forgets that it is the inalienable right of every man ... (Stan interjects, 'or woman') ... or woman, to rid himself ... (Stan interjects again, 'or herself')...or herself.....' At this point. Francis loses the thread of his thought. After a pause, he picks it up again. 'It is,' he says, 'the birthright of every man ... (Stan interjects, 'or woman') ... ' At this point, Reg turns on Stan. 'Why don't you shut up about women, Stan. You're putting us off,' he says, to which Stan replies, sanctimoniously, 'Women have a perfect right to play a part in our movement, Reg.' Francis asks Stan why he is always on about women and Stan comes clean. 'I want to be one,' he says, 'I want to be a woman. From now on, I want you all to call me "Loretta".' Reg is flabbergasted and expresses his flabbergastedness in an explosive, 'What?' Stan continues: 'It's my right as a man.' It seems that Stan wants to be a woman because he wants to have babies, which, he explains, is every man's right. Reg expostulates, 'But ... you can't *have* babies! ... You haven't got a womb! Where's the fœtus going to gestate?! You going to keep it in a box?' Stan starts to cry. Judith, the peace-maker, tries for a compromise. 'Here! I—I've got an idea. Suppose you agree that he can't actually have babies, not having a womb, which is nobody's fault, not even the Romans, but that he can have the *right* to have babies.' Francis agrees with Judith. 'Good idea, Judith!' Turning to Stan (Loretta) he says, 'We shall fight the oppressors for your right to have babies, brother...sister...sorry.' Reg is still manifestly unimpressed. 'What's the point of fighting for his right to have babies when he can't have babies?' he says, not unreasonably, to which objection Francis, in his best Fred Kite voice replies, 'It is symbolic of our struggle against oppression'. Reg mutters, *sotto voce*, 'Symbolic of his struggle against reality!' [YouTube 1979/2007]

In what appears to be a bizarre instance of fact imitating Monty Pythoneque fiction, a politician in the USA appears to have said that he supports the right of transwomen (that is, men) to have abortions! During a debate between Democratic Party Presidential candidates in June 2019, Julian Castro, former Secretary of Housing and Urban Development, was asked by NBC's Lester Holt, 'Secretary Castro, this one is for you. All of you on stage support a woman's right to an abortion. You all support some version of a government health care option. Would your plan cover abortion?' Castro responded, 'Yes, it would. I don't believe only in reproductive freedom, I believe in reproductive justice. What that means is that just because a woman or let's also not forget someone in the trans community, a transfemale is poor, doesn't mean they shouldn't have the right to exercise that right to choose. I absolutely would cover the right to have an abortion.' [see YouTube 2019; also Desanctis; Hutchinson] Perhaps Castro misspoke and didn't really mean to say what he actually said. Or perhaps he's just confused. If he is, who, in the current cultural climate, could blame him?

In the previous chapter, I noted that either sex and gender are the same or they're not. If sex and gender are not the same, they are either related or unrelated. On a common reading of the sex/gender distinction, sex is biological whereas gender is psycho-social. But there is a more radical take on the sex/gender relationship, and that is that sex and gender are not the same, may or may not be related but, in any event, that gender is the more fundamental of the two whereas sex is derivative, or, even more radically, that neither sex nor gender is in any way fundamental. Notwithstanding talk of people being born in a certain way, gender construct theory is meant to release us precisely from the way we were born, whatever that may be. This is particularly evident in one of the most prominent representatives of gender construct theory, Judith Butler, who stoutly rejects the need for any justification for being at variance with one's bodily sex. In contrast to the more common account given of what gender is, Butler believes that gender is not something we observe in ourselves, whether in our bodies or in our innermost feelings. It is, rather, something we *do* to ourselves. It is a groundless act that we perform on ourselves, a sort of self-creation *ex nihilo*. Joanna Williams remarks, 'The application of post-structuralist thinking to ideas about sex and gender led to the view that gendered-performance ... serves as a signifier of their biological sex so that what is being signified (sex) is no more 'true' or 'real' than the performance; both are socially constructed.' [Williams 2020, 5] But this is to get ahead of myself. These issues will be discussed in more detail later in the chapter.

To recapitulate—we can discern at least four possible accounts of the relationship between sex and gender:

1. Sex and gender are exactly the same: to be male is to be masculine; to be female is to be feminine.
2. Sex and gender are not the same. They may or may not be related but, whether this is so or not, sex is biological and fundamental whereas gender is psychosocial and epiphenomenal.
3. Sex and gender are again not the same and may or may not be related, but this time, however, it is gender that is fundamental while sex is, somewhat mysteriously, epiphenomenal.
4. Sex and gender are not only not the same but neither is in any way fundamental or grounded in reality; both are constructed or performed, and float in mid-air like the grin of the Cheshire cat.

Of these various accounts, I think it fair to say that the first is irrelevant to any account of gender dysphoria. The third and fourth accounts are significantly different from the second and are very much more radical and are relevant to the struggle between radical feminists and transgender ideologists. [see chapter 3, § 'Feminism'] The second account, or something close to it, is the one most people will have in mind when discussions of gender dysphoria arise, an account in which gender manifests itself as the complex and often confusing relationship between a person's physico-sexual embodiment and that person's internal sense of self as male or female, or both male and female, or neither male nor female, or any of the very many possibilities adumbrated in the previous chapter. One's gender identity is to be located somewhere on a bewildering spectrum of possibilities, and may be expressed through one's actions, one's choice of clothing, one's hair and make-up, one's voice, or any other mode of personal presentation.

## Gender dysphoria
What lies at the root of one's gender identity? It appears to consist of some kind of privileged, innermost awareness of what one's gender *really* is. What, if anything, is the problem with this? Just figure out your gender identity and get on with the rest of your life. But not so fast. Some people, it seems, suffer from or

experience a condition called gender dysphoria. Gender dysphoria, which used to be known as Gender Identity Disorder, is, it seems, a psychological condition in which individuals experience an incongruence between their sex and their gender identity, together with an experience of distress stemming from such incongruence. It is speculated that gender dysphoria may be the result of hormone imbalance, or perhaps stems from the having of a male brain in a female body or *vice versa*; or it may be an inherited condition, one that one is born with and which is a permanent state; or, on the other hand, it may be a fluid condition that changes moment by moment.

The name change from Gender Identity Disorder to Gender Dysphoria came about in 2013 and coincided with the release of the fifth edition of the bible of the psychiatric profession, the *Diagnostic and Statistical Manual of Mental Disorders*, *DSM-5*. [see Davies 2014, 5-37] It seems that the change in nomenclature was made because the term *disorder* in Gender Identity Disorder was felt to have a stigma attached to it. Ironically, the term *disorder* had itself been introduced for what was felt to be the stigmatising term *mental illness*, in *DSM-3*! But there was a little more to the change in nomenclature than destigmatisation. It also marked a step in the direction of the depathologisation of the condition. Monique Robles tells us that 'Gender dysphoria is presented as a normal variation in human experience, not a mental illness. The distress accompanying gender dysphoria is presented as the result not of patients' psychological difficulties but their lack of social acceptance.' [Robles 2019] For a Butlerian, too, gender dysphoria, while useful as a tool to achieve certain ends, is contemptuously rejected as being in any sense a pathology.

If the cause of the psychological distress is exterior to the sufferer, a matter of dissonance between the sufferer's feelings and society's attitude, rather than the result of dissonance between the sufferer's feelings and their objective biological circumstances, this raises the very obvious question of why the diagnosis of this condition should be retained in the *DSM* at all. Robles again: 'According to one psychiatrist who helped write the criteria for the *DSM-5*, the goal is to maintain gender dysphoria as a psychiatric diagnosis in order to allow continued access to health care services.' [Robles] That such a view is neither new nor even recent can be seen from what Judith Butler wrote in 2004: 'The call to have matters of gender identity depathologized and for elective surgery and hormone treatment to be covered as a legitimate set of elective procedures seems bound to fail, only because most medical, insurance, and legal practitioners are only committed to supporting access to sex change technologies if we are talking about a disorder.' [Butler 2004, 92] As Thomas Szasz notes, 'The definition of disease ... becomes a paramount factor in the calculations of third parties, who hold the money

*Transgender Issues*  47

bag: they are likely to pay for diseases that are in box DX, and will certainly not pay for those that are not in it.' [Szasz 1974, 83] One has to wonder about the ethics of describing something as a disorder that one does not really believe to be a disorder so that insurance companies can be induced to pay for its 'treatment'. I suffer from acute distress caused by my feeling that I should own and drive a BMW and the incongruence of that feeling with my not being able to afford to purchase a BMW. Wouldn't a creative 'diagnosis' of a condition called, let's say, Beamer Dysphoria constrain my medical insurance to pay for the provision of the requisite BMW and the subsequent alleviation of my distress?

On the other hand, if gender dysphoria *is* a pathological condition, one that requires treatment, how can it constitute the ground of anyone's identity? Transgender ideologists insist indignantly that their condition is *not* an illness, but it is hard to see how this conclusion is to be avoided if it's insisted also that it is a condition that must receive medical or quasi-medical treatment. Illnesses that require treatment do not constitute anyone's identity. Being diabetic is an organic condition in which a person either doesn't make insulin or one in which his body cells are unable to use it. If I am unfortunate enough to suffer from diabetes, I do not *identify* as diabetic, as though it made me an entirely new kind of person. Diabetes is a pathological condition I need to treat in order to live and be healthy. I can remember vividly once in hospital, a nurse sticking her head around my room door, and inquiring, 'You're the kidney, aren't you?' It was a little disconcerting to have my whole being reduced to the dimensions of one of my malfunctioning internal organs! If gender dysphoria is a pathology, how is it any different from diabetes?

So, is gender dysphoria a pathological condition that requires treatment or is it not? Which is it? One thing at least is clear, it cannot be both—or can't it?

For the *DSM-5* generation of psychiatrists, it seems that gender dysphoria is a term that now refers not so much or at all to the psychological reasons for a patient's rejection of his or her sex, but rather to the distress in the patient produced by that rejection. If there is no distress, reasons the APA, there is no problem—it is perfectly normal, and not a disorder for a person to refuse to acknowledge the sexual significance of his or her body. With the stroke of a re-definition, the stigma disappears. Despite this, the APA has so far resisted the demands of some transgender activists to de-pathologise the condition completely, for, as we have seen, the absence of a recognised diagnosis means the absence of insurance coverage. So in the professional literature, gender dysphoria occupies something of an borderland area between a psychiatric condition and a normal state of human identity. After all, someone has to pay for these expensive psychiatric treatments and the resultant medical and surgical interventions.

There are, however, some for whom even the change of name from *disorder* to *dysphoria* and the relegation of gender dysphoria to a limbic region is not enough. These people support the declassification of the condition altogether as a mental disorder and, in a startling outbreak of honesty, advocate its complete removal from the *DSM*. In January 2017, for example, the Danish Parliament, moonlighting as psychiatrists, voted to remove not only the term 'disorder' but also the term 'dysphoria' from the description of the condition. Linda Thor Pedersen of LGBT Denmark said that it was important that terms like 'incongruence', 'disturbance' and 'problem' were omitted from the classifications used by the country's medical community. According to Norman Spack, a founder of the gender clinic at Boston Children's Hospital, the new categorisation implies that a mismatch between one's birth gender and identity isn't necessarily pathological. It would seem that the political reclassification of gender dysphoria has gone global, with the World Health Organization's (WHO) decision in January of 2019 to remove the condition from the list of mental disorders and to refer to it as 'gender incongruence'.

It is difficult not to see this linguistic legerdemain as anything other than a quasi-political sham. First, if the mismatch between one's sex and one's gender identity (to accept *gender identity* as a term of art for the sake of argument) isn't pathological, then what's the problem? Why is there any necessity to do anything? Second, the *DSM*'s classification of mental disorders is notoriously subject to political pressures. Physicians don't suddenly decide that renal colic is no longer to be described as a medical condition requiring intervention, but psychiatrists are liable to find that something that up to now has been regarded as a mental disorder is suddenly no longer to be conceived as such. Gail Hornstein remarks that the *DSM* 'is largely a political document—written by a committee, with some categories of disorder decided by vote, its framework so often disputed that a new version of the manual (with a completely different list of disorders) has to be issued every ten to fifteen years.' [Hornstein 2009, 164; see also 191] 'Why,' asks Thomas Szasz, 'do [psychiatrists] sometimes decide that previously recognized mental diseases are no longer diseases? No other medical specialists act this way.' [Szasz 1974, 161, 81] 'The APA,' he notes, 'now has *task forces* and *consensus groups* to make and unmake psychiatric diagnostic categories. That is how, in 1973—under pressure from gay rights groups—homosexuality was deleted from the roster of mental illnesses.' [Szasz 1974, 79] Those attending the 1973 APA Convention were asked to vote on whether to retain the diagnosis of homosexuality as a mental disorder in the *DSM* or to remove it. The decision was less than unanimous: 5,854 voted for its removal; 3,810 for its retention. [see Davies 2014, 14-15]

## Transgender Issues

The American Psychiatric Association validates the diagnosis of gender dysphoria in adolescents and adults if two of the following six conditions are met for at least six months.

1. A marked incongruence between one's experienced/expressed gender and primary and/or secondary sex characteristics (or in young adolescents, the anticipated secondary sex characteristics).
2. A strong desire to be rid of one's primary and/or secondary sex characteristics because of a marked incongruence with one's experienced/expressed gender (or in young adolescents, a desire to prevent the development of the anticipated secondary sex characteristics).
3. A strong desire for the primary and/or secondary sex characteristics of the other gender.
4. A strong desire to be of the other gender (or some alternative gender different from one's assigned gender).
5. A strong desire to be treated as the other gender (or some alternative gender different from one's assigned gender).
6. A strong conviction that one has the typical feelings and reactions of the other gender (or some alternative gender different from one's assigned gender). [*DSM-5*, 452]

It seems somewhat arbitrary to insist on the presence of only two of the six conditions, rather than any of the other four, and for only 6 months rather than, say, for 6 years, but that's what our esteemed psychiatrists, at present, believe. Who knows what they'll believe when *DSM-6* comes out. [see Davies 2014, 16-17] In any event, a diagnosis of gender dysphoria won't be made unless conditions 1-6, in whatever proportion or duration, results in significant distress or impairment. The presence of any or all of the six conditions is not considered by the APA to be psychiatrically problematic unless it is accompanied by distress or impairment.

According to *DSM-5*, somewhere between 70% and 98% of young males and between 50% and 88% of young females who experience gender dysphoria resolve the incongruence by the time they reach early adulthood. 'Rates of persistence of gender dysphoria from childhood into adolescence or adulthood vary. In natal males, persistence has ranged from 2.2% to 30%. In natal females, persistence has ranged from 12% to 50%.' [*DSM-5*, 455] The American Psychological Association's *APA Handbook on Sexuality and Psychology* states that the vast majority of gender dysphoric boys and girls accept their birth/chromosomal sex by adolescence or adulthood. [see Van Mol 2018] Transgender identification, then, would seem to be an transient error that, more often than not, corrects itself. An overwhelming probability of desistance hardly presents a comprehensive scientific case for a politics of transgender identity and for making compliance with its demands mandatory.

In any case, where incongruence is experienced, it can be resolved either by (A), bringing one's beliefs and experiences into line with one's biological reality, or (B), by altering one's primary and secondary sex characteristics to match one's beliefs and experiences. Until recently, treatments of type A prevailed, and those suffering from gender dysphoria were helped to adjust their feelings and perceptions to their biological reality. Now, however, there appears to be a move to switch to treatments of type B, and to treat gender dysphoria by means of hormonal or surgical interventions. If one of these options A or B is more intuitively obvious than the other it is surely A, getting one's beliefs in line with the physical reality of one's sex. If I claimed that I had an overwhelming belief that I was a dog, people might be kind and sympathetic but no one would take my beliefs seriously; I should certainly not be offered hormones or surgery to help me grow an additional pair of legs and a tail.

Levity to one side, the important point here, surely, is that one's feelings, however intense, are not necessarily a reliable guide to reality. 'Many psychologists and psychiatrists think of gender dysphoria as being much like other kinds of dysphoria, or serious discomfort with one's body, such as anorexia,' writes Ryan Anderson. 'These feelings can lead to mistaken and harmful beliefs. The most helpful therapies do not try to remake the body to conform with thoughts and feelings—which is impossible—but rather to help people find healthy ways to manage this tension and move toward accepting the reality of their bodily selves.' [Anderson 2018a, 5] Some of those who believe that they are trapped in the bodies of the wrong sex demand sex re-assignment surgery but this belief, however sincerely and deeply felt, is generated by a mistaken perception of self, and should be appropriately described, if it is to be described in any way at all, as a delusion. Walt Heyer writes, 'Having lived the trans-life as a woman for eight years .... true reality is found in what is called "de-transitioning," which involves coming to terms with and accepting one's birth gender.' [Heyer 2017b] Young people who choose route B will receive what are known as puberty blockers at around age thirteen, receive opposite sex hormones at around age sixteen to prevent or mitigate the development of secondary sex characteristics, and, eventually, they may be the beneficiaries of re-assignment surgery during which breasts and penises are removed, and penises and vaginas, or rather the simulacra of such, are created where there were none before. Of course, such constructed penises and vaginas do not function like genuine penises or vaginas. There is no treatment that can allow a man to menstruate, nor can a woman be made such that she can produce sperm. [but see Johnson 2020]

*Transgender Issues* 51

If treatments of type B are intended to resolve a person's psychological issues, it should be noted that, even if this desirable result were to be achieved (and it's not at all clear that it is), there are significant physical risks and effects associated with the hormonal and surgical aspects of the treatment—decreased bone density, stunted growth, acne, deep-vein thrombosis and infertility. On the psychological side, a study conducted in Sweden in 2011 found that sex-reassigned individuals were likely to attempt suicide by a factor five times higher than a control group and nineteen times more likely to die by suicide. A study of almost seven thousand transgender people in the United States found that 41% had attempted suicide, compared to a national average of 1.6%. Ryan Anderson notes, 'It is widely accepted that [gender dysphoric individuals] disclose a heightened risk for mental health problems. Most striking is the statistic that around 40% of [such individuals] will attempt suicide at some time or other, which is higher than the wider population by a factor of between 9 and 10.' There is no doubt, then, that gender dysphoria discloses a problem; what is in dispute is how best to deal with it. Anderson notes, 'people are suffering from gender dysphoria; they are not generally finding well-being through sex reassignment procedures; and these poor outcomes cannot be explained solely by social stigma.' [Anderson 2018a, 94]

And then there is the painful reality of the transitioning process. Reality TV is the new, cheap way to generate programming for our voracious TV screens, and so it was only a matter of time before we had some reality TV programme focusing on transgenderism. Sure enough, along comes *Transformation Street* on ITV to show us the human side to transgenderism. [see YouTube 2018] It follows the story of certain individuals who are making their trans journey with the help of London Transgender Surgery. The atmosphere we are meant to see is one of normality and good humour. Lucas, transitioning from female to male, was the star of the opening episode. Referring to her/his mother who was with her/him, Lucas said 'She baked me wrong in the oven'. 'Aaaaah,' we all intone, 'how touching'. Then we witness Lucas's chemical mutilation, with testosterone treatment deepening her/his voice, broadening her/his shoulders and giving her/him facial hair. One detransitioner, Walt Heyer, writes, 'cutting off breasts, filling patients with cross-sex hormones, cutting off or refashioning male genitalia, installing a pseudo penis on a female—all of today's transgender treatments are barbaric and need to stop. Someday these matters will be decided in the courts and hopefully the harmful practices will be curtailed, but "someday" is too late for those being ensnared into the trans ideology today .... the trans "treatment" being idolized today should meet the same fate as lobotomies, tooth pulling and colon removal—tossed on the historical rubbish heap of debunked horrific experiments perpetrated on innocent, hurting people.' [Heyer 2019] It is, then,

52 *Hidden Agender*

less than rationally compelling to argue, as some do, that the process of gender transitioning by means of surgery and hormone treatment is a good, still less the best, way of dealing with gender dysphoria. 'What,' asks Paul Dirks, 'does the peer-reviewed research say about the effectiveness of medical transition for gender dysphoria?' This is not an idle question? 'Do puberty blockers, cross-sex hormones, mastectomies, vaginoplasties, and phalloplasties,' he asks, 'successfully alleviate the mental and emotional distress that gender-dysphoric persons face?' As one might expect, studies produce variable results, but 'a careful reading of the literature demonstrates that the best studies show the worst outcomes for those who undergo medical transition.' [see Dirks].

Whatever about choices made by competent adults in respect of surgery or hormone treatment, it is difficult to justify the application of such treatments to those who are legally (and perhaps psychologically) incompetent, especially children. Ryan Anderson and Robert George believe that physical interventions on children to affirm what is taken to be their gender identity are ethically unjustified and should be prohibited. [see Anderson & George 2019, passim] They argue, in my view correctly, that such gender affirmation by physical means 'violate sound medical ethics, that it is profoundly unethical to reinforce a male child in his belief that he is not a boy (or a female child in her belief that she is not a girl), and that it is particularly unethical to intervene in the normal physical development of a child to "affirm" a "gender identity" that is at odds with bodily sex.' [see Anderson & George 2019; Kirkup 2020; Transgender Trend, various]

On the other hand, Tea Uglow, creative director of Google's Creative Lab in Sydney, writes that there are 'people who feel profoundly uncomfortable presenting as the gender they are classified in.' [Uglow 2018] According to Uglow, 'we know that somewhere between 0.3% and 0.5% of the world's population experience gender dysphoria and don't feel they "fit" with a binary model.' Then she goes on to ask, 'Are millions of such people wrong?' What exactly does she mean by asking if they are wrong? Is she asking if what they claim to experience is *not* what they experience? It's hard to know how you could be wrong about that, any more than you could be wrong about your favourite colour, as the study published by Monty Python in *Monty Python and the Holy Grail*, cleverly disguised as satire, has definitively demonstrated. The point of her question 'Are millions of such people wrong?' becomes a little clearer when she goes on to ask, 'Or is the current model wrong?' Model? What model? The scientific theories to which she refers earlier in her piece may have models, models that are revisable in the light of more experience and experiments and new theories, but the binary nature of human sexuality isn't a potentially revisable or disposable model. Are we to understand that because a tiny percentage of people experience a mismatch between their biological sex and what they consider to be their real sex, this calls into question the fact that practically everyone is clearly and unproblematically male or female? The existence of a few, very few, people whose psychosexual development is abnormal doesn't change the fact that human beings are sexually binary. Uglow graciously concedes that 'the ancient model that divides us into two distinct "sexes" is deeply ingrained' but, nevertheless, she believes that it is flawed and broken. There's that term 'model' again, with the suggestion that the binary nature of human sexuality is some kind of theoretical construct that is in principle revisable. She is prepared, in a big-hearted and tolerant way, to allow people to think that men *are* men and women *are* women. In doing this, we are, according to her, exercising a right to our own beliefs and treating people in line with those beliefs. Thank you, Ms Uglow. But she believes we should also be aware that this is a prejudice and acting in this way is discrimination. Oops! Too soon with the thanks.

Strange things are happening, and not just in relation to sex. Some people have their legs amputated not for any medical or therapeutic reason but simply because they have a strong desire to have their legs cut off. According to psychiatrists, these people are perfectly mentally competent. And we are not dealing with one or two isolated cases. One such discussion group has 1,400 subscribers! Why on earth would anyone want to amputate a perfectly healthy leg? Well, it seems that some people are attracted to the idea of being amputees. The term used for this peculiar idea is *apotemnophilia*. What is of interest is cases of apotemnophilia is the way the language of feeling and identity is used, a way that is eerily reminiscent of the way the language of feeling/identity is used in transgenderism. It is as if the body the apotemnophiliacs have is not the one they feel they should have. Are they stuck in a body of the wrong shape, or have they got one or two limbs too many? Bizarre as apotemnophilia may seem to us, its resemblance to those who seek sex-reassignment surgery for gender dysphoria is obvious. Is the removal of a perfectly healthy limb any more bizarre than sex-reassignment surgery? Apotemnophilia may seem weird but then, not so very long ago, the idea that thousands of people would want to have their genitalia surgically altered would also have seemed weird. There are at least two ways to go on this: one is to see both apotemnophilia and sex-reassignment surgery as legitimate forms of body alteration to alleviate feelings of incongruence; the other is to see both as, well, weird. [see Thomas 2020b]

In the previous chapter, we saw Jennifer Gruenke consider the possibility that gender dysphoria was of a kind with other forms of dysphoria, all of them being based on corrigible first-person accounts. Her presentation of the point is worth repeating:

Now, it is worth considering a more principled objection from the conservative front. Some might contend that, if we accept first-person accounts with respect to gender identity, we will have no principled reason to reject them in other cases. For instance, the first-person report is unreliable in the case of anorexia. An anorexic person is convinced that she is overweight, even when she is already underweight. This, it might be claimed, is analogous to the case of a transgender person. A transgender person might sincerely believe that he is female, but that does not mean that he is not mistaken. Indeed, the objector might press that brain chemistry cannot solve this problem. For suppose that an anorexic person *does* have the brain chemistry of an overweight person, and this similarity is accountable in terms of genetic factors; in such a case, we would not say that the girl really is overweight, despite appearances. We'd say that she is really underweight, personal conviction notwithstanding. Anorexia just is a condition characterized in terms of a desire to be thin in spite of already being thin; her brain chemistry and emphatic beliefs don't defeat this. Moreover, the anorexic person is not *correct* merely because her reports match her brain and indeed her brain (if not the rest of her body) developed along pathways characteristic of overweight people. Why, our objector continues, can't a transgender person be similarly mistaken? The fact that a transgender person is making reports in line with her neurological development does not establish that she cannot be incorrect. [Gruenke]

Although Gruenke rejects the analogy between gender dysphoria and other forms of dysphoria, the argument she presents seems to me to be unanswerable. If we are prepared to accept the authority of first-person reports of gender dysphoric individuals, and permit or recommend surgery or hormone treatment to bring their bodies into line with their minds, why do we not do so with anorexics or with those who exhibit body image integrity disorder? The incongruence at the root of gender dysphoria is of a type with that experienced by people who think they're overweight when they're not (anorexics), or who believe that they are disabled and desire to have their bodily being altered to match that belief, a condition known as body integrity identity disorder (BIID). That people entertaining such false beliefs may be stigmatised is a problem, but it's not a problem that can be resolved by pretending that these false beliefs are not false, any more than if a stigma were attached to, say, being a thalidomide victim, it should be resolved by denying that such victims are, in fact, physically damaged.

At first glance, then, and perhaps also at second and subsequent glances, gender dysphoria would appear to line up squarely with other forms of dysphoria (a dysphoria being a state of unease or generalised dissatisfaction with life) such as anorexia nervosa or body dysmorphic disorder or body integrity identity disorder. In all these conditions, there is a mismatch between what one is perceived to be (obese, ugly, disabled) and what one actually is. Is anyone suggesting that those with anorexia nervosa should have surgery to make them obese, or those with body dysmorphic disorder be surgically disfigured, or those with body integrity identity disorder have healthy body parts removed? If such suggestions are not being made, why not? All those who experience various forms of dysphoria are experiencing real distress, but the anorexia nervosa person is not overweight and her treatment shouldn't and doesn't involve forcing her to put on pounds so that there is a correspondence between her beliefs and reality. Nor should the body integrity identity disorder person have disfiguring surgery so that his face may be made truly ugly and thereby conform with his beliefs.

Gender dysphoria is a distressing condition that requires understanding (and perhaps treatment), but the feeling of sex/gender misalignment, however intensely experienced, is simply a mistake. In all these dysphorias, the beliefs of their subjects are genuinely held but they are none the less subjective for all that, and by that I mean that these beliefs do not square with reality. Those who have a genuine experience of themselves as being in some way in the wrong body are experiencing real psychosocial difficulties, but these difficulties are not addressed by surgical mutilation, hormonal assault or a veneer of cosmetics. What we have as the result of any of these treatments are counterfeits, and that counterfeiting is deeply psychosocially problematic. In the cases of bulimia, anorexia and body dysmorphic disorder, while we sympathise with those who hold these beliefs, our sympathy doesn't extend to agreeing that they are correct in what they think, and in these cases, no one would suggest reconstructive surgery as a treatment. When beliefs and reality don't correspond, it is our beliefs that must change, not reality.

As a psychological phenomenon, then, gender dysphoria is real. People who experience it should be treated with compassion, kindness and respect, just like everyone else. Heyer writes, 'I have personally experienced gender dysphoria, and I explored transition in my early twenties. I am aware of the emotional struggle, and I am sympathetic to the sense of frustration and hopelessness. But I am also aware of the empowering realization that I alone control how I perceive the world. Even if I would prefer to be female, I understand that my body is male, and therefore the most effective and healthiest plan of action is to align my sense of gender to that unchangeable state. I have largely been successful, as I feel fully integrated today and am not only comfortable in my male body but find myself enjoying the pursuit of masculine physical progress.' [Greene 2017] But, to anticipate what I'll discuss more completely a little further on, compassion for people experiencing gender dysphoria does not imply that we ought to be morally or legally required to accept a supposedly transitioned or transitioning person as being of the other sex, or that we ought to be legally obliged to use language that is false in addressing or referring to such people. Gender dysphoria, whatever its ultimate nature and whatever its proper treatment, is real; but feelings, however vivid, however distressing, do not change reality.

Most ordinary people are confused about the whole business. They have a laudable desire not to gratuitously offend or cause pain to others, and an understandable fear, in the current hostile climate, of being accused of some dreadful phobia, and so are intimidated into not speaking their minds. People in the main are decent and compassionate and would wish to help or, at the very least, not harm people who think they are members of the opposite sex. But being compassionate is not at all the same as thinking that a person's sex is determined by his feelings as distinct from his biology. Meanwhile, the small band of transgenderist true believers and their cheering section in politics and in the media all subscribe enthusiastically to the new orthodoxy and, filled with evangelical zeal, will brook no dissent, no backsliding. As we shall see later, it is increasingly the case that toleration is not enough. We are called upon to valorise a lie, and our refusal to do so is to be considered a social solecism and a demonstration of bigotry. Even more seriously, a refusal to cooperate in untruth-telling may, in certain circumstances, be deemed a crime.

### I'm in the wrong body!
We have seen that at the root of gender dysphoria is some experience of a mismatch or lack of congruence between one's biological sex and one's inner sense of gender. This incongruence is sometimes expressed as feeling like a man in a woman's body, or a woman in a man's body. What are we to make of such claims? Let's try a thought experiment.

What does it feel like to be a tree? Take this question seriously. Think about it for a little while before reading on.

How did you go about trying to answer this question? Did you screw up your eyes and conjure up an image of a big oak tree, standing alone in a field? But this is simply your remembering or imagining of what you experienced when you see a tree, not what a tree experiences! Can literature help? What about the Ents in Tolkien's *Lord of the Rings*? Not much help here either, and if you're stumped (pun intended) to answer this question, I'm not surprised. You're *not* a tree, so you cannot have a first-hand experience of what being a tree feels like, if, indeed, it feels like anything. Now ask yourself, what does it feel like to be a dog or, if you wish to channel Thomas Nagel, to be a bat? Once again, no human being has that experience and so cannot have the requisite experiential knowledge. We can *imagine* what it would be like to be an tree or a dog or a bat—easier perhaps to imagine we're dogs or bats than trees—things that we are in fact not, but we cannot *have* that experience. Take the bat's ability to navigate by means of a

*Transgender Issues* 57

kind of sonar. We can understand how this works, but the bat isn't checking out signals on an internal mental video screen and making sophisticated mathematical calculations; it simply experiences the world as mediated by its sonar abilities, navigating its way around the world directly by sound much as we do by sight. We can, to a certain extent, *understand* what it is like to be a bat, but we cannot *have* a bat's actual experience.

When a man says he feels like a woman, what does he mean? He isn't a woman and so cannot have the actual experiences that a woman has. At most, he can rely on second-hand accounts from women of what it is like to be a woman, or else he may rely on culturally available stereotypes of femaleness and try to identify with those. But these accounts, or these stereotypes, however extensive and however refined, are not equivalent to actual experience. As Anderson notes, 'many feminists have pointed out, no biological male can really experience what it is like to be a woman, for males can have no embodied female experiences.' [Anderson 2018a, 104] By parity of reasoning, no biological female can experience what it is like to be a male, for females, similarly, can have no embodied male experiences.

If feminism is all about driving a wedge between one's identity and one's body, it should have no difficulty with coming to terms with transgenderism. But, in fact, radical feminists *do* have a problem with transgenderism, and that problem moves them, however reluctantly, towards re-identifying a close connection between body and sexual identity. Their objection tends to be phrased not so much as 'if you haven't got the right body, you can't be female', but rather, 'if you haven't had the right experiences, in particular the experience of patriarchal oppression, you can't be female'. That argument, however, is patently specious as a simple thought experiment will show. If you are female and have been brought up since birth as a princess, the recipient of every good thing, and protected from all possible harm (including male violence), you are a woman. If I am a man who, since birth, has been a consistent target of male violence, I am still a man and not, as the result of persistent male violence, a woman. Contingent experiences cannot make one to be either female or male, either a man or a woman.

What does it mean to have an internal sense of gender? What does gender feel like? What does it mean to say that you have a feeling *of being a man in a woman's body*, or a feeling *of being a woman in a man's body*? These feelings, if they exist, are not like the feeling of being pinched, the feeling of a hot stove on your hand, or the feeling of anxiety. How do you know that *this* feeling that you have is the feeling of being a man as opposed to that of being a woman? What's the point of contrast? If we cannot even experience in all respects what it feels like to be another individual of the same sex, as indeed we can't, still less can we know what it feels like to be a member of the other sex. Indeed, such a feeling would be an odd sort of feeling, for if a given person felt it persistently throughout his life, with no point of contrast, then it would be a background condition of his being and so would be essentially unknowable. It would not be a sort of signal, as our experience of pain is.

Even if we had answers to these questions—and I don't think they have answers—why should our feelings be determinative of reality? It is patently obvious that our feelings change and change frequently—does reality change correspondingly? [see Heyer 2017a] What if I feel I'm black, as Rachel Dolezal apparent did and does? [see below, chapter 4, § 'Transracialism'] Would that make me black? If not, why not? What's so special about my feeling of being a certain gender that in its case, feelings determine reality, but not in other cases?

There is a curiously ethereal aspect to transgenderism. My self, my real self, is given to me by my feelings. I feel as if I were a man trapped in a woman's body, or a woman trapped in a man's body, and my feelings are more real than any mere biological facts. If I have a penis and I feel as if I were a woman, then I am a woman with a penis. If I have a uterus and I feel as if I were a man, then I am a man with a uterus! But what are these feelings of being a man or being a woman if not conformity to existing male and female stereotypes? 'The reason why people can insist they are "trapped in the wrong body",' Andrew Walker notes, 'is that, in the transgender paradigm, psychology dictates ontology.' If self-perception is the criterion of reality, then 'individuals and activists can insist on utter absurdities, such as the claim that men can menstruate, with sober sincerity. It is why *Time* magazine is attempting to make ordinary Americans accept the idea that men can give birth. The transgender movement requires accepting the idea that men who identify as women are *actually* women; and that women who identify as men are *actually* men.' [Walker 2017] It may be that the claim to have these feelings is an oblique way of claiming to have a collection of desires normally manifested by women. Someone inclined to say that he 'feels like a woman' might simply be expressing a desire to wear a dress and high heels, to act as he thinks a woman acts, and to be treated as he thinks a woman should be treated. One significant difference, however, between the transgender person's experience of these desires and a woman's experience of them is that the transgender person experiences these desires *as frustrated* and so, in that respect, he does *not* actually feel as most women feel, for women who want to wear dresses and high heels generally experience those desires as unproblematically fulfillable.

Sometimes, however, transgender incongruence is expressed more radically. It's not so much a *feeling* of being a man in a woman's body or a *feeling* of being a woman in a man's body, but, instead, it is a matter of *being* a man in a woman's body or *being* a woman in a man's body. But just what would it mean to *be* a man in a woman's body or to *be* a woman in a man's body? For this even to begin to make sense, there would have to be a radical distinction between a *me* (which would have to be capable of being a man or a woman) and my *body*. The relationship between these two entities would be contingent so that the real *me* is *in* this (male) *body* but could, conceivably, have been *in* another (female) *body*. Whatever else may be obscure about this position, one point should be obvious. Whatever the *me* is that is not my body, if it has the capacity to inform any living structure, including this or that male or female body, *it cannot itself be either male or female*. What would make it to be one or the other? That is why, in medieval angelology, angels, as purely spiritual beings, are usually considered to be neither male nor female.

There have been systems of thought that have espoused a radical dualism, so that the I—the self, the soul, the *atman*—is what it is, apart from any bodily manifestation, the body being related to it as a vehicle to its inhabitant. This is a view often attributed, not uncontroversially, to Plato. Whatever about that, it is certainly a view that is central to some understandings of Hinduism, where *atman* is contingently related to a body, and persists in another body to which it transmigrates after its current body's destruction, until finally, and desirably, it is completely released from all material attachment.

The idea of other-body-inhabitation is popular in fiction and in cinema and, as might be expected, Hollywood has made some play with the idea of transmigration. In *All of Me* (1984), a dying millionaire, Edwina Cutler, undergoes a process by which she is meant to be detached from her own body and is supposed to transmigrate to the body of a young and beautiful woman. However, as the result of an accident, she ends up inhabiting, together with its original occupant, the body of a lawyer, Roger Cobb. Cue lots of fun and games as the two inhabitants of the single body end up having to sort out this strange *ménage-à-deux*. The villain of the piece into whose body Edwina was supposed to transmigrate ends up inheriting all her estate but, in a bizarre final twist, the self/soul of the villain ends up transmigrating into a horse! Before that happens, Edwina's soul is, at different stages, incorporated within a bowl and inside a bucket of water! In *Heaven Can Wait* (a re-make of *Here Comes Mr. Jordan*), Joe Pendleton, a wannabe American football quarterback, dies in an accident but, as his time was not up, he needs to be re-embodied. For reasons not made entirely clear in the film, this is a matter of some urgency, and if it is to happen at all, there's a limited choice of bodies available to him. One of these is that of a millionaire who has just been murdered by his wife. The problem with this is that the millionaire is old and decrepit, whereas Joe is in excellent physical shape. Joe still wants to play quarterback for his team, but the only way he can do this is to actually buy the team and install himself in that position. His new teammates are understandably sceptical of the quarterbacking prowess of what appears to them to be a decrepit old man, but they come around when this dodderer throws a fifty-yard pass! Now, the problem here is that we, the cinema audience, see a young and vigorous Warren Beatty throwing this pass and that seems entirely reasonable to us; Beatty's teammates, however, see a decrepit septuagenarian throwing the pass and that, to them, is little less than miraculous, as it also would be to us if we thought about it. Both of these films require a hefty suspension of disbelief. Neither is entirely coherent, but that doesn't matter as they are not metaphysical treatises but are meant to be light-hearted entertainment.

The claim, then, that 'I am a woman in a man's body' or 'I am a man in a woman's body' is either incoherent or, at best, analogical. If a boy likes stereotypically girls' toys and activities, does that make him really a girl in a boy's body? Or if a girl likes stereotypically boys' toys and activities, does that make her a boy in a girl's body? What of Georgina in Enid Blyton's *Famous Five* stories who wants to be called George and to be treated like a boy? Is she a boy in a girl's body? Or is she rather a girl who resents and resists the narrow limits of what is presented to her as the acceptable range of female experience and interests, someone, in a word, who doesn't want to be stereotyped?

The ironic paradox of transgender ideology is that it reinforces the very gender stereotypes that other parts of the liberal agenda are industriously trying to erase. I am happy (for once) to enlist Judith Butler on the side of the angels. Speaking of the typical likes and dislikes of young boys and girls, and the fact that some girls like typically boys' toys and some boys like typically girls' toys, she writes, 'But in what world, precisely, do such dislikes count as clear or unequivocal evidence for or against being a given gender? Do parents regularly rush off to gender identity clinics when their boys play with yarn, or their girls play with trucks?' [Butler 2004, 70] Critics of transgender ideology, ironically, appear to be more open to transgressive gender boundaries than its supporters.

Until very recently, the view of humanity in the mass was that our sex was understood to be an intrinsic part of our being and could be known (apart from the rare cases of problematic embryonic development) from an inspection of our bodily structures. Human sexuality is intrinsically oriented towards procreation, and our bodily structures indicate our roles in that process. The desire to change our sex is, at root, a desire to be another person and, implicitly, a desire to cease to be who and what we are. According to the new transgender orthodoxy, you are what you feel yourself to be, so that if you are a man and feel yourself to be a woman, then that is what you are; if you are a woman and feel yourself to be a man, then a man is what you are. The body, as accidental to what I really am, can be moulded to reflect the superior reality of what my feelings reveal me to really

## Transgender Issues

be, although, if my body is really contingent, then it's difficult to see how being either a man or a woman is really me at all.

Let us return to the basic question at the root of all these ruminations. What are we? Are we just lumps of living matter? What is the thing, if it is a thing, that asks these kinds of questions? Am I just my body? And if not, is there something else that I am? Am I a self, a self that is only contingently connected to a body, or is my self, if it is anything at all, just an aspect, a dimension of my body?

These kinds of questions have perplexed mankind for millennia. As I have indicated, one popular answer is to think of the self as what is most real about me, and my body as some sort of vehicle or container for it. Sometimes, this is expressed as a kind of body-soul dualism, where the soul is taken to be what is really me and the body only an accidental carrier to which I am somehow, perhaps temporarily, attached. We find this in certain readings of Plato and, of course, it is a staple of Indian thought. Similar ideas can be found in modern philosophy. Keith Sutherland refers to Iris Murdoch's critique of what she called the 'existential behaviourism' of the 1970s, according to which '"atomised" individuals choose both their identity and moral personality free from natural, social and supernatural constraints. Once the individual has made her sovereign choice this determines both publicly-observable behaviour and inner mental states (insofar as the latter were acknowledged to exist in the academic psychology of the time).' [Sutherland 2020] He goes on to note that 'Philosophy of mind has since undergone both the cognitive revolution of the 1980s and the turn to 'neurophilosophy' brought about by the 1990s 'decade of the brain'. It is now almost impossible to find a serious philosopher prepared to defend the disembodied Cartesian chooser, unconstrained by culture, morality or—indeed—inconvenient factors like biology.' [Sutherland 2020]

Orthodox Christianity speaks of the soul and so it would be understandable if we were to think that it necessarily subscribes to a radical body-soul dualism. But it doesn't. This was one area in which the struggle of early Christianity with those who would turn it in a Gnostic direction was of vital importance. For Gnosticism, what I am essentially is my self or my soul. All that is bodily about me is accidental, something that can be, and at times, should be ignored. Some forms of Gnosticism regard the body as a prison, so that our ultimate goal is liberation from it—*soma sema*, the body is a tomb. The body, not being me, not being what I really am, can be treated in any way that is required. One might be inclined to think that Gnosticism is a matter that would be of interest only to historians of the early Church, but Gnosticism hasn't actually gone away. It has never completely disappeared and it is an ever-present intellectual temptation. [see George 2016]

It must be admitted that some popular forms of Christianity sail close to the Gnostic wind in tacitly supporting some form or other of radical ontological dualism, but orthodox Christianity tends to be somewhat more intellectually austere. [but see Swinburne 2019 and Ward 2010] The pre-eminent Christian theologian and philosopher, Thomas Aquinas, writes in his Commentary on *Corinthians*, 'The human soul is part of a human being but it is not the whole human being; *I am not my soul* [*anima mea non est ego* ], so that though it be accepted that the soul may continue to exist in another life, it is not I nor any other man.' [emphasis added. *In I Cor.* c. 15] On this view of things, human beings are essentially embodied creatures. My body is not some accidental appendage to my real self but a real and necessary dimension of what I am. The human being is an embodied soul or a bodily self. We do not occupy our bodies, and the soul is not, as in Plato's image, like a sailor in a ship. My soul is not adventitiously connected to my body but my soul and body are two dimensions of a single reality. As Aristotle pointed out long ago, in the first book of his *De anima*, the problem with much of what his predecessors had written on the subject of the *psyche* is that it made contingent the relationship between *psyche* (soul) and *soma* (body) whereas, for him, *psyche* and *soma* were two constitutive principles of a single reality.

The Princeton philosopher Robert George explains that transgender ideology is Gnostic in its denial of physical reality in favour of an allegedly overruling knowledge in association with feelings. Similarly, in a letter to the editor of *The Times* of London, N.T. Wright, the eminent theologian and former Bishop of Durham wrote, 'The confusion about gender identity is a modern, and now internet-fueled, form of the ancient philosophy of Gnosticism. The Gnostic, one who "knows," has discovered the secret of "who I really am," behind the deceptive outward appearance ... This involves denying the goodness, or even the ultimate reality, of the natural world. Nature, however, tends to strike back, with the likely victims in this case being vulnerable and impressionable youngsters who, as confused adults, will pay the price for their elders' fashionable fantasies.' [Wright 2017; but see Guyton 2017]

In so far as the treatment of gender dysphoria by hormonal-surgical methods has an intellectual justification, then, that justification seems to depend upon the idea that what I am is my soul or my self. My body is not me, and I am at liberty to create my own identity just by willing it to be so. As Eric Voegelin noted, for the Gnostics, their first principle is the non-recognition of reality. Anyone who has the temerity to point out reality must be silenced—the boy who tells us that the Emperor has no clothes must be shunned. Those who criticise transgenderist ideology are to be silenced by the very effective tactic of name-calling, which immediately puts them on the defensive as possible bigots, and the tactic of linking transgenderism to the struggle for the attainment of civil rights makes it difficult for anyone to resist the movement without seeming to endorse racism. Add to that the usual strategy of highlighting emotionally charged stories of the brave individuals who struggle to achieve their goals, and emotion, as always, trumps reason. In certain respects, then, I don't think it is too far-fetched to say that transgenderist ideology is a belief system that begins to resemble a cult, a kind of latter-day Gnosticism that denies the reality of the world of our experience. What is astonishing to me, and to many others, is that this exotic belief system has now received the official imprimatur of the state, at least in many countries in the West, in the form of Gender Recognition Acts or their equivalents.

If we reject a radical body/soul or self/body dualism, what then are we? Are we merely bodies of quite a high level of complexity? Or can we take from dualism some truth, leaving behind the admixture of error? That is what I believe Aristotle and the Aristotelian tradition does, though I can't argue the point here. It posits that the human being is a unity of two principles: matter (the body—that which is organised) and form (the soul—that which organises). However, for our purposes, we don't need to choose between a form of Aristotelian moderate dualism and a naturalistic monism to account for the human person. It is sufficient to reject the extreme dualism often attributed to Plato and which is characteristic of Hindu thought.

But are we right to reject extreme dualism? Might not the extreme dualistic understanding of the human person be right after all? Perhaps the person (self, soul, *atman*) is not the body, but only inhabits it and uses it as an instrument. Perhaps the real person *is* the conscious and feeling self, the *psyche*, and the body *is* simply a material machine that our real self temporarily animates and in which it temporarily resides. Were the Gnostics (and their latter-day followers) right? Have we erroneously and unreflectively misconceived ourselves as being essentially bodily? Perhaps the Gnostics are right in thinking that the body is a mere machine and the soul or self a kind of ghost that animates it.

But if so, Gnosticism has to account for our seemingly ineradicable experience of ourselves as being essentially one, despite there being pathological circumstances in which we may, on occasion, feel ourselves to be divided into parts. And it has to account for the stubborn and unshiftable experience that our bodies, feeble and fallible as they may be, are *our* bodies, and an essential dimension of what we are, and not prosthetic devices, like a mechanical leg or arm, that we employ but which is, in principle, detachable from us. 'I loved you for your body/there's a voice that sounds like God to me/declaring that your body's really you' [Cohen 2009, 33] It is the one and the same person who thinks abstract thoughts and loves justice and disinterestedly desires the good of others, the one person who sees and hears

64 *Hidden Agender*

and tastes and touches, who eats pizza and who takes up space on a bus. When things happen to my body, they happen to me. To reject extreme dualism, we appeal to experience, one aspect of which is our experience of ourselves as unities, unities of parts, to be sure, but unities nonetheless. Could we be the victims of a systematic illusion in this regard? It is possible, in the thinnest and most abstract sense of possible, but this mere possibility—even if we had any positive reason to think it true (and we don't)—must be placed against the irrefragability of our experience. George again: 'Nothing gives us reason to suppose that experience to be illusory. Even if body-self dualism could be made coherent—which I doubt—we would have no more reason to believe it than we have to suppose that we are now dreaming, or stuck in the Matrix.' [George 2016]

There *are* exponents of ontological dualism in Western thought today but dualism is not the dominant position in the philosophy of mind, not that that makes it false, of course. [see, for example, Unger 2006; Popper & Eccles 1983; Swinburne 1986 & 2019] There are, however problems with certain extreme forms of this position, not least why the ultimately real and ontologically independent self, mind, *psyche* or soul should be associated with a body in the first place! What, we might ask, is a nice soul like you doing in a body like this? The human being, then, is either a natural unity or, as I believe, a psychosomatic unity. [For an elegant and accessible account of the intricacies of the philosophy of mind, see Feser 2005]

There are radical options other than extreme dualism. Nominalism is the doctrine according to which things have no intrinsic natures but can be ordered and moulded to our purposes. This would seem to be the essence of the Butlerian position on sex and gender as performances. The Chinese Government appears to have adopted nominalism as a marketing strategy. China's Aquatic Products Processing and Marketing Alliance (CAPPMA), which operates under the remit of the Chinese ministry of agriculture, has declared that all salmonidae fish can now be sold under the umbrella description, 'salmon'. It is true that both trout and salmon are both members of the group salmonidae, but so are chars, freshwater whitefishes and grayling, so I suppose that they can be sold as salmon as well. The *Guardian* thinks this action of the CAPPMA is bizarre, but if men can be women and women men—claims that *Guardian* writers seem to have little difficulty accepting—than it's hard to see why trout can't be salmon. [Leader 2018] Voluntarism is the doctrine that the will is superior to the intellect. For theological voluntarists, if entities other than God were to have intrinsic natures, this would constitute a limitation on God's will and power. But, for voluntarists, God is an absolute sovereign, able to form and reform reality in whatever way he wishes, subject to no constraints, not even the constraints of logic or coherence.

*Transgender Issues*                                                                                       65

One could argue that transgender ideology combines nominalism and voluntarism to produce a form of immanent nominalistic voluntarism in which human beings occupy a quasi-divine position as self-makers and self-creators, giving effect to the maxim: my will be done. [see Taylor 2007, esp. 97 ff. See also Butler 2004 & 2006 passim] For this nominalist voluntarism, what we are is, in the end, a matter of what we think we are; not a matter of one's biology, or one's genes, or one's upbringing. Human beings are blank pieces of paper on which any script may be written, unsexed beings, contingently stuck in a body of one or other sex (and perhaps not even that), but not required to accept any particular gender. Though unsympathetic to orthodox religion in general, in certain respects transgender ideology appears itself to be quasi-religious. It bears a striking similarity to *goeteia,* a practice that J. Budziszewski describes as "the ancient practice whose goal was to acquire power by 'breaking' nature, unpatterning its patterns, uncreating creation." [see Budziszewski 2011]

These radical positions are ultimately indefensible. Human beings are not indeterminate lumps of flesh that can be transformed either into other beings, or into other sexes. Echoing Reg's comment in the Monty Python sketch with which this chapter began, and expressing it somewhat more formally, we can say that transgenderism is the radical claim that not only can one choose to mirror the sexual identity of a person of the other sex (which one can of course do), but one can assume it in reality. I have no wish to be harsh, but the only way to describe the transgenderist doctrine is as a delusion. The weirdness of the world in which we live is that those who point out this delusion are the ones who are attacked and accused of manifesting a psychologically disturbed condition called transphobia. The attacks come via efforts to blacklist businesses owned by such reactionaries, or pressure put on their employers to fire them, or even of efforts to use or make laws that force them to recant—or else! The efflorescence of what, in 2020, has come to be called 'cancel culture' is merely the latest expression of this targeted hostility. Worrying as these informal methods of intimidation are, even more worrying is that the right to freedom of speech is being increasingly circumscribed by hateful laws prohibiting what is deemed to be hate speech.

In any event, these extreme positions are existentially self-refuting and cannot be lived out. As I wrote some years ago, no theory can be seriously maintained such that, if it were to be true, its very maintenance would become impossible, meaningless, contradictory or self-refuting. Apart from the formal constraints on theories of the necessity for consistency and coherence, and the material constraints of explanatory adequacy and coverage, there is also a self-referential constraint on theories, namely, that theories must not render impossible the conditions of their own statement or the conditions of their being maintained.

66          *Hidden Agender*

If they do so, they are theoretically self-stultifying. In trying to oppose these positions rationally, one feels as if the ground were shifting continually under one's feet. It's like trying to box against the Blob. Rationality requires agreement on ground rules in respect of truth, evidence and argument, but when truth is reduced to opinion, when evidence can be disregarded, and when argument is categorised as simply a form of oppression, then it's difficult to see how one can present arguments against what is, in effect, a surd.

### Detransitioning

One aspect of transgenderism that has perhaps received less attention than it deserves is that of people who have regretted their decision to transition and who wish to reverse their gender-transitioning surgery. Professor Miroslav Djordjevic, a leading genital reconstructive surgeon (he performs around 100 surgeries a year, both at his Belgrade clinic and New York's Mount Sinai Hospital), was first approached about reversal surgery in 2012. Since that time, other would-be reverts have been in touch with him, telling him about the severe levels of depression they experienced *after* their transitions. Based on his experience, Djordjevic, not surprisingly, has concerns about the level of psychiatric evaluation and counselling that people receive before gender reassignment occurs in the first place.

Gender reassignment surgery does not always produce the happy results it is supposed to produce. Robert Winston, emeritus professor of fertility studies at Imperial College London, is reported as warning that 'Many people who change their gender end up with "horrendous" results and are left feeling "badly damaged".' Speaking on the *Today* programme on BBC Radio 4, Professor Winston put some numbers behind his comments, noting that 40 per cent of those who undergo vaginal reconstruction surgery experience complications as a result with many needing further surgery, and that 23 per cent of people who have their breasts removed "feel uncomfortable with what they've done".' [Rudgard 2017]

Research into the negative medical, psychological and social aspects of transgenderism is unwelcome, to put it mildly. The work of James Caspian at Bath Spa University was rejected by his university's ethics committee on the grounds that it might induce criticism of the research on social media, and criticism of the research would be criticism of the university, and that, on the whole, 'it's better not to offend people'. Ethics committees in universities, set up to ensure we wouldn't have Nazi-like experimentation on human subjects, are now assuming the roles of guardians of the 'liberal' faith. Now, even research involving statistics about people can come under scrutiny and interdiction if it leads to conclusions that are not in tune with the *zeitgeist*. No harm can be permitted, not just physical harm or psychological harm to particular individual subjects, but harm to the topic under discussion, to the researcher, to the researcher's institution, and especially to any vocal identity group that might possibly be offended.

When it comes to children, care should be taken before undertaking any form of irreversible chemical or surgical intervention for what we have seen may well turn out to be a transient experience. [see Kirkup 2020] It is easy for parents, concerned about their children's welfare, to have their capacity for impartial judgement affected by the emotional impact of that concern. We can see this in a touching piece by one such parent, Molly Mulready. Ms Mulready writes, 'My son was my daughter until last year, when, after years of hints here and there, and months of him being uncharacteristically tearful and reclusive, he told us he was a boy.' She was cautious at first, advising her daughter, sensibly, as follows: 'Let's not tell anyone at school just yet. You're only 12. I promise I believe that you believe you're a boy right now, but what if you tell your friends and then realise you've made a mistake?' But then she goes on to say, 'What I didn't know then is that people don't just change their minds about this. I've researched and researched and found nothing but evidence confirming that once a person, young or old, comes out, explains their gender isn't all it seems, that's that.' [Mulready 2018] Intending no disrespect to Ms Mulready, it would seem that she hasn't done enough research. That is *not* quite that. People *do* change their minds about it, especially, but not only, the young, and the difficulties of those who attempt to reverse their chemical or surgical alterations is both painful to experience and painful to read about. [see Davies 2014]

Until very recently, the UK's National Health Service (NHS) used to have on its website the following information about puberty suppression. 'If your child has gender dysphoria and they've reached puberty, they could be treated with gonado-trophin-releasing hormone (GnRH) analogues. These are synthetic (man-made) hormones that suppress the hormones naturally produced by the body .... They also suppress puberty and can help delay potentially distressing physical changes caused by their body becoming even more like that of their biological sex, until they're old enough for the treatment options discussed below.' The site then went on to say, 'The effects of treatment with GnRH analogues *are considered to be fully reversible, so treatment can usually be stopped at any time* after a discussion between you, your child and your MDT.' [emphasis added.] That was then, this is now, and now, the information on the page reads:

> Some young people with lasting signs of gender dysphoria and who meet strict criteria may be referred to a hormone specialist (consultant endocrinologist) to see if they can take hormone blockers as they reach puberty. This is in addition to psychological support. These hormone blockers (gonadotrophin-releasing hormone analogues) pause the physical changes of puberty, such as breast development or facial hair. *Little*

*is known about the long-term side effects of hormone or puberty blockers in children with gender dysphoria.* Although the Gender Identity Development Service (GIDS) advises this is a physically reversible treatment if stopped, it is not known what the psychological effects may be. *It's also not known whether hormone blockers affect the development of the teenage brain or children's bones. Side effects may also include hot flushes, fatigue and mood alterations.* From the age of 16, teenagers who've been on hormone blockers for at least 12 months may be given cross-sex hormones, also known as gender-affirming hormones. These hormones *cause some irreversible changes,* such as: *breast development (caused by taking oestrogen) *breaking or deepening of the voice (caused by taking testosterone). *Long-term cross-sex hormone treatment may cause temporary or even permanent infertility.* However, as cross-sex hormones affect people differently, they should not be considered a reliable form of contraception. *There is some uncertainty about the risks of long-term cross-sex hormone treatment. The NHS in England is currently reviewing the evidence on the use of cross-sex hormones by the Gender Identity Development Service.* [see NHS (no date); emphasis added]

Celia Walden, writing in the *Telegraph*, comments satirically, 'On Saturday, new health guidance appeared that pointed out another mistake that we, in all our infinite and superior wisdom, had made—though, of course, without acknowledging it as such. After years of regressive, "hate-filled" voices—mine included—pointed out the dangers of the NHS offering children as young as 11 hormone-blocking drugs and "fast-tracking" young people into changing gender, our health service has quietly done a U-turn. It turns out that the treatments used by NHS gender clinics to halt the puberty of supposedly transgender children "could have long-term consequences for youngsters' brains, bones and mental health". They are not, as parents were assured, either 100% "safe" or "fully reversible." What's that? I didn't quite catch it. Oh: we were wrong.' [Walden 2020]

Sex reassignment, then, is not the holy grail when it comes to dealing with the problem of gender dysphoria. Many of those who have had such interventions still have what would be seen as mental health problems, especially a propensity to attempt suicide. In the rush to be compassionate towards people who experience gender dysphoria, it is sometimes overlooked that there are psychological indicators that suggest that all is not well with such individuals on other fronts. It can hardly be doubted that those who seek to solve their personal problems by changing their sex have a problem or problems that they are trying to resolve—that much is evident—but these may not be problems that can be solved by transitioning. One study showed that just over half of teenagers with gender dysphoria also appeared to have other serious mental health problems, and three quarters of those who manifest gender dysphoria may have other psychiatric problems. As indicated in the NHS's revised statement on the use of hormones in puberty suppression, the hormones can have serious physical and psychological effects.

*Transgender Issues* 69

Some of those who have transitioned have regretted their decision and sought to reverse it, but transitioning, difficult as it may have been, is more easily done than undone. A survey of over two hundred people who de-transitioned showed that many of them had other mental disorders that were left untreated. Ten to fifteen years after surgical reassignment, the suicide rate of those who had undergone sex-reassignment surgery rose to twenty times that of comparable peers. Even among those who don't regret transitioning, many do not appear to have benefitted psychologically from their change. [see Barber 2018]

Jamie Shupe was born in 1963 and grew up in Maryland. He served in the US military for 18 years and retired in 2000. After he retired, Shupe changed his sex to female in 2013 and persuaded the Army to change his military records to reflect his new name and gender. However, in 2016 Shupe rejected his female identity. In June of that year, Judge Amy Holmes Hehn of Multnomah County issued a court order changing his sex/gender from female to non-binary, and in November, he was issued a birth certificate in Washington D.C. with his sex noted as X—indeterminate. [see Mele 2016]

But the story doesn't end there. In January 2019, Shupe announced that he no longer identified as non-binary and now (re)identified as male, claiming that he had been experiencing symptoms of psychosis when he sought a non-binary sex marker. He said he had embraced the lie of transgender identity as a crutch while struggling with deep psychological issues that would better have been addressed by therapy. 'I ended up in the psych ward three times because of hormones. I had blood clots in my eyes because my estrogen levels were 2,585 instead of 200, low bone density, problems controlling my bladder, and emotional instability,' Shupe said. 'Blood tests indicated I was dropping into kidney disease territory (EFGR below 60) for about 18 months, I had chronic dermatology issues and skin reactions to estrogen patches, I passed out on the kitchen floor from Spironolactone.' [see O'Neill 2019] In December 2019, Shupe successfully petitioned the court that had originally ordered his 'non-binary' status to order that the sex on his birth certificate be changed, once again, this time to 'male.' 'The charade of not being male, the legal fiction, it's over,' he said. 'The lies behind my fictitious sex changes, something I shamefully participated in, first to female, and then to non-binary, have been forever exposed. A truthful accounting of events has replaced the deceit that allowed me to become America's first legally non-binary person .... It's an incredibly painful thing to walk back a landmark court decision that made you internationally famous and admit the whole thing was based on lies and deceit.' [see Trinko 2019]

Shupe, of course, is not the only person to have de-transitioned. The founder of the Detransition Advocacy Network [find it at https://www.detransadv.com] is

70          *Hidden Agender*

Charlie Evans, a woman who, having transitioned socially by changing her name, her passport and driving licence to live as a man, refused to go through with the sex re-assignment procedure. Evans was motivated to set up the network after being approached by a girl who told her she had detransitioned and was now shunned by the LGBT community as a traitor. [see Mainwaring 2019; see also Dolgin 2020, and Walsh 2019] Some of those whom Evans is in touch with are people in their late teens and early twenties who have had full gender reassignment surgery that they now wish they hadn't had, as the dysphoria that prompted their decision to transition hasn't been relieved by the surgery.

The doyen/doyenne of de-transitioners has to be Walt Heyer who, like Evans, started a website, this one called Sex Change Regret [find it at https://sexchange regret.com] to support those, like himself, who regret ever having transitioned. The long-term social, medical and psychological consequences of transgender therapy, whether that therapy is social, hormonal or surgical, are less than transparent. While some people who have transitioned seem to be happy with their changed state, many are not. In some cases, this is because the problems that the transition was supposed to solve persist through and beyond the process, not to mention the pain and suffering involved in surgery, and the physical and psychological effects of the hormones required to attain the desired physical characteristics and to prevent reversion to one's natural kind.

The current orthodoxy is to recommend that would-be transitioners must be supported in their decision to transition, otherwise, dire consequences, perhaps even suicide, will result. However, the suicide rate among those who have transitioned doesn't give much comfort to that argument. Some estimates put the rate of suicide attempts among transitioners as high as 41%, compared to that of the general population, which is under 2%. Attempting to become something that one can't really be is just as likely to increase one's difficulties rather than to resolve them, resulting, in some cases, in chronic depression; and the link between depression and suicide is not mysterious.

One transitioner, Thain Parnell, entitles her piece 'Transition is no casual matter, and we need to talk about those who regret it.' [Parnell 2017] Here is her account of her experience:

> Born biologically female, I always had trouble reconciling my gender with my personal identity and expression. Put simply, I was never comfortable with society's expectations of what a woman should be. I was loud, opinionated, undomesticated, a gamer, a nerd, and what might be called a tomboy—much more comfortable in jeans and a t-shirt than in a dress or skirt. I always felt constrained and limited by the gender that had been imposed on me at birth. And then there was the fact I liked girls .... in October 2013, after spending a year researching the process of transition, I decided

to "come out" to my partner, friends, and family .... I spent the next two years living and presenting as male before deciding to take the next dramatic step—hormone therapy. Once I started hormone therapy, changes happened quickly. I got much more muscular as my body fat started to redistribute. My jaw became stronger, squarer, and more defined, and body hair sprouted everywhere. After six months, my voice broke. I was high on becoming the man I thought I was.

But then, the realisation began to dawn on Parnell that all that she had gone through to get what she wanted was not necessarily going to produce the desired results.

But I still didn't feel authentically "me." I felt as if, somehow, I was giving up a part of myself. Late at night I would cry into my pillow for the wounded female me I had rejected. I also don't *feel* like a woman *or* a man—at least not based on current social understandings of those categories. In a perfect world, people like me would just be accepted for who we are—females who behave or appear "masculine." .... I know it's not possible to change my sex—I will always be female, biologically. I'm no longer ashamed—only sad—that society won't accept me for who I am.

Parnell's experience shows a curious thing about the transgender doctrine, which is that it makes it impossible for a girl to like to do typically boy things unless she is prepared to *be* a boy, and for a boy to do typically girl things unless he's prepared to *be* a girl. In short, transgender doctrine reinforces sex stereotypes! Those who reject the transgenderist doctrine are, oddly, much more open to loose, so-called transgressive, gender boundaries than transgender proponents. A girl who likes football and climbing trees? Put her on male hormones, she must be a boy! As if you can't be female unless you enjoy 'stereotypical' female things. A boy who likes clothes and fashion and ballet. Hormones for him until he becomes in fact the girl he so obviously already is. [I owe this point to my colleague Tim Crowley] Despite its intrinsic implausibility, and its socially regressive implications, it is still the case, as Joanna Williams notes, that 'transgender activists continue to promote the idea that people are born with a gender; or, in other words, that humans emerge into the world with a fully formed male soul or female essence—or even a non-binary, genderless essence—that is located within our bodies or our brains. According to this way of thinking, gender is an innate sense we have of ourselves that is entirely independent of both anatomy and social expectation.' [Williams 2020, 12]

I expect that, in the fullness of time, a slew of malpractice suits are likely to be taken against those who have facilitated transitioning. What cannot be stopped, it seems, by common sense, may well be stopped by the prospect of attracting monetary penalties for malpractice. Cometh the hour, cometh the woman!

72 *Hidden Agender*

According to a BBC report, Keira Bell, a 23-year old woman, is taking an action against an NHS gender clinic (the Tavistock) on the grounds that her decision to transition at the age of sixteen should have been more robustly challenged by the Clinic's medical staff. 'I should have been challenged on the proposals or the claims that I was making for myself,' she said. 'And I think that would have made a big difference.' [Holt 2020] When she was twenty, she had her breasts removed. 'Initially,' she said, 'I felt very relieved and happy about things, but I think as the years go on, you start to feel less and less enthusiastic or even happy about things.' She now accepts that she is female but is angry about what happened to her. Jane Robbins notes, 'The lucky ones are those who got out before surgery or other irreversible treatment. As for the others, perhaps the legal system will eventually provide recompense via malpractice suits. Just as liability dissuaded psychotherapists from pushing the "recovered memory" theory with troubled patients, the prospect of substantial payout to GAT victims may cause practitioners to think twice.' [Robbins 2019]

**Conversion therapy**
Gender Recognition Acts are not the only legislative manifestation of transgender ideology. We are now witnessing attempts by legislators sympathetic to transgender ideology to ban what they like to call 'conversion therapies', that is, treatments aimed at the psychological reconciliation of an individual's sex and gender, while, at the same time, they explicitly deny that medico-surgical attempts to reconcile sex and gender are themselves forms of conversion therapy, conversion therapies that are significantly more radical and interventionist than any psychological treatment! In the UK, it has been reported that psychotherapists are 'avoiding challenging children who want to be transgender because they fear being accused of conversion therapy by the NHS.' [Lyons 2020] The staff of the Tavistock and other clinics, were they now to adopt a policy of robustly challenging the claims of those like Keira Bell, might now open themselves to charges of endorsing conversion therapy. [see Kirkup 2020a; Pang et al. 2020]

An older definition of conversion therapy, focused on sexual orientation, was expanded by the NHS in a 2017 memorandum to include gender identity. The result of this change, a culture of non-questioning clinical affirmation of transgender identity, is hardly surprising. One long-serving psychotherapist who doesn't reject medical transitioning received written threats to report him to the governing body of his profession unless he publicly endorsed the new memorandum. He said, 'it concerns me that you can't get a tattoo before 18 even with your parents' permission but you can get puberty blockers.' [Lyons 2020] The adoption of such definitions prohibit psychologists, psychiatrists and psychotherapists from attempting to deal with gender dysphoria by psychological means while permitting its treatment by hormonal or surgical methods. One might be forgiven for wondering why, if psychological conversion procedures are considered so dreadful that they require criminalisation, that hormonal and surgical conversion procedures are considered to be just fine.

The US's Equality Act (2019) mentioned above (and discussed in more detail below) describes what it refers to as the 'discredited practice known as "conversion therapy"' as a 'form of discrimination that harms LGBTQ people by undermining individuals [*sic*] sense of self worth, increasing suicide ideation and substance abuse, exacerbating family conflict, and contributing to second class status.' [2.a 7] Whatever else it may or may not be, it seems a bit of a stretch to describe conversion therapy as a form of discrimination, unless, of course, the term *discrimination* is a non-specific term of abuse.

The Irish Prohibition of Conversion Therapies Bill 2018 seeks to 'prohibit conversion therapy, as a deceptive and harmful act or practice against a person's sexual orientation, gender identity and, or gender expression.' For the purposes of the proposed Act, conversion therapy means 'any practice or treatment by any person that seeks to change, suppress and, or eliminate a person's sexual orientation, gender identity and, or gender expression.' [House of the Oireachtas, s. 1(a); s. 1(b)i] The concept of conversion therapy and the idea that it is necessarily ineffective and demeaning originates in the context of homosexuality, and is used to describe therapies that claim (wrongly, in the eyes of those who disapprove of them) to be able to change a person's sexual orientation from same-sex to other-sex. The definition of conversion therapy, from the transgender charity Stonewall is, 'Conversion therapy ... refers to any form of treatment or psychotherapy which aims to change a person's sexual orientation *or to suppress a person's gender identity.*' [emphasis added]

Whatever the merits or demerits of such therapies in the context of homosexuality, the Irish Prohibition of Conversion Therapies Bill and the US Equality Act extend the idea of the unsuitability of conversion therapy from its original context to that of transgenderism. Attempts to change a person's gender identity is regarded as being as futile and as demeaning as efforts to change a person's sexual orientation. But why should it be ethically (and legally) problematic to attempt to change a person's gender identity? Because, as Dr Louise Theodosiou of the Royal College of Psychiatrists tells us, 'Your sexuality and your gender ID are inherent and there's no evidence base and no therapeutic treatment to change what is simply part of someone's nature.' And here we are, once again, at the great gender divide—the idea that gender is psychosocial, changeable, fluid is trumped by the idea of gender as fundamental, given and immutable.

Let's put all this together. Helping someone who is experiencing gender dysphoria by getting them to adapt their psychological condition to their biological reality is to be prohibited and punished; but helping someone who is experiencing gender dysphoria by adapting their biological condition surgically and hormonally to their psychological experience is just fine. Attempting to treat a person's gender dysphoria psychologically is conversion therapy, but treating a person's gender dysphoria surgically or hormonally is not. In case one might be so crass as to think that medical and surgical interventions are themselves forms of conversion therapy, the Irish Bill hastens to reassure us, telling us that gender identity 'refers to each person's internal and individual experience of gender, which may or may not correspond with the sex assigned at birth, including the personal sense of the body (which may involve, if freely chosen, modification of bodily appearance and, or function by *medical, surgical or other means*) ...' [Houses of the Oireachtas 2018, s. 1 (b) ii. Emphasis added] To the simple-minded observer, it would seem that *both* forms of treatment for gender dysphoria—bringing one's gender identity into alignment with one's biological sex or bringing one's biological sex into alignment with one's gender identity—are forms of conversion therapy. One attempts to change the psychology of a gender dysphoria sufferer to match his biology; the other attempts to change a gender dysphoria sufferer's biology to match his psychology. Yet one of these treatments is deemed to be futile and unethical and, in some cases, is to be made illegal, while the other form of treatment receives the medical, ethical and legal green light.

In the UK, the Government Equalities Office issued a LGBT Action Plan that was signed off by Penny Mordaunt, the Minister for Women and Equalities. [see Government Equalities Office 2018] Describing conversion therapy as an 'abhorrent practice', the Action Plan tells us that the Equalities Offices will bring forward proposals to end this practice in the UK. 'These activities are wrong, and we are not willing to let them continue,' say the authors of the Action Plan. Under the leadership of the Government Equalities Office, 'we will fully consider all legislative and non-legislative options to prohibit promoting, offering or conducting conversion therapy. Our intent is to protect people who are vulnerable to harm or violence, whether that occurs in a medical, commercial or faith-based context.' [4: 15] The 30-page plan promises to improve police response to LGBT hate incidents, remove deep-seated prejudices in our communities, appoint a National Adviser to lead improvements to LGBT healthcare, tackle homophobic, biphobic and transphobic bullying in schools, support local pride events across the UK, support countries that want help to repeal laws discriminating against LGBT people, give more support to LGBT students and teachers, and to improve gender identity services for transgender adults. It's good to know that the

*Transgender Issues*

Government has its priorities straight. Why should the police bother themselves about such mundane and unexciting crimes like burglary when they can focus on LGBT hate incidents and, indeed, hate incidents of every kind. Read this delightful and exhilarating document for yourself and, if you are a UK citizen, rejoice to see how £4.5 million of your money is to be spent. [see Government Equalities Office 2018]

But what exactly is the problem with conversion therapies? Are people being physically coerced into undergoing such therapies, dragged unwillingly into conversion clinics and forcibly treated? If not, what's the problem? We have all kinds of alternative therapies available to us; if people want to offer these therapies and others want to avail of them, then so be it. We are told by those who disapprove of them that conversion therapies are not only abhorrent but also harmful. Indeed? Harmful in the way that reconstructive surgery and puberty blockers and hormonal interventions are harmful?

# 3. Transgenderism in Practice

*For they have sown the wind, and they shall reap the whirlwind*
—Hosea

*Dieu pardonne toujours, l'homme parfois,*
*la nature—jamais!*
—Anon

Let's step back for a moment from the theoretical issues of sex, gender and gender dysphoria to take a look at some ways in which transgender ideology plays out in practice. There are many areas from which I might have chosen but, to keep the presentation within reasonable bounds, I have selected just four: feminism, education, sport and medical services.

## Feminism
TERF wars have erupted over who is and who isn't a woman. And no, TERF is not a misspelling of TURF. TERF stands for *trans-exclusionary radical feminist*. It is a term of abuse used by transgender activists and directed against feminists, even such iconic feminists as Germaine Greer, who think that men can't become women simply by declaring themselves to be women, or even by the generous application of hormones or reconstructive surgery. According to Greer, 'The insistence that man-made women be accepted as women is the institutional expression of the mistaken conviction that women are defective males.' [see YouTube 2015; also Hodges & Jalsevac 2015] For saying this, Greer has been accused of transphobia. No one, not even the greatest and the best, is allowed to make the outrageous claim that men are not women and women are not men, or, indeed, any remark that might seem to be ever-so-slightly sceptical of trans-related claims, unless they are prepared to attract heavy, and often quite vicious, criticism.

J. K. Rowling, the author of the phenomenally successful *Harry Potter* series of books, was, it seems, a little miffed by reading a headline that talked about creating a more equal post Covid-19 world for people who menstruate. 'People who menstruate,' she mused. 'I'm sure there used to be a word for those people ... Wumben? Wimpund? Woomus?' [Swerling 2020a; but see Lamnisos] Rowling was immediately accused of—yes, you've guessed it—transphobia, and informed by some not-so-kindly souls, speaking *de haut en bas*, that trans men who haven't transitioned can menstruate, as can non-binary people. Rowling should be grateful to have her astonishing biological ignorance so unkindly remedied but, in a comment made after her original tweet, it would seem that the wizarding author remains intransigent (pun intended) and is resisting the attack of her very own dementors, saying, 'If sex isn't real, there's no same-sex attraction. If sex isn't real, the lived reality of women globally is erased .... It isn't hate to speak the truth.' [Swerling 2020a]

In the days that followed Rowling's fall from grace, a veritable avalanche of commentary, some supportive, some dismissive, descended upon her. [see, for example, Ditum 2020, Moore 2020, Singh et al. 2020, Stanford 2020, and Thomas 2020. See also Hay 2020] A writer in the *Telegraph*, a newspaper that would normally be considered sympathetic to conservative opinion, described Rowling's views on transgenderism as 'strident', a word that, according to the *Oxford English Dictionary*, means 'loud, harsh and shrill'. [see Goldsbrough 2020] A digital advertisement in Edinburgh's main railway station that proclaimed, 'I ❤ JK Rowling' was removed by Network Rail on the grounds that it was likely to cause offence. [Daisley 2020] The president of Robert F. Kennedy Human Rights, an organisation that presented Rowling with the Ripple of Hope Award in December 2019, said in August 2020 that she was dismayed by what she termed Rowling's deeply troubling transphobic tweets and statements, which, according to Kennedy, had the effect of degrading the lived experiences of trans people. In her statement, Kerry Kennedy went on to say, referencing Anne Fausto-Sterling, 'The science is clear and conclusive: Sex is not binary'. [Kennedy 2020; see Flood 2020] In what would appear to be an idiosyncratic effort at literary intimidation, some authors who shared the agency that handles Rowling's literary affairs, the Blair Partnership, left the agency in dudgeon, some of them accusing it of 'declining to issue a public statement of support for transgender rights.' [Waterson 2020] Three of the authors who left issued a joint statement in which they declared, sanctimoniously, 'Freedom of speech can only be upheld if the structural inequalities that hinder equal opportunities for underrepresented groups are challenged and changed.' [Waterson 2020] A weighty pronouncement, no doubt, if (a) we only knew what it meant, (b) if it were true, and (c) if it had any relevance to Rowling's tweets. I suspect that what it means is that the authors believe that freedom of speech is conditional and should be available only to those who hold approved views, but I may be wrong in being so cynical. To their eternal credit, the Blair Partnership

## Transgenderism in Practice

79

responded to this contemptible attempt at intimidation by declining to sign a statement of PC-faith, saying, 'it could not compromise on the "fundamental freedom" of allowing authors the right to express their thoughts and beliefs,' and that 'it was not willing to have staff "re-educated" to meet the demands of a small group of clients.' [Waterson 2020; see also Singh 2020a]

Rowling is just one of a number of people who have incurred the wrath of the trans activist establishment. It was reported in June 2020 that Graham Linehan, whose TV credits include *Fr Ted*, *The IT Crowd* and *Black Books*, had been permanently suspended from Twitter for allegedly breaching the site's rules on banned words. Linehan was, it seems, accused by Twitter of repeatedly violating their rules against hateful conduct and 'platform manipulation', having tweeted 'men aren't women tho' in reply to a post from the Women's Institute wishing their transgender members a happy Pride. [see Blackall 2020; see also Hayton 2020] This is not the first time that Linehan has been in such trouble. In 2018, he was given a verbal warning by the police, following a complaint by a transgender activist who reported him for transphobia. The complainant, Stephanie Hayden, has a record of complaining, having previously described the University of Sussex as 'a temple of transgender hate' and campaigned to have a billboard company in Liverpool remove a poster that said the definition of 'woman' was an adult female, on the grounds that this was offensive. [see Halliday 2018]

From the famous and the relatively famous to the not-at-all famous. In late 2017, the teenager Lily (formerly Liam) Madigan, was elected as the women's officer for a Labour Party branch in Kent. His/her election caused a bit of a kerfuffle. Anne Ruzylo, a lesbian feminist Labour Party women's officer in a different constituency, who wasn't, to put it mildly, enthusiastic about this development and made her opinion known, was accused of transphobia by Madigan, and although Madigan's complaint was not upheld, Ruzylo stood down from her position. The executive committee of Ruzylo's branch resigned in protest at the treatment Ruzylo received. Whether or not it makes sense to have a position such as 'women's officer' in a political party is moot but, if there is to be such a role, and if one thinks that its operational effectiveness requires one to have had the lived experiences of being a woman, it doesn't seem unreasonable to insist that it be filled by someone who actually *is* a woman. What we can see in this affair is that there is no one, not even those with the most impeccable woke credentials, who cannot be trumped by someone who ticks a higher-ranking identity box. As a woman, a feminist and a lesbian, Ruzylo ticks three identity boxes; Madigan ticks just one identity box, transgender, but it outranks all of Ruzylo's. Writing in *Spiked*, Ella Whelan probably speaks for quite a few women and not a few men when she says, 'I don't care if I get called a transphobe: Lily Madigan is not a woman.

80            *Hidden Agender*

At 19, he is barely even a man. Of course, Liam should be perfectly free to call himself Lily and wear whatever the hell he wants. Most polite people who come to know him will probably agree to refer to him by his new name and by female pronouns. But should society at large, and political and social institutions, have to do likewise, and even grant people like Madigan access to what have traditionally been women's public roles?' [Whelan 2017] If feminists protest that trans women are men who are now telling feminists what they may not say or think, then they incur the dreaded censure of being called—transphobic. Part of me can't help feeling a *soupçon* of *schadenfreude* (a feeling immediately suppressed) as the wind sowed by radical feminists by their strategic adoption of the notion of gender to further their own ends returns as the whirlwind of transgenderism to blow them away. [see Jeffreys 2014, passim]

But what is sauce for the goose is, apparently, *not* sauce for the gander, or maybe it's the other way around—it's so easy to get confused! In 2018, David Lewis put himself forward as a candidate for a position in his Constituency Labour Party Branch in Basinstoke, UK. Nothing unusual or newsworthy in that, you might think, except that Lewis is a man and the position he applied for is that of Women's Officer, and in order to be eligible for consideration, candidates have to 'self-identify' as women. So far, so like Lily Madigan. So that's just what our David did, claiming, tongue firmly in cheek, that he self-identifies as a woman on Wednesdays between 6.50 a.m. and midnight. And why not, say all of us? Why should one's identity be limited by anything as flimsy as temporal considerations? The Labour Party has officially ruled that people who self-identify as women are allowed to be added to all-women's shortlists and to stand as women's officers. These roles are open to men who now identify as women and no medical certification is required to attest to this transition. According to Labour Party Policy, 'All Women Shortlists are open to all women, including self-identifying trans women. Similarly, women's officers and minimum quotas for women in the Labour Party are open to all women, including self-identifying trans women.' Mr Lewis said his application for the post was intended to highlight problems with self-identification, specifically to demonstrate what happens 'when you say that someone's gender depends only on what they say and nothing else'. Despite their avowedly liberal and progressive transgender policy, the Labour Party, channelling Queen Victoria, was not amused by Mr Lewis's application, and his membership of the Party was suspended.

And then, there is Julia Beck, a lesbian, who was booted out of the LGBTQ Commission in Baltimore, Maryland for the violence she had perpetrated. What awful act had she committed? Did she punch the Committee Chairman in the face? Haul off with a baseball bat on the unsuspecting heads of her fellow committee members? Alas, what she did was far more terrible if considerably less dramatic. It seems that she refused to use female pronouns for a jailed male rapist who continued to rape female prisoners in the women's prison to which he had been sent. She was forced off the commission by its chairman, a man who presents as a woman and considers himself a lesbian. Joan Robbins writes,

> Feminists are beginning to recognize the threat of transgenderism not only to fair competition in athletics but to women as a whole .... If a male is allowed to join the female sex simply by declaring he feels like a woman, is there really such a thing as women? Is there any basis for protecting women in private spaces (such as restrooms and locker rooms), colleges, dormitories, even prisons? Is there any way to ensure that programs designed to help women, such as dedicated loans or set-asides in government contracting, are restricted to actual women? Transgender radicals are so concerned about the resistance from feminists, especially lesbians, that they have created their own slur to describe the leftist dissidents: Trans-Exclusionary Radical Feminists, or TERFS. The name-calling, however, has not deterred these feminists, who realise that enshrining legal rights based on gender identity rather than sex "would eliminate women and girls as a coherent legal category, worthy of civil rights protection." [Robbins 2019]

The word *war* in 'TERF wars' is not entirely metaphorical. A confrontation between transgender activists and radical feminists took place at a meeting at Speakers' Corner in Hyde Park in October 2017. A woman who was filming what was termed a 'gender recognition talk', called to support proposed changes to the Gender Recognition Act, had her camera taken from her, was knocked to the ground and then was punched and kicked. Maria MacLachlan, aged 61, a gender critical feminist, had been struck by 26-year-old Tara Wolf. Second-wave feminists have been less than happy at the proposal to eviscerate the concept of woman, pointing out the dangers of allowing anyone to define their gender on a whim. If men can decide to be women simply by filling out a form, they would thereby be entitled to have access to women's changing rooms, women's sporting competitions, women's refuges and the like. Tara Wolf is not only considerably younger than the woman she assaulted but is also, despite the name, not of the same sex! The judge in the case suggested that Ms MacLachlan might refer to the defendant as 'she' while giving evidence. Ms MacLachlan replied to this suggestion, not unreasonably, 'I'm used to thinking of this person who is a male as male.' Wolf was convicted and fined £150. I never thought that I would feel sorry for radical feminists, but the spectacle of an elderly woman being beaten up by a man masquerading as a woman has managed to squeeze an ounce of sympathy from my hard heart. [see Humphery 2020]

82 *Hidden Agender*

A particularly charming battle in the TERF wars took place in 2018 at the San Francisco Library. [see Vigo 2018a] The Library sponsored a show entitled 'Degenderettes Antifa Art' and in so doing, according to the report, it 'allowed a group of misogynist males to take over public space in order to promote violence against women as an art form. To some radical trans activists, "TERFs"— a slur for females who critique gender ideology—deserve to be murdered for denying that someone with a man's body can really be a woman.' [Vigo 2018a] It appears that the Library exhibit included shirts with the slogan, 'Your apathy is killing us' and 'I punch TERFs.' Weapons were displayed throughout the exhibit, 'including a large cardboard sculpture of a skeleton with phallus holding an axe, six brightly-colored baseball bats, and a series of weapons labelled a "femme sledgehammer" and "trans labrys (axe)".' Vigo concludes her piece by writing, 'The Degenderettes invert power relations by allowing men claiming to be women to craft an identity based on fictional oppression by feminists. In reality, their gender politics is merely misogyny in drag. It's a twist on the older paradigm of sexist males telling women to get in "their place." Today, men on the left are instructing women that they "are on the wrong side of history." Trans activists even go so far as accusing lesbians of discriminating and creating a "cotton ceiling" if they refuse to have sex with biological males who identify as women.' [Vigo 2018a]

Dame Jenni Murray is one of those awful TERF people who, it seems, are intent on oppressing poor innocent trans people. What was her crime? Dame Jenni, who is the presenter of BBC Radio 4's *Woman's Hour*, wrote in the *Times* that a sex change can't make a man into a real woman. [Murray 2017] The BBC reprimanded her, telling her she should remain impartial on the subject, since impartiality, apparently, requires one to deny reality. [see York 2017] Rachel Cohen, the executive director of Stonewall, a transgender charity, questioned Murray's right to question other people's identities, and said that Murray's comment had been 'reductive' and 'hurtful'. Cohen said, somewhat gnomically, 'Whether you are trans or not, your identity is yours alone. I do not question your identity Jenni, and in return, I wouldn't expect you to question mine—or anyone else's. What right would you have to do so?' I'm not quite sure what questioning someone's identity is, but let us press on. Cohen again: 'Trans women have every right to have their identity and experiences respected too. They are women—just like you and me—and their sense of their gender is as ingrained in their identity as yours or mine.' Cohen's claim that trans women are women just like you and me is just a little bit question-begging. If trans women were women just like Murray and Cohen, there wouldn't *be* an issue. It's precisely because they are not women 'just like' Cohen and Murray that there is an issue to be resolved. Moreover, Cohen's notion of gender identity as something that is 'ingrained' would seem to

*Transgenderism in Practice* 83

make gender not something ephemeral, not something socially constructed, but something essential to the person, something a bit like, well, like one's sex, actually. I believe that Dame Jenni got things right but for the wrong reason. She appears to think that the reason a sex change can't make a man into a real woman is simply that men grow up with masculine privileges and so can't have the experiences of real women. That would make being a man or a woman a matter of contingent experience, which, of course, is nonsense. No, Dame Jenni, the reason men can't be women (or women, men) has nothing to do with privilege (whatever that may be) and everything to do with biology. [see Murray 2020a; on the feminist fantasy of male privilege, see Casey 2019, 62-72]

As one might expect, not all feminists are TERFs. In the dim and distant past of 2012, Roz Kaveney, writing in the *Guardian*, took her feminist sisters to task for what she regarded as their 'anti-intellectualism, emphasis on innate knowledge, fetishisation of tiny ideological differences, heresy hunting, conspiracy theories, rhetorical use of images of disgust, talk of stabs in the back and romantic apocalypticism', all of which, she thinks (with some justice if true) amounts to something less than feminism and more of a cult. [Kaveney 2012] I couldn't have put it better myself, Ms Kaveney. Despite her scolding of her sisters, however, I suspect that Ms Kaveney doesn't dissent much if at all from the minutiae of radical feminist dogma. What gets up her nose is that her TERF friends aren't all that keen on having transgenderists invading their turf. They would prefer feminists to be either women who have suffered the slings and arrows of outrageous fortune in being born female and living through the trauma of repression by the patriarchy, or men who, for whatever reason, believe (or pretend to believe) the usual radical feminist nonsense about patriarchal oppression. What they most assuredly *don't* want is men disguised as women jumping on their victimhood bandwagon. David Green tells us, just in case we didn't already suspect it, that 'Victimhood as a political status is best understood as the outcome of a political strategy by some groups aimed at gaining preferential treatment.' [Green 2006, 1]

More recently, Libby Purves was of the opinion that 'The sisterhood is crazy to bar its door to trans women'. Purves objects to the rejection by such as Murray of the claim that transgender women are real women. Purves objects, in my view correctly, to the arguments that transwomen, because they have had the privilege of being men, or because they haven't gone through the pain of puberty, PMT or menopause, they can't be women. She is absolutely right to reject the male privilege and non-persecution arguments as unfitting men to be women, but, she concludes wrongly, employing a delightful but surely inadvertent understatement, that 'the differences between genders are not extreme, or even absolute, except in reproductive feasibility.' [Purves 2017] Most people would not consider

84                          *Hidden Agender*

'reproductive feasibility' to be an insignificant difference between the sexes. The difference between genders is, well, who knows what? On the other hand, the difference between the sexes is precisely extreme and absolute, except in the very limited case of intersex individuals.

Zoe Williams is yet another non-TERF feminist. She believes that feminist solidarity empowers everyone and that the feminist movement must be trans-inclusive. According to Williams, 'Feminism ... takes the side of the oppressed. That is our raison d'etre.' [Williams 2020] Let's see how this argument might run: 'Feminism is a movement in support of the oppressed; Trans people are oppressed; therefore, Feminists should support trans people.' If we are to take this argument at face value, we might wonder why feminism is called feminism and not rather, say, anti-oppressionism. Willliams believes that the mainstream feminist view is, in fact, trans-inclusive and she concludes her piece, ringingly: 'Solidarity is boring to talk about, but fascinating and empowering to live. Solidarity is not exclusive or pedantic; it is compassionate and fights oppression where it finds it. That is its lifeblood. That is why trans women are women, or womxn.' All very compassionate and sensitive and all very much beside the point. After all, it seems perfectly possible, as Dame Jenni thinks it is, to support the rights of trans people to be trans, without having to accept the claim of some (not all) men who have transitioned that they are, in fact, fully and completely and really women.

The in-house argument between TERFs and non-TERFs lines up something like this. According to TERFs, to be a woman is necessarily to have experienced the oppression and prejudices that women experience. But if what prevents a trans woman from really being a woman is his lack of the requisite experience of oppression and prejudice, then, by parity of reasoning, a biological female who had not, in fact, experienced such oppression and prejudice wouldn't be a woman either. This argument has the charming property of poisoning the wells! We can see a version of this argument in the writing of Chimamanda Ngozi Adichie. Adichie, a Nigerian novelist and feminist, thinks that we cannot equate the experience of those who've lived as men, with all the privileges that she believes is accorded to them, 'with the experience of a woman who has lived from the beginning in the world as a woman, and who has not been accorded those privileges'. [Gbadamosi 2018] So, her argument appears to run: women are victims of oppression; you've been a man and thus not a victim of oppression; so you can't now consider yourself a woman because you haven't been oppressed as women have been. On the other side of the argument, someone like the transactivist Raquel Willis concedes that while Adhichie is correct in saying that women are oppressed, Adichie ignores the fact that women are privileged inasmuch as they have been accepted in their female gender since they were born, unlike trans-

*Transgenderism in Practice* 85

gender women, who have had to struggle against—you've guessed it—oppression to get to where *they* are! Much the same point was made by Diana Thomas in his/her series 'My transgender diary' in the *Telegraph*, when he/she writes, 'while women are underprivileged when compared with men, they have a huge privilege compared to transwomen. I'm not sure they understand, or acknowledge, that privilege, though the hurtful comments often presume it.' [Thomas 2020a] And now we witness a struggle to assert one's superior victimhood: your privilege is superior to mine; my oppression trumps your oppression. As Willis remarks, 'If you want to play the Oppression Olympics, sorry cis women, you're going to lose more often than not. That's why this conversation isn't productive. If that were the case many of your rich, white faves wouldn't be "real women" either.' [Willis 2017; for an amusing fictional example of the oppression/diversity Olympics, see *Modern Family*, S2E5]

On the centrality and importance of the experience of oppression as constituting what it is that one really is, the trans activists and their non-TERF feminist allies and the TERFs are all agreed, but in making this claim central to their arguments, they are sublimely missing the point. Are they seriously suggesting that the essence of what they are consists in their being victims? The TERF's denial that trans women are women should be based on the fairly obvious fact that, however they present themselves, whatever form of hormonal or surgical alterations they undergo, men cannot ever become women because it's simply not possible for that to happen. The TERF argument doesn't appear to be based, as it should be, on the impossibility of changing one's sex, but rather on the fact of what they perceive as sexual oppression, which, if it exists at all, is surely a contingent rather than a necessary phenomenon. Leaving to one side the intellectual lack of hygiene in using contingent experience as a necessary condition of ontological status, on a point of strategy alone, if TERFs want to play the victimhood game on the pitch of oppression, then, as Raquel Willis has indicated, they are inevitably going to lose out to the transgenderists whose home ground oppression is.

Some academics have come under attack for their non-subscription to the new normative environment. One of these is Professor Selina Todd of Oxford who specialises in the history of working-class women and feminism in modern Britain. [see Woods 2020] Professor Todd was no-platformed by an event she herself had helped to organise, and was accused of transphobia because of her involvement in women's rights advocacy and her teaching of feminist history. [see Turner 2020] Other female academics who have come under attack are Reading's Professor Rosa Freedman and Sussex University's Professor Kathleen Stock. [Turner 2019]

Whatever the sins of their academic superiors, it is reassuring and gratifying to know that the intellectual calibre of our students is as strong as it has ever been.

86            *Hidden Agender*

In a series of tweets in 2018, the LGBTQ group at Goldsmith College (London), wielding their weapons of mass instruction in up-to-the-minute-wokeness, said, 'The ideas of TERFs and anti-trans bigots literally *kill* and must be eradicated through re-education.' [see Freiburger 2019] Strong stuff! Rejecting the idea that men can become women and resisting the use by such transitioned or transitioning men of women's toilets and other female-only spaces *literally* kills, eh! Perhaps slightly hyperbolic, you might think? Maybe a tad hysterical? Just a wee bit over the top?

Not content to rest on their laurels, the LGBTQ group suggested that a certain Claire Graham should be sent to the gulag. What was Ms Graham's heinous offence? Counter-revolutionary terrorism? Stealing candy from little children? Womansplaining? No, she had written to object to the LGBTQ's threat to target feminist academics who, they claimed, were prejudiced against transgender individuals. Once again, perhaps just a little over the top, even if meant hyperbolically. But no! Our doughty LGBTQ warriors were anxious to reassure those astonished by the suggestion that Soviet Gulags were benign places whose involuntary residents received education and training and participated in sport and theatre, a kind of Butlin's in Siberia, as it were. So much fun were the residents of these Gulags having that, by conservative Soviet estimates, over a million of them died, probably from an over-enthusiastic weigh-loss programme rather than from deliberate starvation.

In a rare outbreak of sanity, the Goldsmith Students' Union suspended the LGBTQ group and withdrew its support for its activities. Commenting on this jaw-dropping piece of sheer stupidity in *First Things*, Carl R. Trueman wrote, 'what raises this silliness to the level of malevolent absurdity is that the students, after their proposal was criticized, attempted to justify it by claiming the gulags were compassionate educational institutions. The incident reveals catastrophic cultural and historical ignorance. This should not surprise. The humanities have been subject to ruthless politicization and concomitant trivialization over the years. I doubt those recommending the gulags have ever studied them. And I doubt they have taken the time to read Solzhenitsyn's novella, *One Day in the Life of Ivan Denisovich*, or his magisterial *Gulag Archipelago* trilogy. Why would they bother when their teachers have told them the history that portrays the gulags as morally significant has been constructed by white conservative males—men with a vested interest in rewriting history to disguise their own imperial atrocities?' [Trueman 2018]

Trueman goes on to argue that the historical (and literary) ignorance displayed by the refusal of the LGBTQ group to recant is not a mere piece of bloody-minded stupidity, but something that characterises the relationship between

## Transgenderism in Practice

sex and identity that lies at the heart of transgenderism. Transgenderism is, in part at least, a massive effort of self-induced ignorance that denies not just the biological reality of the would-be transgenderist but also his or her birth and his or her life-before-transition. In my own courses on political philosophy, I gradually realised that a hefty dose of history was a necessary prerequisite to any grounded consideration of more theoretical and abstract issues, if for no other reason than to demonstrate the falsity of what I call 'presentism', the view that the way things are is not just the way things are but the way they have to be. 'It is not surprising,' Trueman writes, 'that the transgender activists of Goldsmiths should prefer historical solecisms to Solzhenitsyn. History has only two functions for them: It is either an account of oppression to be overcome, or it is just another plastic body of evidence that can be twisted to fit any particular identity or policy which catches their fancy.' [Trueman 2019]

In 2018, the Quakers, that most pacific of all religious organisations, was accused of hosting a transphobic feminist meeting in Oxford organised by A Woman's Place UK (WPUK). Protesters from the LGBTQ Campaign of the Oxford Student's Union said, 'This event is predominantly about curtailing transgender people's rights, and invites exclusively cisgender people to speak on this ... This kind of trans-exclusionary feminism cannot be condoned.' [see Marshall 2018] The members of WPUK have been labelled as TERFs, and WPUK has been described by the protesters as a hate group. The University of Oxford Student Union said: 'We firmly oppose discrimination/harassment on the basis of gender identity. As such, we chose to co-sign statement (*sic*) to challenge groups, such as a Women's Place UK, and stand as a united community against hate speech.' [Marshall 2018]

Some women who attended a Women's March in Washington in early 2020 were asked, 'What is a woman?'. Their answers were revealing, revealing that is, of a deep-rooted intellectual confusion. '"A woman is anything that she wants to be defined as," said one. "A woman is someone who chooses to express themselves," said another. "That's a trick question," said still another. Two other women who *were selling uterus pins* told [the interviewer] that they don't think having a uterus is what makes a person a woman!' [see Stonestreet & Morris 2020] Other women, with perhaps a clearer understanding of what a woman is, hold the seemingly reactionary view that the self-declared gender laws that may eventually end up in force in the UK, as they have in other countries, will do nothing less than render the word 'woman' meaningless, with all that that implies for equality and freedom and, well, civilisation as we know it. How could they possibly think that! Some seem to think that you can't *become* a woman, because being a woman is a matter of biology. Others, as we have seen, argue that being a woman essentially involves the socialisation and experience that only those born to it can have. For these women, if the law dictates that a man can attain to womanhood simply by signing a few forms, the concept of womanhood becomes empty and women, as women, lose any standing in society.

All those who believe that men can't become women, whether for reasons of ontology or experience, agree that if being a woman becomes a matter of self-declaration, then all-women shortlists in politics could be infiltrated by transwomen (that is, by men who claim to be women). The same is true, of course, of women's sports. If we accept the idea that people can define their own gender/sex without external check or scrutiny, we are committed to accepting that the purely subjective and unverifiable supersedes the objectively biological nature of sex as a significant socio-legal category. All the fuss about gender representation, a favourite trope of feminists, requires that there can actually *be* a finite number of different and distinct genders, not an infinite number of them. If you can't clearly and definitively identify groups A and B, you cannot determine the relative proportions of As and Bs in the population. If you can slip back and forth between being a man or a woman simply by virtue of making a claim, then any possibility of equal representation becomes meaningless, even if it were otherwise desirable! If it becomes ever easier for men to become women, then mandatory quotas and all-women shortlists and the like could—and this is a feminist's nightmare—come to be colonised by 'former' men!

Dr Nicola Williams of the organisation Fair Play for Women is concerned that the ultra-rapid expansion of laws and social practices relating to transgender women is endangering what she regards as hard-won rights for women by compromising women-only spaces and women-only activities. If people want to live as though they were members of the opposite sex, she accepts their right to do so, but there is, she thinks, 'a fundamental conflict between the demands some trans lobby groups make and the rights of another vulnerable group—women and girls. What this amounts to is that 'if someone who still has their full male anatomy wants the right to enter women's changing rooms, or refuges, or to compete against women and girls in sports, and women have no choice about that, that takes away women's most fundamental right: the right to say no to male-bodied people entering our spaces.' She believes that the effects of changes in the law that would allow for self-identification have not been properly thought through and she calls for a rational discussion on these matters. As she explained, 'Data isn't "transphobic". Evidence isn't "hateful". Facts are just facts, and the plain fact is that the proposed policy of "self-identified sex" would have a huge impact on women and girls.' But she notes that those who call for such a discussion are being categorised as transphobic and their actions as hateful, and in some cases their efforts

*Transgenderism in Practice*                                   89

are met with threats and even with physical violence. Self-identification would, she believes, 'punch a huge hole in the hard-won system of women's legal rights that allow us to say no to male-bodied people being in our spaces. There would be no official way to tell who was male for purposes of single-sex overnight sleeping accommodation, for women's refuges, or for single-sex sports.' [Williams 2019a]

And so, the interesting-to-watch mudwrestle between the old guard feminists and the men in dresses carries on. But the trans chaps are not taking the resistance from the feminists lying down. Oh no! They know where their enemies live and, as someday it may happen that a victim must be found, they've got a little list. On that list is Labour Party stalwart Linda Bellos, self-described black, Jewish, lesbian, radical feminist and one-time leader of Lambeth Council, but now, it seems bizarrely, too right-wing for the Shiny New Labour Party! Bellos who, as a black, Jewish, lesbian, radical feminist, would surely seem to rank highly in the victimology charts on at least four counts, was disinvited from speaking at the University of Cambridge's Beard Society because she intended to ask some questions about the direction that gender politics is currently taking. The Beard society, which had invited her, told her in their disinvitation, without any evidence of blushing, that while they believed in freedom of expression, 'Peterhouse is as much a home as a college. The welfare of our students in this instance has to come first.' [see Heuchan 2017] It's not immediately clear how the welfare of Peterhouse's students would be adversely affected by Bellos's questions, though the nauseating cant of claiming to believe in freedom of expression while simultaneously disinviting a speaker is hard to take, even for a stomach as case-hardened as mine. Of course, Bellos is just following in the footsteps of Germaine Greer who encountered protests when she tried to speak at Cardiff University in 2015. She too was accused of transphobia. And on that list too is Emma Salmon, who is one of those who argued for proper all-women shortlists. She's had enough and she's not going to take it anymore. 'We've had serious, perpetual aggression,' she said. 'When we state our point of view we're told we are Nazis, no better than Hitler.' [see Liddle 2018] Should anyone who is not a card-carrying member of the SNLP (Shiny New Labour Party) care about the outcome of this domestic squabble between the transgender activists and the old-guard radical feminists? Probably not. Still, there is a certain sanguinary (if guilty) pleasure to be had from sitting in the Coliseum watching the professional victims of identity politics slaughtering each other in gladiatorial combat. But if I had to choose sides—and I don't—I would come down on the side of the women, the real women, that is.

The dispute between the TERFs and the transgender activists hinges on their take on the relationship between sex and gender. One feminist take on this topic is to hold that while sex may be biological and in some sense a given, gender is a matter of social construction. This is the perspective of second-wave feminism-lite. But there is an inner tension within feminism on this very point, however, for second-wave feminism-heavy, (following Beauvoir and Millett), and third-wave feminists, such as Judith Butler, have in fact provided the theoretical basis for what would become transgender theory. [see Yenor 2017] One way to think of the struggle between radical feminists and transgender activists for supreme victimhood status is to see it as a kind of family quarrel which, like many family quarrels, is characterised by a degree of nastiness not normally seen in afamilial human hostilities!

Second-wave feminism-heavy is precisely the source of the division between sex and gender appropriated for their own purposes by transgender activists. Simone de Beauvoir was one of the earliest of the second-wave feminists to separate sex from gender and to posit culture alone as determining the significance of sex and the female body. Kate Millet in her *Sexual Politics* (1970) took matters a stage further, advocating the end of male supremacy, the elimination of specific gender roles in child-rearing, women's complete financial independence from men, and the liberation of women from their children by the ingenious strategy of liberating children from their parents. Even more radically, Millett proposed an active embrace of what, up to then, had been sexually taboo, the complete removal of all sexual inhibitions. Millett made it possible for feminists to embrace queer theory, the view that how one expressed one's sexuality was, in the end, a matter of social construction, and so not fixed and determined, but fluid and changeable. The radical second- and third-wave feminists take on the subversion of sexual norms allowed queer theory to segue to transgenderism. 'Transgenderism is consistent with the philosophical premises of second-wave feminism (i.e. divorcing one's body from one's identity) ...' [Yenor 2017] Butler herself writes that transgender theorists are 'carrying on the legacy of Simone de Beauvoir: if one is not born a woman, but rather becomes one, then becoming is the vehicle for gender itself.' [Butler 2004, 65]

Some commentators, however, see a significant difference between the gender theories of second-wave and third-wave feminists. Joanna Williams remarks, 'Rather than sex preceding gender, Butler argues it is our social and cultural views on gender that construct sex .... Today, following Butler, sex has been rejected by many radical thinkers as an outdated concept that has no more basis in material reality than gender. As a result, the performance of gender floats freely from biology: both are considered equally arbitrary. Gender can now be conceived as fluid and multiple. People are not assumed to be born male or female but randomly assigned membership of a culturally prescribed sex category in an act of symbolic violence conducted at the moment of birth.' [Williams 2020, 6-7] It is not without

## Transgenderism in Practice

a certain sardonic humour that one notes that the transgender approach to gender, differing in direction as it does from some conservative feminist approaches to gender, nonetheless ultimately derives from the introduction and popularisation of gender as a strategic weapon of deconstruction by radical feminists. 'Efforts to separate transgender theories from radical feminism mistake their common roots,' writes Scott Yenor. 'Transgenderism pushed against the door that second-wave feminists opened: it extends the philosophical premises of second-wave feminism and fosters its political project. Efforts to roll back one roll back the other, while efforts to further one further the other.' [Yenor 2017]

Wherever the precise point that the radical theory of sex and gender is to be located in feminist theory, the transgender activists, latching on to the dogma of the more radical feminists on gender and running it for all that it is worth, hold that gender is a given and that sex is something constructed and ultimately unreal. How gender comes to hold this position for transgender activists is a bit of a mystery, and quite how gender can be what they take it to be without a subscription to gender stereotypes is also a little opaque. The trans narrative asserts that gender is biological and inherent and *not* a product of social circumstances, family, and culture. If a young boy dresses in a tutu, this implies that his body is actually female. Boys who like stereotypical girl's activities are now considered to be trans-girls. Girls who like climbing trees and construction are to be considered trans-boys. [see Ruse 2019] 'These trans activists,' writes Julian Vigo, have created a narrative that 'attempts to remove the specificity of female *biology* by claiming it is a "social construct" while asserting that *gender* is biological.' This last is a complete reversal of what doctors and social scientists know to be true. Yet any disagreement with this proposal results in one's being told that she is "denying the existence" of a transgender person.' [Vigo 2018a]

Some forms of feminism took us from the not unreasonable position of attacking inflexible gender stereotypes so that women would have the freedom to make their own decisions, to the ever-so-slightly less reasonable idea that there were no important differences between men and women at all. The claim that men and women are essentially identical is difficult to reconcile with the idea that changing one's sex/gender makes a real difference; after all, if men and women are essentially the same, what's the point of going through the trauma of hormonal or surgical interventions to change from one to the other? Most people would, I think, be prepared to accept that there are a range of sensible positions to take between, on the one hand, the extremes of rigid gender roles and, on the other hand, total androgyny. It comes down, as it so often does, to choice. If men and women have different needs and desires and inclinations, then, under the rubric of the zero-aggression principle, they should be legally free to satisfy those needs, desires and inclinations. You may not approve of what others choose to do with their freedom, but then again, they may not approve of your choices either!

## Education

The school around the corner's not the same as it was in the good old days. Remember those mind-numbing æons in school when the clock seemed to run backwards, and you were forced to learn history (actual dates in sequence, kings and queens, battles and revolutions—how crazy was that?) and geography (the rivers, mountains, bays, harbours, towns, and major industries of our own countries and others) and grammar (what's grammar?) and mathematics (mental arithmetic, the multiplication tables, long division, elementary trigonometry)? Well, you'll be glad to know that now, in Scotland at least, the boring lives of pupils will be enlivened by tales from the world of transgressive sex. Yes, the kinds of things we used to whisper about and hope the teachers didn't overhear, will now be the very things the teachers will be only too keen to tell us all about. The *Guardian* reported in 2018 that Scotland is about to become the first country in the world—in the world!—'to embed the teaching of lesbian, gay, bisexual, transgender and intersex rights in the school curriculum, in what campaigners have described as a historic moment.' [Brooks 2018] An historic moment indeed. If only the pupils had some idea what history actually is they might appreciate this pivotal moment. Jordan Daly, the co-founder of TIE (Time for Inclusive Education) described this policy as 'a monumental victory for our campaign, and a historic moment for our country.' [Brooks 2018] In addition to working to eliminate those dreaded mental derangements, homophobia and transphobia, state schools will be obliged to teach all about the history of LGBTI, as well as instructing their pupils in LGBTI identity. Should a school or its teachers wish not to inflict this material on their pupils, well, that's too bad since no one will be allowed to avail of an exemption or an opt-out. So much for tolerance and a respect for conscience. [see Kuby, passim]

And it's not just Scotland. In England too, in 2018, the Government was urged—by the Royal College of Paediatricians and Child Health (RCPCH) no less—to go the full Monty in the sex and relationship classes that will become compulsory in 2020. In these classes, pupils should be taught 'what it means to be lesbian, gay, bisexual or transgender', sensitively and age-appropriately to be sure. Speaking for the RCPCH, Dr Davie said, 'We have got a strong commitment against discrimination on LGBT and we need to commit to that.' [Donnelly 2018] The UK's Department for Education says it wants 'all children to grow up to become happy, healthy and safe, which is why we are making Relationships Education compulsory for all primary schools as well as Relationships and Sex

# Transgenderism in Practice

Education (RSE) compulsory for all secondary schools.' [Donnelly 2018] I'm sure we're all happy to know that the Department for Education wants our children to be happy, healthy and safe, but precisely what the causal connection is between that eminently desirable outcome and the compulsory teaching of Relationships (and Sex) Education to vulnerable young children is not immediately evident.

And, of course, it will be compulsory. The Department's website tells us that 'There is no right to withdraw from Relationships Education at primary or secondary as we believe the contents of these subjects—such as family, friendship, safety (including online safety)—are important for all children to be taught.' [see Gov. uk] In the first instance, the Department encouraged schools to include LGBT content but this was not required and schools could opt out. Now the Department says that 'Pupils should receive teaching on LGBT content during their school years. Teaching children about the society that we live in and the different types of loving, healthy relationships that exist can be done in a way that respects everyone. Primary schools are strongly encouraged and enabled to cover LGBT content when teaching about different types of families.' The required consultation with parents is effectively pointless, of course, since parental objections will not be allowed to veto whatever it is that the school decides to teach. [but see Southworth 2020]

It's good to know that a Conservative government doesn't feel any obligation to defer to tiresome, hidebound ideological commitments to actually be, ahem, conservative. [see Sidwell 2020; 2020a] In December of 2017, guidance for head teachers was issued that advised that primary schools should include in their curriculum, books that feature transgender parents. The advice was issued by the National Association of Head Teachers (NAHT) in conjunction with Stonewall, the LGBT Rights Charity, and was endorsed by the Department for Education. [see NAHT & Stonewall 2017] School leaders were told that they must 'celebrate' transgender people and encourage their staff to teach children about trans issues, thereby ensuring the visibility of trans perspectives in the classroom. What is it, precisely, to *celebrate* transgenderism? I know what it is like to celebrate a birthday or a graduation or a wedding, but I haven't a clue how to celebrate transgenderism. Cake for everyone, perhaps? Camilla Turner tells us that schools have indeed been told to 'give transgender pupils a cake to celebrate their transition'. [Turner 2017] Terry Reed, founder of the Gender Identity Research and Education Society told teachers at the Association of Teachers and Lecturers Conference that they should send an upbeat message to students who no longer identify with their sex, but, to those of us whose baking skills are less than perfect, she conceded that it doesn't absolutely have to be done with cake. She also advised schools to avoid separating boys and girls to bring about what she termed 'gender blurring'. Not

94          *Hidden Agender*

surprisingly, she wants schools to make it clear that there is 'zero tolerance for transphobic behaviour.' [Turner 2017]

Schools and teachers are warned against entertaining complaints from parents or others that might interfere with the commitment of the schools to create an inclusive environment for transgender people. School leaders have a role in 'Forbidding complaints (or fear of complaints) from parents, governors or staff members to interfere with their commitment to an inclusive school environment—any more than they would allow complaints to interfere with their commitment to supporting black, Asian or minority ethnic (BAME) or disabled staff. It is important that all staff members are clear that they will be supported and defended by the school's leadership team in such matters.' [NAHT & Stonewall 2017, 5] If we were to coin a slogan, it might be: Don't pay any attention to these reactionary fuddy duddies. Paul Whiteman, General Secretary of the NAHT, says, 'We haven't made as much progress as we should on LGBT+ rights in schools. We need to change that. We need to break down the fear: school leaders who aren't sure of the rules have feared causing offence.' [Turner 2017a] School leaders are encouraged to 'ensure the school celebrates diversity by inviting external speakers and by marking events that celebrate diversity, for instance, Trans Day of Visibility on 31 March and LGBT history month in February. Consider joining Stonewall's school champions programme, which enables members to access visits from LGBT role models who are trained to speak to pupils about celebrating different identities.' [NAHT & Stonewall 2017, 11]

In a related development, Pearson, a company that publishes thousands of school textbooks in the UK, intends to make all its teaching materials LGBT inclusive. To help them in their ambition to be woke they have sponsored the production of a Stonewall handbook entitled *Creating an LGBT-Inclusive Curriculum: A Guide for Secondary Schools*. In this handy little production, teachers can find advice on how to make the curriculum more welcoming for LGBT students. [Stonewall 2018] In a foreword to the *Guide*, Stonewall's Chief Executive Ruth Hunt writes, 'For every young person to be prepared for life in modern Britain, it's vital that their curriculum reflects the full diversity of the world they live in. When pupils are supported to understand diversity and celebrate difference, they can develop accepting attitudes towards those who are different to them, and feel proud of the things that make them different themselves.' Unless, presumably, the difference of any given child consists in not wanting to celebrate transgenderism, in which case, this is presumably not a difference that the child should feel proud of. In the teaching of English, the *Guide* suggests that lessons might

1. Introduce LGBT authors and themes: Study works of fiction by LGBT authors. Discuss how their LGBT identity and the culture they lived in might have influenced

## Transgenderism in Practice 95

their writing, and include LGBT themes in discussions about representation in literature. 2. Compare depictions of LGBT characters and themes in different contexts: Look at texts with LGBT themes and characters from different nations, eras and walks of life. Contrast the representation of LGBT characters in contemporary literature with older texts. What has or hasn't changed? How does this reflect societal change? 3. Explore representations of gender: Support pupils to consider and discuss representations of masculinity, femininity and androgyny in writing. Talk about traditional gender roles and stereotypes (the basis of much anti-LGBT bullying) and why it's OK not to live up to them. 4. Set up speeches, discussions and writing activities on LGBT topics: Support pupils to discuss topics such as same-sex marriage, or why it's important to challenge gender stereotypes. Set persuasive writing tasks relating to LGBT topics—for example a letter to the local council arguing against the closure of local LGBT services. 5. Include LGBT topics in teaching on grammar and language: For example, when discussing pronouns, highlight their importance and what they tell us about a person's gender, linking to respecting people's choice of pronouns (including gender-neutral pronouns such as they/them). Explore how the English language has changed over time by planning a lesson on word etymology, using the word "gay" as one example. [Stonewall 2018, 7]

In such ways, the teaching of English is to be LGBT-colonised. It is not difficult to see how the teaching of literature and other humanities subjects lend themselves to such colonisation, but surely some subjects, Science and Mathematics, for example, are intrinsically less receptive to permitting the required LGBT makeover. But no! When it comes to the teaching of mathematics, for example, the *Guide* suggests that lessons could

1. Include references to LGBT people and different family structures in teaching: For example, "Mr X & Mr Y want to know how much it will cost to have a holiday in Italy if...", "Lila's mums are trying to calculate..." 2. Use research into the experiences of LGBT people: As part of your work on statistics, percentages and fractions, use Stonewall's research into the experiences of LGBT people (such as School Report 2017 and Unhealthy Attitudes 2015). Look at the ways data is collected, presented and used in different settings and around the world to advocate for different issues, including LGBT equality. 3. Highlight LGBT mathematicians: Make reference to the contributions of LGBT mathematicians and LGBT figures in related disciplines, such as Alan Turing (mathematician and code-breaker), Tim Cook (CEO of Apple), Sophie Wilson (British scientist and computer engineer) and Lynn Conway (American scientist). 4. Examine arguments for and against capturing data on sexual orientation and gender identity: Use documents published by different bodies, including the Office for National Statistics (ONS), to discuss: Why doesn't our census currently capture people's sexual orientation and gender identity? What would be the advantages of capturing this information in future censuses? What are some of the potential barriers to collecting this information? [Stonewall 2018, 9]

And there is much more in the same vein in respect of Art, Geography, History, Music and Sport, all subjects that are to be colonised by LGBTIP2SQQAPKA (lesbian, gay, bisexual, transgendered, intersex, pansexual, two-spirit, queer, questioning, asexual, polyamorous, kinky, and allies). There will be no means of escape for schoolchildren from this deluge of propaganda, no matter what the actual subject that is supposed to be being taught.

Of course, there are those benighted people who refuse to get on board with the latest trends. One of these is Chris McGovern, a former Government advisor and the director of the Campaign for Real Education, who said that indoctrinating children about what he termed the 'politically correct anxieties, passions and neuroses of adults' had no place in schools, but I presume the complaints of people such as Mr McGovern are precisely what the NAHT guidelines encourage us to pre-emptively reject. As I've just mentioned, the NAHT wants its members to 'forbid' complaints about the policies recommended in their guidelines from busybodies such as parents or governors or members of staff from interfering with the commitment of schools to create what it regards as inclusive environments for transgenderists. In what can only be regarded as a disturbing, even a sinister, development, the NAHT's guidelines suggest that 'It may be useful to develop a detailed contract of inclusivity that everybody signs, including new staff members, parents, governors and pupils.' [NAHT & Stonewall 2017, 9] What happens if you do not want to or cannot conscientiously sign such a latter-day statement of faith?

Some woke people woke up earlier than others and are leading the charge. In late 2017, it was reported that Andrew Fisher, the headmaster of the co-educational 'progressive' school, Frensham Heights, in the UK, had given permission for a girl to sleep in the boys' boarding house, albeit in her own room. The reason for this was that the girl in question had disclosed doubts about her gender identity. Mr Fisher said, 'In the past, girls identifying as boys would simply have been called tomboys, and boys who felt more like girls would have been described as effeminate. The ability to medically transition [using hormones and surgery] has changed the whole conversation.' [Anon 2017a] No, Mr Fisher, with all due respect, it hasn't changed the conversation. All it has done is to take a transitory psycho-social phase in a young person's life and attempt to mould his or her biological reality to that, with consequences that haven't really been explored. It seems that two teenage girls at Frensham Heights who play football on the boys' teams have adopted male names and have asked to be addressed as 'him' rather than 'her'. Really? Girls liking sports must *be* boys? That's meant to be progressive? Isn't it rather the ultimate stereotypical 'boys and girls must be a certain way and fulfil certain roles, and let's have no nonsense about it'? Fortunately, not all headmasters are equally prey to the whims of the latest gender fashion. Andrew

*Transgenderism in Practice* 97

Halls, who is the headmaster of King's College School, Wimbledon remarked, 'We have to be careful. There is evidence that some people who have done the full transgendering have regretted it. We must avoid a headlong rush into a void of ignorance. This is like a new science no one fully understands.' [Leader 2017] To be fair to some who find themselves in charge of co-educational schools, the prospect of falling under the wheels of juggernaut laws such as the Equality Act 2010 might explain some of their actions as a defensive strategy.

As might be expected, the universities are not to be found at the rear of this assault on reason. Since 2017, Murray Edwards College, a women-only college at Cambridge, has accepted applications from any person who, at the point of application, identifies as a woman. (They don't tell us what would happen if a student, once admitted, ceases to identify as a woman.) The College's Council issued a statement saying that it is sympathetic towards the idea that gender isn't binary and that what it terms 'narrow gender identities' are damaging to wider society. Quite how such narrow gender identities succeed in damaging society is a bit of a mystery, but let that pass. The College's decision has been criticised by Germaine Greer, who said, 'If [Murray Edwards] really don't believe that gender is binary, then they really shouldn't be a single sex college. Their position is ridiculous. The only sane thing for them to do is to cease discriminating on the basis of assigned gender of any kind.' [Yorke et al. 2017] It is difficult to see how Greer's criticism could be rebutted but, give them credit, the authorities of Murray Edwards try. One senior tutor at the College, Juliet Foster, said, 'Our position is very clear: we want to be open to all outstanding young women, and we felt that society is changing and there is greater understanding of the complexities surrounding gender.' She went on to say, 'We felt that it was therefore in line with our values to accept all women, including transgender people who identify as female.' Ms Foster's point was echoed by the College's President, Dame Barbara Stocking, who said, 'In order that we remain true to our mission of being open to all outstanding young women we recognise that it is right for anyone who identifies as female, regardless of their born gender, to be able to apply to study with us.' [Yorke et al. 2017] If I might make a small point, Ms Foster and Dame Barbara: as most people whose minds haven't been corroded by a university education know full well, trans women are not women. Would it be very rude of me to suggest, echoing Greer, that if you can't tell the difference between men and women, you probably shouldn't be in charge of a women's college?

It's just great when universities get on board with the sex/gender mystification. It must be particularly gratifying when Catholic universities, which might be expected to be resistant to the latest effusions of the gender-fashionistas, throw off the shackles imposed by their religious affiliation and get with the programme. 'But

98 *Hidden Agender*

Dad, all the kids are gender-questioning today!' At Marquette University, students are offered the option of identifying both a legal gender and a chosen gender. The legal one is limited to two options, male and female, but the chosen one can be selected from a drop-down menu which includes 'intersex', 'transgender', 'non-binary' and others. Of course, there will be those bigots and reactionaries who will suggest that Marquette's endorsement of gender-speak might possibly be at odds with Catholic teaching on the creation by God of human beings as either male or female [*Genesis* 5: 2], but we can ignore these Neanderthals or, if necessary, intimidate or even fire them.

## Sport

Sex segregation in sport is designed to benefit women, not men. Men don't need men-only sporting competitions. In sports involving strength, endurance and speed, the best woman will never outperform the best man. The men's 100 metres was run in 10.8 seconds in 1891 in Paris by Luther Cary. This dropped to 10 seconds in 1967, a time achieved by various athletes. Currently, the record is 9.58 seconds and is held by Usain Bolt (2009). One hundred and thirty nine men have run the 100 metres in under 10 seconds. In contrast, the women's 100 metres was run in 13.6 seconds by Marie Mejzlíková in Prague in 1922. The current record is 10.49 seconds, held by Florence Griffith-Joyner, and was set in 1988 in Indianapolis. This time was achieved by men between 1912 and 1921. Perhaps the difference between men and women in the 100 metres is explained by its being a sprint, so let's look at records over a longer distance. Maxie Long ran the 400 metres in New York in 1900 in 47.8 seconds. The current record is held by Wayded van Niekerk (2016, Rio de Janeiro) and stands at 43.03 seconds. The current 400 metres record for women was set by Marita Koch in Canberra in 1985 and took her 47.6 seconds. This time was achieved by men in 1924. Still too much of a sprint you say? Very well, let's look at the 5,000 metres. The first record we have of this event was set by George Touquet-Saunis in 1897 in Paris and it took him 16 minutes and 34 seconds to cover the distance. The current record of 12 minutes and 37 seconds is held by Kenenisa Bekele and was in Hengelo in 2004. The current women's record is 14 minutes and 11 seconds, set by Tiranes Dibaba in 2000 in Oslo. This time was achieved by men between 1932 and 1939. It would be tedious to go through all the various sporting categories. Suffice it to say that much the same differences can be found in the field events of long and high jump, pole vault, shot putt and discus as are found in track events.

There is a reason for this consistent difference between the sporting performances of men and women, and the reason is not hard to find. In the aggregate, men are stronger than women, are heavier, taller, have a greater lung capacity, have

## Transgenderism in Practice

99

greater upper-body strength, and have significantly greater skeletal muscle mass. Perhaps even more significantly, men's muscle fibres have a larger cross-section. Men run faster than women; the fastest woman in the world wouldn't meet the men's qualifying standard for the Olympics. Men can lift heavier weights than women, and throw the javelin, discus and shot put further than women. All this is blindingly obvious, unless, of course, you're wilfully blind.

One can argue about the merits of having sporting events that are exclusive to women. In some cases, where the aggregate physical differences between men and women are obvious and are decisively tilted in favour of men, if there were no women-only events, women would never be in a position to win anything, and so a reasonable case can be made for competitions that are exclusive to them. In other competitive events, such as chess or darts or snooker, there's no obvious reason why men and women cannot compete directly against each other, and no rational case can be made in such sports for women-only events. [see White 2020] At the moment, for example, in chess, there are women-only tournaments, women-only titles (requiring significantly lower achievements) and women-only funding. Why? No great upper-body strength is needed to lift the chess pieces, and women and girls are as capable of sitting in chairs for long periods of time as any man or boy. Sex-segregation in chess exists exclusively to benefit females in a way that male chess players are not benefitted.

But even in those events in which women can reasonably be expected to compete on comparatively level terms against men, their best achievement is rarely if ever to reach the top, and such success as is attained is invariably celebrated as an historic and newsworthy occurrence. Fallon Sherrock won some matches (matches, please note, not the tournament) at the Professional Darts Corporation World Championship match in London in 2019 and the event was reported in *Time Magazine*, *The New York Times* and many other print and electronic outlets. [see Reilly 2019, Mather 2019; see also White 2020] I was waiting to see my doctor on the day after this earth-shaking occurrence and I saw news of it continually looped on news channels, and heard the victorious Ms Sherrock being interviewed on national TV while I sat, captive, in the doctor's waiting room. That such a media fuss was made about Ms Sherrock's real, albeit modest, achievement shows clearly just how rare such sporting success is for women, even in those areas where, as I indicated above, speed and strength are not important factors. When at some time in the future a woman wins the Dart's World Championship or a professional snooker championship and it is reported in the sports pages (not the news) as a victory just for her and not for womankind as a whole, then we shall know that women have achieved parity in those sports for which sex segregation cannot be justified except as a custom. Jim White's headline in the *Telegraph* read: 'Women are taking men on at their own game ... and beating them: Increase in awareness and funding has allowed female athletes to close the gap in sports like snooker, horseracing and darts.' [White 2020] The first part of this sentence is relatively unproblematic; the second half is peculiar inasmuch as darts and snooker players, skilful as they may be, cannot by any stretch of the imagination be described as athletes, and jockeys would be athletes only if they carried their horses over jumps and not the other way around. So, to repeat my point, sex differentiation in sport is designed to facilitate women, not men, completely in respect of athletics and football and rugby and the like, and practically in respect of sports such as snooker and darts and chess.

At the beginning of this book, I gave a preliminary account of the achievements of the weight-lifter Laurel Hubbard and cyclist Rachel McKinnon. Here are the full stories.

In 2017, Hubbard won the Women's over 90kg division at the Australian international in Melbourne, setting four unofficial national records in the process. Gavin decided to transition to female in his/her 30s and to compete in athletics under his/her newly reassigned gender. He/she was allowed to compete in a competition supervised by the Commonwealth Games Federation on the grounds that they support fairness, non-discrimination and inclusion. Hubbard, who had set junior male records before transitioning, lifted a combined total of 268kg, 19kg better than silver medallist Luniarra Sipaia of Samoa. Samoa's head coach protested, with some justification one might think, that a man is a man and a woman is a woman. 'I know,' he said, 'a lot of changes have gone through, but Laurel used to be a male weightlifter. The strength is still there, and for all females it's unfair. Can we expect to see Laurel/Gavin competing the women's weightlifting in Tokyo 2020? More generally, can we now expect to see women's competitions systematically invaded by former men so that the no-hopers in the men's divisions can suddenly shine as women?" [Brown 2019] As it happens, it seems that you don't even have to have been a former male weightlifter to shine in the women's division. The rapper Zuby claimed to have broken the women's dead lift record of 238 kg without, as he modestly put it, 'really trying'. [McManus 2019] To rub salt into the wound, Zuby tweeted, 'P.S. I identified as a woman whilst lifting the weight. Don't be a bigot.' [McManus 2019]

Canadian Rachel McKinnon, who was born male, came in first in a women's cycling championship at the UCI Masters Track Cycling Championship in Los Angeles in October 2018. Many have praised his/her achievement, but some say it was cheating, since he/she is a man. [see Kearns 2019a] McKinnon's victory attracted some criticism, with some people pointing out the disparity in size between McKinnon and the other competitors, all of whom were actually female.

## Transgenderism in Practice

One Twitterer was less than impressed and wrote, 'Amazing! I was so enthused at reading this, I went out and challenged two 8 year olds to a 100m race. Guess what, I ONLY WENT AND F***ING WON. First time running in a 8 year old's race too!' Others made the same point less sardonically. Madeleine Kearns wrote an article entitled, unequivocally, 'Rachel McKinnon Is a Cheat and a Bully.' 'Rachel McKinnon,' she wrote, 'is a man. I'll repeat that so my meaning cannot be misconstrued. *He is a man.*' She went on, 'by pretending that McKinnon is not a man, we have allowed him to cheat at sports at the expense of his female competitors. Because McKinnon being a man is directly relevant to the argument that he should not compete against women, in calling him something other than a man, we obfuscate that argument—and all for the sake of a very recently invented set of blasphemy norms (e.g. "misgendering" and "deadnaming") that don't apply to us non-believers.' [Kearns 2019a; see Jones 2019] Jen Wagner-Assali, who came third to McKinnon at the UCI Masters Track World Championship in 2018, tweeted: "it's definitely NOT fair." Under pressure, Wagner-Assali apologised to McKinnon. *She* apologised to *him/her*! But that wasn't enough for the ungracious McKinnon who responded, 'The apology is not accepted: she still thinks what she said. She merely apologizes for being caught saying it publicly.' [Kearns 2019a] It's not only such as McKinnon who treat the objections of women to the participation of men in their competitions with contempt. Hannah (formerly Callum) Mouncey, an Australian who played for Australia's men's handball side before he transitioned, described the objections of the female players to having a man in their changing rooms and showers as 'frankly ludicrous'.

Some years ago, when the transgender issue first began to become a matter of public discussion, I half-jokingly asked on a radio programme if we could expect men-now-women to participate in women's events, so that, say, a male tennis player ranked 250th in the world could enter Wimbledon, compete in the women's events and win! This feeble attempt at a humorous *reductio* argument was met with responses that were variations on 'Of course not!' and 'Don't be silly!' Oh well, that'll teach me to be facetious.

It's not only the unfortunate Wagner-Assali who thinks the participation of trans women (i.e. men) in women's competitions is cheating. Martina Navratilova, the multi-time Wimbledon singles champion, caused some controversy when, in 2019, she wrote that it's 'insane' and 'cheating' to permit biological males who declare themselves to be trans women to compete against women in women's sports. She wrote: 'A man can decide to be female, take hormones if required by whatever sporting organisation is concerned, win everything in sight and perhaps earn a small fortune, and then reverse his decision and go back to making babies.' [see Fink 2020]

The *Telegraph* reported in 2019 that two thirds of Britons regarded the participation of transwomen in women's sport to be cheating. I'm astonished that the figure is as low as two thirds. The main reason given for this judgement was that such athletes would have unfair physical advantages. This is true in the aggregate but misses the essential point, as does the headline to the piece that reads, 'Two thirds of British public think it is cheating for women born male to compete in women's sport, says poll.' [Tominey 2019] Trans women, despite what the headline writer in the *Telegraph* seems to think, are not women-born-male; they're simply not women at all. There *are* no women-born-male. Whether or not allowing trans women to participate in women-only events is cheating is a secondary issue. In some sports, transgender athletes are now being allowed to compete in women's events provided their testosterone is below a certain level but, again, this misses the point completely. They're not women! (If you would like to witness the intellectual gymnastics of those who, like the Sports Council Equality Group, seem incapable of grasping the simple fact that men are not women, see Various 2020.)

World Rugby is, it seems, having second thoughts on its policy of allowing trans women (that is, men) to play women's rugby. A draft document produced by World Rugby notes the significantly greater risk of injury that women run when tackled by someone who has gone through male puberty. The working group notes that those whose puberty and development is influenced by androgens/testosterone 'are stronger by 25%-50%, are 30% more powerful, 40% heavier, and about 15% faster' than those whose puberty and development is not influenced by androgens/testosterone (that is, women). Whether or not trans women (that is, men) reduce their testosterone levels by means of medication, they still retain significant physical advantages over biological women. 'Current policies regulating the inclusion of transgender women in sport are based on the premise that reducing testosterone to levels found in biological females is sufficient to remove many of the biologically-based performance advantages,' the draft report says. 'However, peer-reviewed evidence suggests this is not the case.' When it comes to transgender men (that is, women) competing in men's rugby, the report recommends that they be allowed to do so, provided they undergo a physical assessment and produce a therapeutic-exemption certificate and are willing to put their names to a statement that they understand they risk greater injury. Here is a draft version of the waiver that transgender men (that is, women) may expect to sign: 'I acknowledge and accept the injury risks associated with transgender males playing contact rugby with males who are statistically likely to be stronger, faster and heavier than transgender males, as described in the World Rugby Transgender Guidelines which I have read and understand.' [see Ingle 2020; see also Morgan 2020a]

## Transgenderism in Practice

At present, in athletics, we have men's events and women's events, not high testosterone events and low testosterone events. Male/female is binary; testosterone level lies on a continuum. There is no non-arbitrary cut-off point on such a scale. Why have competitions for competitors only above a certain level or below a certain level? Why not multiple levels? Can we expect to hear someone touted as the testosterone level 6 world champion, and another as the testosterone level 1 world champion? If not, why not? We already have a system not unlike this in Special Olympics and Paralympics, and it is standard in boxing. So if we're going to go this route, let's get rid of the designations 'Men's ....' and 'Women's ...' and just use the testosterone levels to sort people into various categories. Helen Joyce write, 'Males were first permitted to compete in women's Olympic events in 2004, provided they had transitioned surgically. That rule never made much sense: most of the male sporting advantage is due not to the testosterone produced every day by the testicles, but to the legacy of male puberty. This includes a larger heart and lungs, stronger bones, a narrower, more ergonomically efficient pelvis and more high-twitch muscle fibre.' She goes on to note, however, 'But the small number of people who undergo transition surgery, and the fact that until recently it was usually sought in middle age, meant that male athletes did not enter women's elite sports in noticeable numbers. That is starting to change. Since 2015 male athletes have needed merely to take medication that lowers their testosterone levels for 12 months (to a level still far higher than seen in women) in order to compete in the Olympics as women.' [see Joyce 2020]

Rachel McKinnon accused his/her critics of bigotry and transphobia (what a surprise) and went on to argue that transgender women should be allowed to compete at the Olympics without being required to maintain their testosterone at a certain level. Of course, if we're going to accede to the demands of such as McKinnon, then it might be more sensible just to abolish separate sporting events for men and women altogether. This would result in a situation where no woman is likely ever to win a sporting or athletic event again, but it seems we're heading in that direction anyway so why not just bite the bullet and get the agony over with? On the other hand, we could keep male and female events for actual males and females, with special categories for those who are demonstrably intersex.

Putting all this together, a number of possibilities suggests themselves. First, stick to existing male and female events, with entry controlled by evidence of internal and external biological markers. Intersex individuals can be allocated to male events by default, or to events regulated by level of testosterone, or to a special category of intersex events. Second, create a system of testosterone-specified levels, as per the weight systems used in boxing, wrestling and weight-lifting, ignoring the residual physical advantages that accrue to men because of their somatic develop-

104 *Hidden Agender*

ment. Or third, make all sporting events open to everyone without restriction, thus ending forever the problem of sorting out who goes where. If this option is chosen, then no woman will ever again win any athletic or sporting event where men's dimorphic physiology systematically advantages them, but why should we worry about that? 'When sport becomes gender blind,' writes Joanna Williams, 'women find themselves relegated to the sidelines.' [Williams 2020, 42] Men don't need men-only sports events. If all sports were 'open', that wouldn't affect men's ability to compete. It is women who require women-only sports events. If these events can be colonised by trans-women, then the notion of women-only events becomes functionally meaningless and they might as well be jettisoned.

**Medical services**

A booklet produced by Public Health England entitled 'Information for trans and non-binary people' is a masterpiece of official PC-gender Newspeak. Here's a glimpse of what is contained in the booklet. In regard to breast screening, it tells you that if you are a trans man or a non-binary person assigned female at birth aged 50 to 70 who is registered with a GP as female, you *will be* routinely invited for breast screening, whereas if you are a trans man or non-binary person assigned female at birth aged 50 to 70 who is registered with a GP as male, you *won't be* invited for breast screening. [NHS 2019, 6] On the other hand, if you are a trans woman or non-binary person assigned male at birth aged 50 to 70 who is registered with a GP as female, you *will be* routinely invited for screening, whereas if you are a trans woman or non-binary person aged 50 to 70 who is registered with a GP as male, you *won't be* invited for breast screening. [NHS, 2019, 7) Are you clear on what this means? No? Let me try again.

What this appears to mean is that if you are a woman claiming to be a man but are registered with your GP as a woman, you'll be invited for breast screening. But if you are a woman claiming to be a man and are registered with your GP as a man, you will not be invited for breast screening. On the other hand, if you are a man claiming to be a woman and registered with your GP as a woman, you will be invited for screening, but if you are a man claiming to be a woman but registered with your GP as a man, you won't. Is that all clear to you now?

When it comes to cervical screening, the situation is similar. If you are a trans man or non-binary person aged 25 to 64 who is registered with a GP as female, you *will* routinely be invited for cervical screening. But if you are a trans man aged 25 to 64 who is registered with a GP as male, you *won't be* invited for cervical screening. [NHS 2019, 12] In a rare burst of common sense, the booklet informs us that if you are a trans woman aged 25 to 64, you do not need to be screened as you don't have a cervix. [NHS 2019, 13] Despite this, if you are a trans woman or

# Transgenderism in Practice

non-binary person assigned male at birth and registered with your GP as female, you *will* routinely be invited for cervical screening, whereas if you are a trans woman or binary person assigned male at birth and registered with your GP as male, you won't be invited for cervical screening. [NHS 2019, 13]

Again, in what I hope is more comprehensible language, what this means is that if you are a woman claiming to be a man but registered with your GP as a woman, you will be offered cervical screening. If you are a woman claiming to be a man but registered with your GP as a man, you won't be offered cervical screening. In short, putting it all together, women registered with their GPs as women will be offered screening; women registered with their GPs as men won't; men registered with their GPs as women will be offered screening, men registered with their GPs as men won't. I hope I've got all that straight. I might have mixed things up since I've been laughing so much. How can any normal person read this nonsense and not think it is utterly insane? Are government administrators populated entirely by women's studies graduates? I imagine the final, completely non-discriminatory and totally safe legal solution to this 'problem' will be to ensure equality in all services that the NHS provides so that everyone, male or female, will be offered breast tests and cervical smear tests and invitations to prostate examinations. What's that? You haven't *got* a prostate? No matter. We don't want to be seen to act in a discriminatory manner. Men protesting that they do not need a cervical check, or women denying their need for a prostate examination will be at risk of being labelled transphobic and treated accordingly, that is, with official contempt

In the UK, the Equality and Human Rights Commission [EHRC] has threatened the National Health Service [NHS] with legal action if it doesn't start to offer fertility treatments routinely to transgender patients. Such patients should be offered the chance to have their eggs or sperm stored. The chief executive of the EHRC, Rebecca Hilsenrath said: 'A choice between treatment for gender dysphoria and the chance to start a family is not a real choice.' [Doward 2018] In a related report in the *Telegraph*, we are told that the British Fertility Society has informed the NHS is that it must offer transgender men egg storage so that they can be parents. [Knapton 2018] Some of these transgender men, in case you're confused, are women who have voluntarily chosen to have hormone treatment and/or surgery that can, in many cases, destroy the chance of their having children. The supposed requirement incumbent on the NHS to offer the transgender men egg storage facilities is based on the grounds of equity. Transgender men have, it seems, the right to become parents, even though the unsympathetic amongst us might think that they have voluntarily ceded that right. Some people have suggested that the money required to pay for this supposed right might be better spent on basic healthcare. Josephine Quintavalle, from the organisation Comment on Reproductive Ethics, said: 'The cash-strapped NHS should be concentrating on offering good basic healthcare to women or helping them beat their cancer, and not get side-tracked with these kinds of novelties.' [Knapton 2018] Just so.

It was reported in 2018 that the UK's Cancer Research has taken out the word 'women' from its campaign for smear test screening so that transgender men will not be deterred from taking the test. [Horton 2018] The charity used to urge women between twenty five and sixty four to have the test; now it encourages all those with a cervix to sign up. Fiona Osgun from Cancer Research UK said: "Cervical cancer develops in anyone who has a cervix. This includes women as well as people with other gender identities such as trans men.' An announcement from Cancer Research reads, 'Cervical screening (or the smear test) is relevant for everyone aged 25-64 with a cervix.'

The *Times* reported in 2017 that a woman who asked for a female NHS nurse to perform her cervical smear test was somewhat taken aback when the person who offered to undertake the procedure had a deep voice, lots of tattoos and facial stubble. The nurse insisted he wasn't male but was transsexual. Not surprisingly, the woman declined the examination. She complained and received an official apology from the NHS. In her letter of complaint, the patient remarked that 'People who are not comfortable about this are presented as bigots and this is ... kind of how I was made to feel about it.' [Hellen 2017]

In 2016, the British Medical Association published its booklet entitled 'A guide to effective communication: inclusive language in the workplace'. The booklet manages to be simultaneously patronising (or should that be matronising?) and ignorant (of the grammar and history of language). It contains many possible targets for satire but the winner must surely be this one: 'A large majority of people that have been pregnant or have given birth identify as women. We can include intersex men and transmen who may get pregnant by saying 'pregnant people' instead of 'expectant mothers'. [British Medical Association 2016, 5] It would be gilding the lily to comment on the spectacular stupidity of this advice.

In a scene from the 1960's romcom *Pillow Talk*, Brad Allen (Rock Hudson), not wanting to meet Jan Morrow (Doris Day) as they walk towards each other along an office corridor, ducks into a conveniently located doctor's office. The doctor happens to be an obstetrician but Allen doesn't know this. The nurse-receptionist directs an inquiring look at him and Allen asks for an appointment. 'For your wife?' asks the nurse. 'No,' says Allen, 'I'm not married. For myself.' The nurse is understandably perplexed. 'The doctor should examine you?' she asks, eyebrows raising. Allen replies, 'I'm not feeling too well. Maybe just an upset stomach, but a guy can't be too careful.' The nurse goes into the surgery to tell the doctor about this strange phenomenon, and the doctor emerges from the surgery in a highly

## Transgenderism in Practice

excited state to witness this phenomenon for himself but Allen has already left. 'Where is he?' the doctor asks the nurse. 'He must have just gone,' she replies. The doctor is understandably frustrated. 'Excuse me,' he says, 'a man said he was going to have a baby and you let him go?' The nurse replies, defensively, 'He was obviously a psychopath.' 'And if he wasn't?' asks the doctor. Later in the film, Allen follows Morrow into the Ladies' Room next to the doctor's office and, as he is being ejected, bumps into the same nurse on the office corridor. Once again, she alerts the doctor, who rushes into the corridor. No sign of Allen. 'Where did he go?' he asks. 'I don't know,' replies the nurse, but (pointing to the Ladies' Room) she says, 'he came out there.' 'You let him go again?' says the doctor. The nurse begins to ask, 'You don't believe ... ?', to which the doctor replies, 'A prejudiced view never advanced the cause of science. Somewhere there may be a man who's crossed a new frontier.'

That was then, when the idea of a man's being pregnant was a subject of farce; this is now and it's not farcical any more, or rather it *is* farcical but in quite a different way. The *Telegraph* reported that not one but *two* British men have given birth! [Knapton 2017] But hold the presses! It seems that the two men in question, Hayden Cross and Scott Parker, were both born women who hadn't yet undergone gender reassignment surgery. What the newspaper headline *should* have read is something like this: 'Two British women who think they're men have given birth,' which is more a case of 'Dog bites Man' than 'Man bites Dog.' Parker apparently requested that s/he be registered as 'father' on her daughter's birth certificate but was told that s/he could only be registered as her mother. In a rare moment of insight, Cross remarked, 'It's a very female thing to carry a baby and it goes against everything I feel in my body.' Just so, Ms/Mr Cross, just so. It is indeed a very female thing to carry a baby. One might even think it is a quintessentially female thing.

But perhaps not such a female thing anymore. It now seems that there is no anatomical reason why a transgender woman (i.e. a man) could not receive a womb! Dr Richard Paulson, President of the American Society for Reproductive Medicine, is of the opinion that the medical technology is already available to allow women who began life as men to receive donated wombs. Womb transplantation has been undertaken with women but the procedure is long and complicated. [see Serena 2017; Bodkin 2017] Not everyone is as ecstatic about the prospect of men receiving wombs via surgery as is Dr Paulson. Professor Julian Savulescu of Oxford University comments, 'Uterine transplantation represents a real risk to the foetus, and future child.' While the procedure is technically possible, he believes that one would need to be confident that the uterus would function normally during the pregnancy. 'Uterine rupture,' he said, 'could cause the death or permanent disablement of the foetus.' [see Bodkin 2017] Given all this, it's not, perhaps, surprising that Professor Savulescu thinks that public resources should not be used to fund the womb-transplant procedure for transmen. If a baby is ever born from such a womb-transplant, the headline can truly read—'Man gives birth!'—and then it *would* be a case of 'Man bites Dog!' and not merely 'Dog bites Man!'.

Jenni Hempel, writing in *Time* magazine in 2016, tells us about her brother's pregnancy—yes, that's what you just read, her *brother*'s pregnancy. The story, which, I suspect, is meant to be touching and to elicit a sympathetic 'Aaaaah' from readers is, I would suggest, more likely to elicit an 'Aaaaagh' from those who can make it through to the end, especially when they read about 'chest' feeding with a profusion of body hair and a beard. I suspect the overall feeling many will experience when reading this story is one of deep sadness.

Her brother Evan, Hempel tells us, 'was born female,' and 'had wanted to be a parent since he was very young, when he played with dolls just a bit longer than the other kids. He'd helped pay for college by nannying triplets. And when he first came out to friends as transgender at 19, changing his name and beginning his long physical transformation, he didn't stop adding to the list of baby names in the back of his journal: Kaya, Eleanor, Huxley.' [Hempel 2016] I don't want to be crassly sexist or to carelessly stereotype anyone, but some might think that a person who plays with dolls longer than others, wants to be a parent from an early age, makes money by nannying, and keeps baby names at the back of her journal might, just might, be more likely to be female than male. Whether or not this is stereotypical female behaviour, it's certainly not stereotypical male behaviour.

In any event, Evan became pregnant, not an unusual occurrence for a human female but, as the *Pillow Talk* episode illustrates, somewhat out of the ordinary for a male. Hempel asks the obvious question: ' ... what if you are born into a female body, know you are a man and still want to participate in the traditionally exclusive rite of womanhood? What kind of man are you then?' [Hempel 2016] Once again, a crass and unfeeling but obvious response might be, 'Not any kind of man at all!' but that, I suspect, would not be the response that Hempel is hoping to elicit. The question Hempel doesn't ask is: what exactly does it mean to be born *into* a female body? Indeed, what does it mean for anyone to be born *into* a body, as if there were a *you* prior to your embodiment and a subsequent insertion of that *you* into an organic structure that might be other than it actually is. And what does it mean to claim to *know* that you are a man, apart from having the customary physical indicators? Is knowing you're a man the result of having some kind of irrefragable inner experience that is unchallengeable in a way that having an inner experience that one was a duck wouldn't be irrefragable? I was talking to a neighbour recently and, having gone through what I like to call 'the organ

## Transgenderism in Practice

recital', a comparison, often boastfully exaggerated, of our various ailments, I told her I would soon be seventy. She remarked, very kindly but untruthfully, 'You don't *look* seventy'. Being the smart-aleck I am, instead of taking the compliment gracefully, I responded, 'I don't *feel* seventy either!', a response that is completely vacuous, since the only experience I have of being the age I am is the experience I actually have—there is no possible experiential point of contrast.

Hempel describes Evan's transition which, even though it did not include reconstructive surgery, was not a matter of waving a magic wand, but was still rather a gruelling and painful process. 'I watched his body change,' she tells us. 'He started binding his chest with a thick bandage wrap. His hair began to thin. His hips disappeared and were replaced by thick muscles around his chest. But mostly, I remember his hands. We both have the same small hands, the same indelicate, stubby fingers. I watched the hair grow thick over his knuckles, which were my knuckles. I felt sad that, feature by feature, I was losing my doppelgänger .... Before his pregnancy, he injected hormones into his thigh once weekly to lower his estrogen while boosting his testosterone. He elected not to have top surgery, the double mastectomy that many trans men undergo, because he is allergic to most antibiotics. Also, he knew he might one day want to nurse a baby. So he wears two compression-tank binds made by a company called Underworks beneath his shirt. "It hurts, but I've gotten used to it," he told me. "I imagine it's like some women getting used to high heels." [Hempel 2016]

One of Evan's friends who is also trans became pregnant a year before Evan. During this pregnancy, this friend felt, what Hempel describes as, 'a traumatizing disconnect between his masculinity and the female attributes of his body.' I suspect that many readers will find Evan's friend's experience of a traumatising disconnect totally unsurprising. What of Evan? Did he feel a corresponding disconnect? Hempel asked her/him if giving birth to a child had changed what he thought about his gender? 'Were you always a boy trapped in a girl's body, I wanted to ask him, or are you really a girl who got lost for a decade? "You know, people who are not trans talk about being 'trapped in a body.' But that's not really the way my friends talk about it," he said. "I was always Evan. I always had these parts. I always just felt like me, and like I was a guy." [Hempel 2016] I see—or rather I don't see. Saying 'I always just felt like me and like I was a guy' tells us absolutely nothing.

Ms Hempel, do you *really* believe that you have a brother who has managed the physiologically impossible feat of gestating another human being? Or do you believe that you have a sister, a troubled and confused sister, who did what many other women have done since time began, and that is to have a baby?

# 4. Transgenderism and the Law (1)

*'I reject your reality and substitute my own'*
*—Dungeonmaster*

*In regard to all civil acceptations, an Act of Parliament can do any thing ...*
*it may make a woman mayor or justice of the peace,*
*for they are the creatures of men,*
*but it cannot alter the course of nature.*
—Mr Justice Wilde (1671)

The problem that many people, including myself, have with those who believe that they are not the sex they patently are, or who desire to be the sex that they aren't, isn't primarily with their non-standard beliefs or desires, nor is it with their wanting to have or actually having surgery or hormone treatment to give effect to their beliefs or desires. The problem we have isn't with what *they* do or want to do, it is with what I and others who do not and cannot believe that people can change sex are being legally and socially forced to do. People can believe what they like, desire whatever they wish, however improbable or impossible the objects of those beliefs and desires may be, but, as Brendan O'Neill points out, 'The problem with the gender-recognition tyranny is that it doesn't only say "identify however you please"—it also cajoles public institutions, and by extension the public at large, to accept an individual's self-identification. And it cannot be long before we will face punishment for refusing to do so.' [O'Neill 2017]

### Gender Recognition Acts

How did we arrive at this point? To get some idea, let's travel back in time to 2002 to visit the seminal case of *Christine Goodwin v. The United Kingdom*, heard before the European Court of Human Rights. The applicant in this case, Christine Goodwin, was a post-operative male to female transsexual. Goodwin complained that he/she was receiving discriminatory treatment in respect of employment, pensions, social security and an inability to marry as he/she chose, and he/she sought relief under articles 8, 12, 13, and 14 of the European Convention on Human Rights. The Court agreed with Goodwin that his/her human rights had

112                                    *Hidden Agender*

been violated under article 8, the right to respect for private and family life, and under article 12, the right to marry and to found a family.

Despite extensive references to gender throughout the *Goodwin* judgement—there are at least 30 paragraphs in which this term occurs—I was unable to find a definition of it. Moreover, starting a trend that, as we have seen, was to continue, *sex* and *gender* are either insufficiently distinguished from one another or are simply conflated. The following random citations illustrate this conflation or lack of clear distinction. To make the point clear, I've italicised the terms *sex* and *gender*. In §52 of the *Goodwin* judgement, we find, 'It was for Parliament, not for the courts, to decide at what point it would be appropriate to recognise that a person who had been assigned to one *sex* at birth had changed *gender* for the purposes of marriage.' §57 has the following passage: 'As regarded the eligibility of post-operative transsexuals to marry a person of *sex* opposite to their acquired *gender......*'; and §97 notes, 'The Court recalls that in the cases of Rees, Cossey and Sheffield and Horsham the inability of the transsexuals in those cases to marry a person of the *sex* opposite to their re-assigned *gender* ... '

Responding to the *Goodwin* judgement, the UK Parliament passed the Gender Recognition Act in 2004. The key section of the Act states, 'Where a full gender recognition certificate is issued to a person, the person's gender becomes for all purposes the acquired gender (so that, if the acquired gender is the male gender, the person's sex becomes that of a man and, if it is the female gender, the person's sex becomes that of a woman'. [UK Parliament 2004, s. 9.1] Note the-quickness-of-the-hand-deceives-the-eye shuffle between the terms *gender* and *sex*. Let's look at this passage again, this time, with the term *gender* italicised and the term *sex* bolded: ' ... if the acquired *gender* is the male *gender*, the person's **sex** becomes that of a *man* and, if it is the female *gender*, the person's **sex** becomes that of a *woman*).'

In his *A Second Miscellany-at-Law*, Sir Robert Megarry notes that 'The statement that "parliament can do every thing, except making a woman a man, or a man a woman" is nearly always attributed to de Lolme ... What is less well known is that the saying was well over a century old in his day. In 1648 the Earl of Pembroke and Montgomery is reported as attributing it to his father, Henry Herbert, second Earl of Pembroke: "My father said, that a Parliament could do any thing but make a man a woman, and a woman a man". Some years later, in 1671, Mr Justice Wilde, recognising that the powers of Parliament were limited by nature, said, 'In regard to all civil acceptations, an Act of Parliament can do any thing ... it may make a woman mayor or justice of the peace, for they are the creatures of men, but it cannot alter the course of nature.' Alas, Lord Pembroke, thou shouldst be living at this hour, when Parliament has done precisely what you said it could never do. Alas, Mr Justice Wilde, what would you say now that Parliament claims

# Transgenderism and the Law (1)

to have the power to alter the course of nature that you said it didn't have? Come back Francis (of the People's Front of Judea), all is forgiven. Your struggle against reality has been legally vindicated.

But the UK Parliament is not the only legislature that appears to have been invested with quasi-Divine powers. In Ireland, it wasn't possible for transgender persons to alter their birth certificates until the passage of the Gender Recognition Act in 2015. Lydia Foy took an action in the Irish High Court in 2002 to have his/her birth certificate altered, an action that was unsuccessful, as the Court deemed birth certificates to be historical documents. Foy instituted new proceedings in the High Court, relying, *inter alia*, on *Goodwin*, and his/her case came on in October 2007. After judgement had initially been reserved, the Court eventually found in Foy's favour, holding that the Irish State had failed to respect Foy's rights under article 8 of the European Convention of Human Rights by not providing any mechanism for Foy to obtain a new birth certificate in his/her female gender. If it had been relevant, the Judge also said he would have found Foy's right to marry under Article 12 of the Convention had also been infringed. Moreover, the Judge held that parts of the Civil Registration Act 2004 were also incompatible with the Convention.

The Irish Gender Recognition Act allows all individuals over the age of eighteen to self-declare their own gender identity. Those who wish to change their gender make an application to the Minister for Social Protection by completing a Statutory Declaration in which they affirm that they have 'a settled and solemn intention to live in the preferred gender of male/female' for the rest of their lives, understanding the consequences of such a declaration and are making the application of their own free wills. The Irish Act bears a suspiciously striking resemblance to the UK's Gender Recognition Act save that, in the case of the UK's Gender Recognition Act, applicants are required to provide medical or psychological evidence to support their applications. That requirement, as we shall see, is currently under review, and the latest indications are that it may continue to be a requirement, at least, for the present. [see Jones 2020a]

Many statutes contain a preliminary section in which key terms are defined. It is noticeable that the Irish Gender Recognition Act contains no such section. The nearest we get to it is section 2, 'Interpretation', in which we are told what terms such as *endocrinologist, medical practitioner*, and *psychiatrist* mean. The definitions of *gender* or *sex* are conspicuously absent from the section. The term *gender* does appear in two instances, the first telling us what a gender recognition certificate is, the second telling us that preferred gender means 'the gender a person applies to have specified or which is specified in a gender recognition certificate.' The term *sex* does not appear at all in the preliminary section.

114 *Hidden Agender*

The key section of the Act reads: 'Where a gender recognition certificate is issued to a person the person's gender shall from the date of that issue become for all purposes the preferred gender so that if the preferred gender is the male gender the person's sex becomes that of a man, and if it is the female gender the person's sex becomes that of a woman.' [Irish Statute Book, §18 (1)] It is easy for the eye to glide over material like this, but read this passage again and note, as in the case of the UK Gender Recognition Act, the sudden and unexplained (perhaps inexplicable) change from 'gender' to 'sex'. To make the point clear, I have once again italicised the word *gender* and bolded the word **sex** in the passage: 'Where a *gender* recognition certificate is issued to a person the person's *gender* shall from the date of that issue become for all purposes the preferred *gender* so that if the preferred *gender* is the male *gender* the person's **sex** becomes that of a *man*, and if it is the female *gender* the person's **sex** becomes that of a *woman*.' You will notice five mentions of *gender* at the start of this passage with no mention of *sex*, and then, mysteriously, at the end of the sentence, the sudden appearance of *sex*. This would seem to be either a spectacularly careless piece of legal draftsmanship, or a deliberate conflation of terms that refer to different realities. The practical effects of this piece of word-magic are wide-ranging. Those who acquire a Gender Recognition Certificate as female will have the right to access female-only spaces and services such as domestic violence shelters, sports teams, single-sex schools, changing rooms, jobs reserved for women, and can be imprisoned in female gaols.

Of course, if, appearances to the contrary notwithstanding, gender and sex are *not* the same thing, then, depending on what gender-not-sex is taken to be (often the self-presentation of a male as female or vice-versa), a change of gender may well be possible (even if it is of no great social or moral significance) and, if so, as a libertarian, I believe that people should free to change their genders. But if sex and gender are not the same thing, then one wonders what relevance gender has in law and, in particular, one wonders why there should be such pieces of legislation as Gender Recognition Acts. After all, a basic principle of law is that it does not concern itself with trifles [*de minimis non curat lex*] and if gender isn't the same thing as sex then, barring evidence to the contrary, it would seem to fall squarely into the category of the trifling. As a libertarian, I believe that, coincident with people's choice to change gender, where gender is not the same thing as sex, there should be no obligation upon others, whether that obligation be social, moral or legal, to 'recognise' that change of gender, especially not a legal obligation, anymore than there are obligations to 'recognise' anything else another may choose to represent himself as, such as the greatest composer in South County Dublin, or a gazelle, or Edmund Spenser, or Red Rum. On the other hand, if gender and sex *are* taken to be the same thing, as seems to be the case in both the English

## Transgenderism and the Law (1)

and Irish Gender Recognition Acts, then it is all the more necessary that there should be no obligation upon others, whether that obligation be social, moral or legal, to 'recognise' that change of gender. Furthermore, if gender and sex are effectively the same thing, a problem arises. There are only two sexes, so, given the functional equivalence of sex and gender, there can only be two genders. But as anyone who's been following the latest developments in transgender ideology will know, there are many more than two genders. What if someone claims to be possessed of a gender not equivalent to either the male or female sex? This problem worries the Transgender Equality Network Ireland [TENI] which says that 'TENI will continue to advocate for the meaningful inclusion of young, intersex and non-binary people in the Gender Recognition Act.' [TENI 2020] And why should they not? In the US in 2018, Massachusetts state representative Jim Lyons opposed the introduction of a bill that would allow people to list their genders as simply 'X' on their drivers' licences and other forms of ID produced by the state. His opposition to the Bill, perhaps somewhat mischievous, was that it was discriminatory in permitting only three possibilities—male, female and X—leaving out, and thus discriminating against, the many other genders that people could choose to be. Responding to a reporter who wondered why he torpedoed the Bill, Lyons replied blandly, 'Are you saying you want to leave some genders behind?' [Carr 2018]

**Validation**

As I mentioned in the Introduction, tolerance is not enough, for toleration implies a negative judgement by the tolerators of the actions or words that are tolerated. What is demanded of us is not our toleration, but our active validation and valorisation of transgender ideology; anything less is unacceptable to trans activists. It is not enough to obey our Big Brothers & Sisters—we must also learn to love their commands. As Winston Smith is advised, 'Do not imagine that you will save yourself ... however completely you surrender to us. No one who has once gone astray is ever spared.' [1984] Transgender activists do not simply want freedom for their sex and gender performances. Judith Butler writes, 'We are not carving out a place for autonomy if by autonomy we mean a state of individuation ... apart from any relations of dependency on the world of others.' [see Yenor 2017] One's transgender identity is not fully real until it is endorsed by public authorities and recognised—*recognised* is the key word—by one's fellows. This fragile identity is not self-existent but requires 'continual validation and confirmation from an external audience. All critical discussion is a threat to this public validation and it is often effectively curtailed.' [Williams 2020, vii; see also the discussion in chapter 5, § 'A *Grimm* reality']

It's madness and most people know it's madness. Ask any normal, decent member of the public if Dave, 32, born a boy, still in possession of a penis, and a five o'clock shadow on a rough weekend, is a man or a woman, and I bet you they will say: 'Man.' Not because they are prejudiced or 'transphobic'—the latest phobia slur designed to pathologise dissent—but because they understand reality. And truth. And biology and experience. They know that in order to be a woman, you first have to have been a girl. They know womanhood is not a pose one strikes in front of the mirror but is biological, relational, cultural and social. They know the man who wears a dress is a man who wears a dress. [O'Neill 2017]

So, if we all know that Dave is a man and not a woman, why don't we say so when the necessity arises? Because the trans activist lobby has managed to persuade the political establishment, and in particular a compliant liberal media, that claiming that there are two and only two biological sexes is passé, when it's not actually a form of hate speech, so that it has become a form of secular blasphemy to deny the dogma of trans-transubstantiation.

O'Neill again: 'Like Winston Smith in *Nineteen Eighty-Four*, beavering away at the past-altering Ministry of Truth, we are made to lie. Trans agitators' greatest accomplishment has been the institutionalisation of lying.' [O'Neill 2017] If some man wants to claim to be a woman, or some woman wants to claim to be a man, most of us will shrug our shoulders and go on our way, wondering. But what is at issue is not Dave's or Jill's bizarre claims to be something they aren't, it is the demand that the institutions of the state support those claims and make it mandatory for the rest of us to recognise them, or risk incurring legal sanctions if we don't.

Why should men who think they are women or women who think they are men need and demand official recognition of this supposed fact? Such a demand reveals a deep insecurity that 'is exposed by their rhetoric of "recognition" and demand to be acknowledged by society, or the demand to be addressed according to their new sex or gender using the correct pronoun. Wrongly call a "he" a "she" and you will be met with tearful tantrums and complaints of being "hurt".' [West 2017]

Women who are inclined to be sympathetic to male-to-female transitioners, seemingly the majority of women, should reflect that the logical implication of accepting the trans activist dogma is effectively to accept that being a woman is more or less a matter of fashion—and so we would have to  say goodbye to biology, to women's experience and to women-only spaces and institutions. To be soft-hearted is to be compassionate and caring and that, we can all agree, is a good thing; but to be soft-headed is to be, well, just stupid, and that, most emphatically, is *not* a good thing.

## Self-identification and the UK's Gender Recognition Act

As already mentioned, the UK Gender Recognition Act, unlike the Irish Gender Recognition Act, requires the production of evidence in support of applications. These requirements include, among other things, 'a report made by a registered medical practitioner practising in the field of gender dysphoria and a report made by another registered medical practitioner (who may, but need not, practise in that field)' or 'a report made by a [registered psychologist] practising in that field and a report made by a registered medical practitioner (who may, but need not, practise in that field).' [UK Parliament 2004, s. 3 (1) (a) & (b)] These reports are to include details of the diagnosis of the applicant's gender dysphoria.

Those who are experienced in the ways of social agitation suspected that it would be only a matter of time before these requirements would be taken to be onerous, and so it has proved. This alleged experience of onerousness is a very common and effective strategy for producing radical social changes in the face of opposition. The first iteration of any proposed change to a law, or introduction of a new law, is said to be extremely limited and is hedged around with all sorts of restrictions, so that its effect on innocent bystanders is said to be little or nothing. Then, after some time has passed, the restrictions are said to be onerous and unjust, and agitation to have them removed mounts until, eventually, the radical change desired from the beginning stands revealed in all its undisguised glory as a *fait accompli*. This has been the strategy, for example, with divorce. We went from a situation in which there was no divorce, to divorce by Act of Parliament, to divorce for serious causes (desertion, adultery), to divorce for less serious causes (mental cruelty), to no-fault divorce with significant time requirements, to no-fault divorce with minimal time requirements, etc. etc. We might call this the Boiling Frog strategy—turn the heat up gradually and the frog won't jump out of the pot. The ultimate goal of transgender activists is legal (and social) recognition of gender/sex changes based solely on the wishes of those who desire such changes without any need for them to have recourse to surgery, or hormone treatment, or even a diagnosis of gender dysphoria. [see Williams 2020, 24]

It was announced in the summer of 2017 that the Conservative Government in the UK planned to reform the Gender Recognition Act to allow people to specify their gender on their birth certificates without benefit of medical opinion or surgery. The then British Prime Minister Theresa May, in her previously unadvertised and presumably moonlighting role as psychiatrist/medical practitioner, told us that her Government would seek to streamline the process for changing gender because, as she so pithily put it, 'being trans is not an illness and it shouldn't be treated as such.' [Various 2017] She made this announcement at an event called the Pink News Awards! But credit must be given to the Leader of the Liberal Democrats, Jo Swinson, for placing the proposed reforms to the Gender Recognition Act firmly on the political agenda in the run-up to the 2019 general election. A matter of great concern to many women was the issue of the single-sex exemptions enshrined in the UK's 2010 Equality Act, such as the legal right to have women-only shelters. When Ms Swinson was asked about this, she waffled, asking the interviewer why, since such shelters admitted lesbians, they should not also admit trans women. A less polite interviewer might have pointed out to Ms Swinson that lesbians don't have penises, whereas non-surgically-altered trans women do. When asked by a caller to the BBC *Radio Five Live* programme the seemingly simple question, 'What is a woman?', she found this a surprisingly difficult question to answer. When asked about the reality of biological sex, she could only suggest that she didn't think things were as binary as they were often presented. On *Newsnight*, the politically born-again Liberal Democrat Sarah Wollaston, a medical doctor, disclosed that she didn't think a baby's sex is revealed at birth, but rather that its gender is a matter of assignment—once again, the sex/gender two-step. When asked if gender self-identification would be abused by predatory men, Dr Wollaston replied, 'There will be, of course, a very tiny number of individuals who will seek to exploit this to behave as violent criminals towards women and you need a separate route for these people.' All very well, perhaps, except that, as Janice Turner points out, self-identification means that people *are* whatever sex those persons say they are so that there can *be* no separate route. [Turner 2019; Kirkup 2019a]

The Conservative Party in the UK would appear to have given up any pretentions to be conservative, unless conservatism consists in the conservation of the changes made by the Labour Party. The Government's online page requesting feedback on the Gender Recognition Act read: 'The government ... seeks your views on how to reform the legal recognition process. The consultation focuses on the Gender Recognition Act 2004 ... This consultation does not consider the question of whether trans people exist, whether they have the right to legally change their gender, or whether it is right for a person of any age to identify with another gender, or with no gender. Trans and non-binary people are members of our society and should be treated with respect. Trans people already have the right to legally change their gender, *and there is no suggestion of this right being removed.* This consultation simply asks how best government might make the existing process under the Gender Recognition Act a better service for those trans and non-binary people who wish to use it.' [UK Government 2018; emphasis added] The Gender Recognition Act that gave people the right to legally change their gender/sex was introduced by a Labour government. Why then is there no

# Transgenderism and the Law (1)

suggestion of its being repealed in whole or in part by a Conservative government, especially now that the UK's divorce from the European Union has been ratified? I know that the European Court of Human Rights [ECHR] is not an organ of the European Union, but one might think that it is in the spirit of Brexit to return complete legislative power to Parliament, and that would include whether or not to be bound by decisions of the ECHR, such as that of *Goodwin*.

In respect of the Conservative's proposed changes to the Gender Recognition Act, James Delingpole puts the matter pithily: 'The fact that senior echelons of the [Conservative] party can even countenance such stupidity suggests to me that the Conservatives are now so ideologically enfeebled, so burdened with over-promoted no-talents, so out of touch with where ordinary, real people are, that they are quite beyond the point of redemption'. He continues, 'For me this is one of those pivotal moments in the decline of western civilisation. The barbarians are at the gate and here's Justine Greening pushing the doors wide open: "C'mon in guys, gals—or however you want to define yourselves! The city is all yours. Or is that zirs?"' There is a joke, an old one but a good one, which ran, 'With friends like this, who needs an enema!" We might adapt the format to read: with Conservatives like this, who needs the loonie Left?' [Delingpole 2017]

This proposed liberalisation of the law appears to have broad political, judicial and ecclesiastical support, even though a YouGov poll revealed that while 28% of the general public were in favour of making the process of changing gender easier, 47% were opposed. [Swerling 2020d] There is little doubt that the right to self-identification will ease its way through the Commons, eventually, if not in the short term, and become law, just as it has in Ireland. For the immediate and mid-term future, the substantive law on this issue is as close to being settled as makes no difference. All that said, it seems that, wonder of wonders, the post-May Conservative government [2020] might not be quite so gung-ho to press ahead with the liberalisation as the previous Conservative administration. Celia Walden, in the *Telegraph*, writes, 'leaked government plans [have] itemised a series of grievous mistakes made around gender and personal safety. Due to be published next month [July 2020] as part of No 10's official response to a public consultation on the Gender Recognition Act, which has been in the long grass since 2018, these plans will prevent people from being allowed to change their legal identities simply by "self-identifying" as a different sex, without any medical diagnosis .... safeguards will henceforth be put in place to protect "safe spaces" for women. That's after, and not before, female inmates and prison officers were raped and assaulted by fellow inmates claiming to be trans. Who had allowed these perpetrators into our "safe spaces"? Those who knew better: the enlightened, the progressives, the righteous.' [Walden 2020; but see Jones 2020b] Even if what Walden writes is correct, however, there will be nothing to prevent the next Labour Government, should it ever arrive, from liberalising the law and then, when next a Conservative Government comes to power, it will perform its usual party trick of conserving Labour's innovations. A report published by the thinktank Civitas in July 2020, authored by Joanna Williams, has argued that public institutions have been captivated by the ideology of transgenderism, and she called for a moratorium on all projected reforms of the Gender Recognition Act by the UK Government and the Scottish Parliament for at least the duration of the current Parliament. [Williams 2020; see Tominey 2020; but see also Castricum 2019]

While it seems then that the issue of altering the UK Gender Recognition Act to make it more like the Irish Gender Recognition Act is still undecided, in other parts of the UK matters are more advanced. In 2019, Simon Johnson reported that the Scottish Executive proposed to allow those over the age of sixteen to change their genders without any of the onerous requirements of having to produce evidence. [Johnson 2019] Also in 2019, The First Minister of Scotland, Nicola Sturgeon, was questioned about the implications of adopting such a policy for the single-sex exceptions in the Equality Act that allow for the existence of women-only spaces and services. The First Minister's response was to assure her questioner blandly that her concerns about single-sex exceptions were misplaced. Quite why and how these concerns were misplaced was not immediately clear from the First Minister's response. [see Kearns 2019]

The UK Gender Recognition Act, whether as it stands or as it is proposed to be amended, could be regarded as just so much woke legislative absurdity; so too the Irish Gender Recognition Act. What gives these Acts real teeth, however, is their linkage to various equality and anti-discrimination laws. As Gaby Hinsliff, writing in the *Guardian,* noted, 'It was discrimination law, not the recognition process, that came under scrutiny in Canada after serial sex attacker Christopher Hambrook attacked two women in domestic violence shelters in Toronto, which he'd entered dressed as a woman.' [Hinsliff 2018]

### Official forgery

Those in possession of a Gender Recognition Certificate may have the details on their birth certificates altered. The Irish Birth Certificate has printed, in bold, at its foot: 'To alter this certificate or to use it as altered is a serious offence'. [*Is cíon tromcúiseach é an deimhniú seo a athrú nó é a úsaid agus é athraithe.*] Similar warnings are to be found on British Birth Certificates: 'Any person who (1) falsifies any of the particulars on this certificate, or (2) uses a falsified certificate as true, knowing it to be false, is liable to prosecution', and 'There are offences relating to falsifying or altering a certificate and using or possessing a false certificate.' Now,

# Transgenderism and the Law (1)

by a process of what looks to the unbiased eye very much like a species of official forgery, the government can alter such documents by legislative and administrative fiat. It should be noted that the Irish Birth Certificate asks for information not about one's gender [*inscne*] but about one's sex [*gnéas*], so too, the British Birth Certificate. Since the ultimate effect of the issuance of what is called a Gender Recognition Certificate, then, is not only to change a person's gender (whatever *that* may be) but to change that person's sex, we might think that the Gender Recognition Acts are somewhat reticently named. They should really be called Sex Recognition Acts, unless, of course, in the eyes of the law, gender and sex are the same thing. That would solve the problem of the apparently reticent nomenclature, but it would leave unsolved the mystery of how Acts of the Irish and British Legislatures are able to bring about a change of sex.

So there you have it. All it takes in Ireland and the UK to bring about a sex change is the issuance of a certificate by the proper authorities, and its effect is not only prospective but retrospective. The powers of the Irish and British legislatures are mighty indeed. Even God can't change the past, but such a feat is not beyond the powers of those who make Irish and British laws. It seems that they inhabit a *1984*-ish world where, as the unfortunate Winston began to comprehend, 'The past was alterable .... Anything could be true. The so-called laws of Nature were nonsense.' [Orwell] It might be well to remember that *1984* was meant as a warning and not as an instruction manual. Brendan O'Neill notes the Orwellian implications of the proposed liberalisation of the GRA. 'Britain is going full Orwell,' he writes. 'The Tory government is proposing to include in the Gender Recognition Bill the 'right' to alter the sex on one's birth certificate.'

> Like Winston Smith in *Nineteen Eighty-Four*, beavering away at the past-altering Ministry of Truth, we are made to lie. Trans agitators' greatest accomplishment has been the institutionalisation of lying .... To okay the rewriting of birth certificates is to nurture a new Orwellian era in which past events can be altered upon the whim of contemporary prejudice or hysteria. Just as Big Brother sanctions the shoving of inconvenient historical documents into a memory hole and their replacement with 'improved' versions of history—so that 'the lie passed into history and became truth'—so the Tories are proposing a system in which key documents, the very registry of life in Britain, could be edited. Forever. A document that once told us a boy was born on 18 August 1985 would now tell us a girl was born on that day. It would lie to us, and to future generations. Shouldn't this concern us, this official approval of misinformation? [O'Neill 2017]

Yes, Mr O'Neill, this official approval of misinformation should concern us; it should concern us deeply. Untruths are untruths, no matter who states them, or how often, or with what authority. An old conundrum has a boy asking his father, 'Father, how many legs would this calf have, calling the tail a leg?' 'Why, five, my son,' replies his father. 'No, father, he would not,' says the boy, 'he would only have four.' 'But didn't you say, "calling the tail a leg," my boy?' 'Yes indeed, father,' replied the boy, 'but calling the tail a leg does not make it so, you know.'

Readers won't be surprised to learn that in several jurisdictions in the USA the sex/gender switch on birth certificates is available. In Alabama, a birth certificate can be altered if it is appropriately certified that the sex of an individual has been surgically altered, although the new certificate will note that the designation of sex has been changed. In California, reflecting the laid-back nature of California culture, all that it takes for the issuance of a new birth certificate is for the applicant to submit an affidavit in which he or she attests that the request for the altered birth certificate is not for any fraudulent purpose, but is sought to bring the applicant's legal gender into conformity with the applicant's gender identity. The application will set you back a mere $23. The law in Massachusetts is, as one might expect, rather stuffier about all this than in California, requiring more in the way of paperwork but, in the end, the result is pretty much the same. Provided you have had your sex reassignment surgery and had your name legally changed, your shiny new birth certificate can be issued with your new name and new sex on it for all to see. The law in Delaware is similar to that in Massachusetts, requiring an affidavit from a licensed medical or mental health professional stating that the applicant has undergone surgical, hormonal or psychological or other treatment for the purpose of gender transition, after which the applicant can collect his or her new birth certificate that will have his or her new sex emblazoned on it. If the state of California is laid-back, the state of Washington is almost fully recumbent. For Washingtonians, no substantiating documentation at all is required, merely a request from an adult or emancipated minor applicant to have the applicant's birth certificate changed to F, M or X. But, as might be expected, there's always one holdout, one person who wants to spoil the party. The state of Tennessee insists, unfeelingly and uncompromisingly, that the sex of individuals will *not* be changed on birth certificates, even after sex-change surgery.

In Australia, you had to have had sex-reassignment surgery to have your sex changed on your birth certificate. But no longer. Since 2019, all it takes in five of Australia's states to make the change is to make an official request. Even children may make such a request provided they have their parents' permission and a statement from a doctor or psychologist. The dispensation from the requirement to have had sex-reassignment surgery broadly follows the proposed UK reforms. The Attorney General of Victoria, Jill Hennessy, said 'These overdue reforms will ensure that trans and gender diverse people can have a birth certificate which

## Transgenderism and the Law (1)

reflects their true identity.' She commented that the requirement of having to have sex-reassignment surgery sent 'a painful and false message that there is something wrong with being trans or gender diverse that needs to be "fixed"—that's why we're removing this cruel and unfair barrier.' Not everyone was as tender-hearted as Ms Hennessy, however. The opposition Liberal Party objected to what they saw as the new policy's conflation of sex and gender and its subversion of the whole point of having birth certificates in the first place. Their leader, Michael O'Brien, said 'A birth certificate is supposed to report somebody's biological sex, but gender identification is a different concept.' [Banger 2019]

In permitting the alteration of official documents, Ireland and the UK and other Western countries are not the only ones to engage in what amounts to a quasi-official collusion in forgery. Pakistan joined the official forgery club in 2018. The Transgender Persons (Protection of Rights) Act allows people to choose their gender and to have that gender recognised on official documents, such as national IDs, passports and driver's licences. The bill also outlaws discrimination in schools, at work, on public transit and against those in receipt of medical care. One activist who helped to draft the Bill that became the Act said, 'This kind of development is not only unprecedented in Pakistani history, but it's one of the most progressive laws in the whole world.' Oh well, that's all right then; if it's progressive, it must be good. Here are some questions I'd like to have answered. If I can change my gender (for *gender*, read *sex*), can I also change my place of birth (POB)? If not, why not? Or my date of birth (DOB)? If not, why not? My DOB and POB are much more contingent than my sex. My mother could have been somewhere else at the time I was born, and the actual day on which I was born can often be a matter of minutes either way, as we know from the annual contests to determine the first newborn of the New Year.

If I suffer from gender dysphoria, believing that I am a woman trapped in a man's body or a man trapped in a woman's body, the government is willing to give legal effect to my feelings. Since feelings appear to determine reality, the question now arises; suppose I suffer from chronodysphoria, a strong feeling that I am much younger than my birth certificate currently reveals, why should my birth certificate not be changed to recognise this 'feeling-fact'? Likewise, if I suffer from locodysphoria, a strong feeling that I was born in the wrong place, why shouldn't my birth certificate reflect *this* 'feeling-fact'? As it stands, my birth certificate states I am a male, born in 1951 in Cork, Ireland: the revised document giving effect to all my feelings might now state that I am a female, born in 1973 in San Francisco, USA. If my sex can be changed at the stroke of a pen by a government invested with powers greater than those that belong to God, why not my age and my birthplace?

I originally wrote the foregoing passage on official forgery in 2018 and, as I hope is apparent, it was intended to be satirical. Sadly, subsequent events have shown how difficult it is to be satirical in a world gone, to use a technical term, completely bonkers. In November 2018, it was reported that Dutchman Emile Ratelband had started legal proceedings to have himself declared 20 years younger on the grounds that at his current age, 69, he is being discriminated against on a dating app. Emile, bless his little cotton socks, who describes himself modestly as a young god, doesn't feel his chronological age and is no longer comfortable with his actual date of birth. His argument? If I can change my sex, why can't I change my age? Emile has a point. Pull one loose thread on the fabric of reality and the whole thing begins to unravel.

The judge in his case had to admit that the ability to change one's gender (sex) was a development in law that not so long ago would have been thought impossible, and he appeared to be somewhat nonplussed in figuring out how to respond to the bold Emile's appeal. It seems the best he could come up with—and you don't have to be Emile to find what the judge said rather feeble—was to ask our young god how his parents would feel if 20 years of his life were to be wiped out by administrative fiat. By the same token, you might imagine a judge asking a transgender applicant how his parents would feel about their son's desire to become their daughter or *vice versa*. As it happens, while we know that some parents of would-be transgenderists would be just fine with their child's decision, others might not be quite so happy, but their discomfort wouldn't be allowed to stand in the way of their child's transgender transition. At the end of the hearing our young god made this pronouncement: "It is really a question of free will." And there, Emile, *rem acu tetigisti*—you have touched the sharp point. It *is* a question of will, your will in contest with a hitherto recalcitrant reality. Reality says it's this way but you, by your will, determine it shall be that way. Thy will be done or, more likely, thou will be done—by the judge.

As expected, the Dutch court rejected Emile's request, saying 'Mr Ratelband is at liberty to feel 20 years younger than his real age and to act accordingly. But amending his date of birth would cause 20 years of records to vanish from the register of births, deaths, marriages and registered partnerships. This would have a variety of undesirable legal and societal implications.' Indeed, that is true, but the fact that changing one's sex (sorry, sorry—gender) might have a variety of undesirable legal and societal implications isn't permitted to stand in the way of those who wish to make *that* change, which tends to undermine somewhat the judge's rationale for his decision.

The response of some defenders of transgenderism to our Emile's antics has been to adopt the Victorian strategy of not being amused. Writing in the *Guardian* in

## Transgenderism and the Law (1)

November 2018, Ellie Mae O'Hagan is inclined to take what Mr Ratelband did as part of a 'rather sad tradition of men pursuing frivolous lawsuits that undermine LGBT rights.' [O'Hagan 2018] Her response to Ratelband's petition to have his age changed on the grounds that if one's gender can be changed so too can one's age, is simply to assert that his claim presupposes that one's gender is something that can be chosen and, apparently, according to Ms O'Hagan, it can't. Can't genders be chosen? I thought that was the whole point about them? Apparently, Ms O'Hagan hasn't got the memo from the gender theorists. Mr Ratelband may not be able to change his age legally but he can derive some consolation from his being at liberty to freely choose whichever one of the 300+ genders that are on offer today takes his fancy, with perhaps more options on the way tomorrow.

But the bold Emile is not without some support. One Joona Räsänen, from the University of Oslo published a paper in *The Journal of Medical Ethics*, arguing that individuals should be allowed to change their ages. Apparently channelling Ratelband, Räsänen asks, 'Suppose that someone feels his age is not correct and wants to make himself legally 20 years younger on the grounds that he is being discriminated against due to his old age ... Should he be allowed to change his legal age?' Mr Räsänen is anxious to assure us that this question 'is not a joke'. [Mastrangelo 2019] He posits three situations in which age change should be possible. First, where one's emotional age, the age one feels oneself to be, differs from one's chronological age; second, where one's biological age differs significantly from one's chronological age; and third, where, as Mr Räsänen puts it, 'age change would likely prevent, stop or reduce ageism, discrimination due to age, he would otherwise face.' This last scenario should be music to our Emile's ears.

It appears, then, that we can have three ages: chronological, emotional and biological. It is true that, informally, we can distinguish between a person's chronological age and his emotional or intellectual maturity. We know that some people are in better physical shape for their age than others, but even if the notions of biological and emotional ages are not totally incoherent, it is difficult to see what relevance this might have for legal purposes. One's biological age is a physiological attribute and has no obvious legal significance, and taking the notion of emotional age seriously in a legal context might cause some problems. Is a fourteen-year-old who feels twenty-one to be allowed to drink, or a girl of six who feels eighteen to vote? Can a defence to a charge of statutory rape be offered on the grounds that the girl while chronologically twelve was emotionally twenty-five?

### Transracialism

One might think, with some reason, that the protestations of Emile Ratelband lack a certain *gravitas*. But there are analogues to transgender identity that are not so lightly to be dismissed. In late 2018, the question of racial identity—specifically the question, 'What does it mean to be black?'—took a bizarre twist when a British theatre director, Anthony Lennon, or Anthony Ekundayo (formerly David) Lennon to give him his full name, was given a job that was intended to promote diversity by increasing black representation in the theatrical profession. I won't comment on the absurdity of this notion of group representation since I've already done that elsewhere [see Casey 2019], but what made the choice of Lennon problematic wasn't anything to do with the absurdity of group representation just as such, or at least, not directly, but that Lennon is, or appears to be, white! Lennon has sometimes been taken to be a mixed-race person, and has described himself as 'African born-again' because, at least in part, he believes that he experienced the struggles of a black man despite having had two white Irish parents. His comment about going through the struggles of a black actor was prefaced by his saying, 'Although I'm white, with white parents ... ' [Bulman 2018]

Was this racial identification a genuine, born-again experience, or was it sheer opportunism? If the timing is anything to go by, it seems that the born-again experience occurred after Lennon had been signally unsuccessful as a white actor. That doesn't mean his experience wasn't genuine, but it does raise the spectre of opportunism. Writing in *The Spectator*, Ron Liddle expressed the scepticism of those who suspect Mr Lennon of opportunism. Liddle writes, 'I hope similarly to gain financially from my remarkable discovery, at the age of 58, that I am in fact black. Like Anthony I was teased as a child on account of my appearance. I also have a very strong sense of rhythm and am usually cheerful, both qualities which my mother told me were associated with people of African-Caribbean descent. My denial of my blackness I put down to the pressures imposed by a white supremacist society in which I have struggled to survive for so long. I am black—get over it. And gimme the money.' [Liddle 2018a]

Some of those who are unambiguously black were less than impressed with Mr Lennon's 'born-again' experience, and regarded as perverse the award to him of funds that were supposed to be dedicated to 'artists of colour'. Paula Akpan, writing in *The Independent*, said that Lennon's claim of being 'African born again' wasn't how race works, while Luke Elliot, a black actor, said that Mr Lennon was 'taking up the little [*sic*] resources' awarded to black artists. But not everybody was critical. The theatre Mr Lennon works for, Talawa, and the Artistic Director Leadership Programme (ADLP) that awarded the traineeship funding are both satisfied that Mr Lennon is mixed-heritage. The ultimate source of the grant, the Arts Council, said of the Lennon case that having taken into account the law in relation to race and ethnicity, they did not think it undermined the support they provide to black and minority ethnic people within the theatrical profession.

## Transgenderism and the Law (1)

Defending himself in the *Guardian*, Lennon conceded that, yes, he had white parents but he claimed that he had African ancestry too. Given that it has been postulated that the earliest humans emerged from East Africa, Lennon's claim to have African ancestry might well be true but not, perhaps, in any significant way, for if the postulation is correct, we would all have African ancestry. 'I have never,' Lennon writes, 'made any secret of the fact that I was born to Irish parents, and that my parents and grandparents are white. But my identity is different. It's there for all to see in *Chilling Out*, a documentary I took part in back in 1990. As I said then: "When I'm alone in my bedroom looking in the mirror, thinking about stuff I've written down, thinking about my past ... I think I'm a black man."' What? He *thinks* he's a black man so that makes him black? Later in the piece he writes, 'in my mind there is no doubt that I have some African ancestry.'

I hope I will not be thought to be hyper-critical if I ask how he knows this remarkable fact, apart from there being no doubt in his mind? [Lennon 2018] There have been times in the lives of some denizens of psychiatric institutions when there was no doubt in their minds that they were Napoleon or Jesus Christ or some other exalted person but alas, not doubting a proposition does not make it to be true. Some insensitive souls have opined that Mr Lennon cannot be black because, well, he isn't black! But why should mere factuality matter? Doesn't he feel himself to be black, and isn't that enough? After all, that's the criterion we are now to apply to whether someone is a man or a woman. And the odd thing is that one's maleness or femaleness is more easily and more definitively assessable than one's race. Sex is binary, race, at least in the matter of skin colour, lies along a continuum. [see Wright 2019b]

Thus Mr Lennon. What of Rachel Dolezal who became mired in controversy in 2015 over her claims of racial identity? Ms Dolezal claimed to be black for almost ten years before she was revealed as not being black. In her defence, she makes the point, a not unreasonable point it seems to me, that race is less biologically grounded than gender so that, just as we have the category of transgender, we must, all the more so, allow for the category of the transracial. She remarked, 'Gender is understood—we have progressed, we have evolved into understanding gender is not binary, it is not even biological but what strikes me as so odd is that race is not biological either and actually race has been to some extent less biological than gender.' [Pasha-Robinson 2017]

Why might it not be acceptable to change your race? One answer might be that race is determined by one's biology, whereas one's gender isn't. Even if both race and gender were both biological at root, race appears to exist on a continuum whereas gender, if by gender we mean sex, is binary and has two values—male and female (the vanishingly small number of intersex individuals to one side). Taking

128 *Hidden Agender*

skin colour as the primary marker of race, we have not just white and black and yellow and brown, but a whole spectrum of skin colours on display. Of course, if by gender we don't mean sex but something else—a desire for particular forms of clothes, a fascination with one's personal appearance (or not!), a liking for football (or not), and so on—then gender too runs along a continuum, but then, why should anyone care about it?

The sympathy and understanding with which Mr Lennon's claims have been received, contrast sharply with the treatment accorded to Ms Dolezal. She lost one job with the Spokane chapter of the NAACP, and another job where she taught something called 'African Studies' at Eastern Washington University. And to add insult to injury, she was accused of cultural appropriation by *both* blacks and whites. Justin Wm. Moyer in the *National Post* rejects Ms Dolezal's call for 'racial fluidity' and states that the cases of transgenderism and transracialism are not at all alike, but nothing in his piece supports this naked assertion except perhaps the claims that you can't be black unless you've carried the burden of being black. But then, as we've seen, some feminists claim you can't be a woman unless you've carried the burden of being a woman. That claim, of course, is nonsensical, so, by parity of reasoning, the claim that you cannot be black unless you have carried the burden of being black would appear to be equally nonsensical. Terry Glavin makes the point that Dolezal has consistently lied about almost everything to do with her personal history. But so what? Pointing out this no doubt reprehensible fact doesn't address the conundrum her situation poses: if transgenderism is possible, why not transracialism? Why can't Dolezal be black if that's what she wants to be and what she declares herself to be?

Someone who supports Dolezal's position on transracialism is Rebecca Tuvel. Ms Tuvel is a liberal-feminist philosophy professor (is there any other kind?) and she thinks, just like Ms Dolezal, that if a man can be a woman, and *vice versa*, then a white person can be black. If we can have transgenderism, it seems perfectly reasonable to suggest that we can have transracialism. Indeed, of the two forms of trans, transracialism would seem to be significantly more antecedently plausible than transgenderism for, as I just mentioned, skin colour runs along a broad range while sex is binary. Let's take a closer look at Tuvel's controversial piece 'In Defense of Transracialism' in which she argues that the 'considerations that support transgenderism extend to transracialism. Given this parity, since we should accept transgender individuals' decisions to change sexes, we should also accept transracial individuals' decisions to change races.' [Tuvel 2017, 264]

On the face of it, this argument doesn't seem to be absurd. If transgenderism is an intellectually coherent process, then why not transracialism? Tuvel accepts the legitimacy of transgenderism and so, following the logic of her argument, claims that we should be prepared to accept the intellectual coherence of transracialism. We might express Tuvel's central claim as a conditional proposition: if we should accept the decision of transgender individuals to change sex, then we should accept the decision of transracial individuals to change race. I accept Tuvel's central conditional claim but, instead of affirming its antecedent as she does ('we should accept the decision of transgender individuals to change sex') and thereby affirming its consequent ('we should accept the decision of transracial individuals to change race'), I deny its consequent ('we should *not* accept the decision of transracial individuals to change race') and therefore also deny its antecedent ('we should *not* accept the decision of transgender individuals to change sex'). Tuvel's critics, on the other hand, as we shall see, deny her central claim.

*Tuvel's central conditional claim*
if (A): we should accept the decision of transgender individuals to change sex, then
(C): we should accept the decision of transracial individuals to change race.

*Tuvel's argument:*
(A): we should accept the decision of transgender individuals to change sex, therefore
(C): we should accept the decision of transracial individuals to change race

*My argument:*
not (C): we should *not* accept the decision of transracial individuals to change race, therefore not (A): we should *not* accept the decision of transgender individuals to change sex

I should make it clear once again that what I am rejecting is not the freedom of individuals to believe that these changes are possible, nor am I suggesting that we should legally prevent those who wish to make them from attempting to make these changes, whether sexual or racial; rather, I am rejecting my (or others) having to accept that these attempted changes are what they purport to be on pain of legal sanctions.

'Generally,' writes Tuvel, 'we treat people wrongly when we block them from assuming the personal identity they wish to assume.' [Tuvel 2017, 264] Why should we accept this principle? It's truth is not immediately evident to me. In Tuvel's article, the only relevant identities discussed are those about sex and race. But what of nationality? Is that not a matter of personal identity? If someone born and raised in Britain to British parents and who had never left the country were to, let us say, assume the identity of an Azerbaijani, would it be wrong to 'block' them, that is, to deny that they are, in fact, Azerbaijani? If so, why? I can remember being extremely puzzled when I first visited the United States to meet people who told me they were Irish but who, when questioned about this claim, turned out not to have been born in Ireland, or from parents who were born in Ireland, and who had never even visited Ireland, still less lived there for any period of time.

In respect of her central claim, Tuvel asks, 'Is it even possible to feel like a member of another race similar to the way one can feel like a member of another sex?' Note, she appears to think that being able to feel like a member of another sex is unproblematic, and that the problem, if there is one, is with race. She continues, 'I do not know whether it is possible to feel like you belong to a different race. Indeed, Dolezal's claim that she saw herself as black as a child and drew self-portraits with the brown crayon instead of the peach crayon do strike me as decidedly odd. But I cannot say whether they seem odd because they are false, or because we are not routinely confronted with such claims. Indeed, I imagine it was once just as odd to hear people say they felt like they belonged to a sex other than the one that they were assigned at birth.' [Tuvel 2017, 265] Well, if it's just a matter of getting used to it, then time will eliminate the appearance of oddness of transracial claims, as it appears to have done in the case of those who claim to be transgender. If, on the other hand, the oddness derives from its being intrinsically incoherent, then custom, while it cannot stale the infinite variety of psychological shocks of hearing such claims, would not eliminate its conceptual incoherence. Whether or which, she remarks, I believe correctly, that 'it is not clear how one can affirm that it is possible to feel like a member of another sex but deny it is possible to feel like a member of another race.' [Tuvel 2017, 265] Exactly so, Ms Tuvel.

Tuvel presents four objections against the possibility of transracialism and shows, I believe, persuasively, that three of these objections, if valid, would apply just as much to transgenderism but, since she believes transgenderism to be coherent, then these objections must be rejected, and transracialism accepted as a possibility. I, on the other hand, do not believe that transgenderism is coherent, and so accepting the cogency of her objections, I reject the coherence of transracialism as well. What are Tuvel's objections to transracialism?

'First, someone might object that a person like Dolezal cannot identify as black because she did not grow up with the experience of anti-black racism .... Since Dolezal has never experienced what it is like to be black, she therefore cannot claim to be black.' [Tuvel 2017, 268] As it happens, a version of this argument is used by feminists to insist that transwomen cannot be women because they haven't experienced the systematic misogyny that they believe all women experience. Dame Jenni Murray believes that a sex change can't make a man into a real woman because men grow up with masculine privileges and so cannot have the experiences of real women. Tuvel, however, notes that, 'if true, this objection would also apply to trans women who transitioned later in life but did not grow

# Transgenderism and the Law (1)

## 131

up knowing what it was like to experience sexism. Yet despite not having grown up with this experience, we do not rightly suggest that a trans person cannot, for this reason, now identify as a woman.' [Tuvel 2017, 268] Who are the *we* that Ms Tuvel blithely assume her auditors are all part of? Ms Tuvel, allow me to introduce you to Dame Jenni.

The second objection that Tuvel presents holds that 'Dolezal cannot identify as black because of the way society currently understands racial membership', and one way society does this is on the basis of ancestry. [Tuvel 2017, 268] Dolezal just doesn't have the right ancestry to be black. Citing Cressida Heyes, Tuvel remarks, because sex-gender has been understood to be a 'property of the individual's body,' the possibility of changing one's sex-gender through bodily modification is acceptable in our society. However, because race has been understood to be a matter of "*both* the body and ancestry," one cannot alter one's body to become a different race. [Heyes 2009, 139, cited in Tuvel 2017, 269; Tuvel's emphasis] The problem with this argument, as Tuvel points out, is that 'it dangerously appears to limit to the status quo the possibilities for changing one's membership in an identity category,' and, making the transgender connection, she notes that 'Indeed, American society has not always granted recognition to those who felt their gender did not align with their sexed bodies.' Would it not be a consequence of Heyes's argument that, 'during this time, a person born with male genitalia, but who identified as a woman, would not be permitted to affirm her self-identity, because the available social resources were not yet in place?' Or, she continues, 'imagine a transgender person born in a country today where such forms of identification are not tolerated, because the understanding of sex-gender identity is firmly restricted to the genitalia one possesses at birth. Would that person be justly forced to renounce her felt sex-gender, because she was born into a society where "beliefs about the kind of thing [sex-gender] *is* shape the possibilities for [sex-gender] change" [Tuvel 2017, 269, citing Heyes 2009, 142]

And then there is the objection that whereas white people like Ms Dolezal can, employing white privilege, discard their race, black people cannot. Tuvel cites Tamara Winfrey Harris as saying, 'Ms. Dolezal's masquerade illustrates that however much she may empathize with African-Americans, she is not one, because black people in America cannot shed their race ... I will accept Ms. Dolezal as black like me only when society can accept me as white like her'. [Tuvel 2017, 270, citing Harris 2015] But, as Tuvel points out, ' ... the same argument would problematically apply to a male-to-female (mtf) trans individual who could return to male privilege, perhaps especially if this individual has not undergone gender confirmation surgery,' adding ' ... it is difficult to see how giving up one's whiteness and becoming black is an exercise of white privilege. Rather, it seems like the ultimate renunciation of white privilege, if by white privilege we understand an unearned system of advantages conferred onto white bodies.' [Tuvel 2017, 270; 271]

Despite Tuvel's evident wokeness and acceptance of transgenderism, and despite that, as she later noted, 'My article is an effort to extend our thinking alongside transgender theories to other non-normative possibilities', she came in for some severe criticism. One Nora Berenstain posted on Facebook that 'Tuvel enacts violence and perpetuates harm in numerous ways throughout her essay.' [see Weinberg 2017] Oh my goodness, that's bad. Can you imagine it; enacting violence, and doing it with words? What terrible violent things did Tuvel say? Berenstain obligingly tells us: 'She deadnames a trans woman.' Oh my goodness! Tuvel also 'uses the term "transgenderism".' Eh? I'm not sure I quite grasp the force of this criticism. What term was Tuvel supposed to use? Whatever. Let us move on to some of Berenstain's other criticisms of Tuvel.

According to Berenstain, Tuvel 'talks about "biological sex" and uses phrases like "male genitalia".' Well, any reasonable person would have to admit that this is beyond the pale in polite or even in academic society. Not just talking about sex, but talking about *biological* sex (what other kind of sex is there other than biological?), and I think we would all agree that the mentioning of male genitalia should be *verboten* in all and every circumstance. Tuvel, says Berenstain, 'focuses enormously on surgery, which promotes the objectification of trans bodies.' Bad, bad, very bad, Ms Tuvel—take a slap on the wrist. '[Tuvel] refers to "a male-to-female (mtf) trans individual who could return to male privilege," promoting the harmful transmisogynistic ideology that trans women have (at some point had) male privilege.' Well, as it happens, not a few feminists make precisely this point, but who could deny that misogyny is systematically outflanked by transmisogyny. And last, but certainly not least, 'In her discussion of "transracialism," Tuvel doesn't cite a single woman of color philosopher, nor does she substantively engage with any work by Black women, nor does she cite or engage with the work of any Black trans women who have written on this topic.' Well, well, you have to admit that it's pretty arrogant to think that one's arguments should stand or fall on their merits instead of relying on the skin colour or sexual/gender identity of possible interlocutors.

Other criticisms of Tuvel followed, and the result was a nauseatingly cringe-inducing apology from *Hypatia*'s Board of Associate Editors. I present you with a substantial chunk of this pearl of prose because if I merely précised it, you would, I think, be disinclined to believe me. The last sentence of the passage I am about to cite, with its elegiac mention of mourning, is worth the price of admission alone.

## Transgenderism and the Law (1)

We, the members of Hypatia's Board of Associate Editors, extend our profound apology to our friends and colleagues in feminist philosophy, especially transfeminists, queer feminists, and feminists of color, for the harms that the publication of the article on transracialism has caused. The sources of those harms are multiple, and include: descriptions of trans lives that perpetuate harmful assumptions and (not coincidentally) ignore important scholarship by trans philosophers; the practice of deadnaming, in which a trans person's name is accompanied by a reference to the name they were assigned at birth; the use of methodologies which take up important social and political phenomena in dehistoricized and decontextualized ways, thus neglecting to address and take seriously the ways in which those phenomena marginalize and commit acts of violence upon actual persons; and an insufficient engagement with the field of critical race theory. Perhaps most fundamentally, to compare ethically the lived experience of trans people (from a distinctly external perspective) primarily to a single example of a white person claiming to have adopted a black identity creates an equivalency that fails to recognize the history of racial appropriation, while also associating trans people with racial appropriation. We recognize and mourn that these harms will disproportionately fall upon those members of our community who continue to experience marginalization and discrimination due to racism and cisnormativity.' [see Weinberg 2017]

Tuvel later noted that 'so much wrath on electronic media has been expressed in the form of ad hominem attacks .... So little of what has been said, however, is based upon people actually reading what I wrote. There are theoretical and philosophical questions that I raise that merit our reflection .... Calls for intellectual engagement are also being shut down because they "dignify" the article. If this is considered beyond the pale as a response to a controversial piece of writing, then critical thought is in danger. I have never been under the illusion that this article is immune from critique. But the last place one expects to find such calls for censorship rather than discussion is amongst philosophers.' [see Weinberg 2017] But, Ms Tuvel, philosophers ain't what they used to be. If you didn't know that before, you know it now. Let us leave the suitably chastised and chastened Ms Tuvel and move on.

Caitlyn Jenner was valorised for his/her bravery in coming out and saying he/she felt like a woman. He/she received congratulations from the President of the USA and started being referred to widely as 'she'. Rachel Dolezal, on the other hand, was decidedly *not* valorised for saying she felt black. She was fired, shunned, and attacked on social media. If we are going to define gender/sex as a personal choice, how can we deny the claims of those who do not accept the race they were 'assigned' at birth? It has been said, as by Glavin, that Dolezal lied in saying she was black whereas, it seems, Jenner didn't lie when he/she claimed to be female?

But Dolezal is unrepentant. If we accept that gender is non-binary, the same should apply to race. She says, 'It's very similar, in so far as: this is a category I'm born into, but this is really how I feel.' And, of course, as we all know by now, or should know by now, feelings determine reality, psychology trumps ontology. And if gender identity is fluid, racial identity is, if anything, even more fluid. The transgender lobby are not happy with the comparison but why should that matter? In the end, Dolezal seems to be making the point that if anything goes, then *anything* goes. In an interview, Democratic National Convention Senior Advisor Zac Petankas was asked if racial identity was fluid. Mr Petankas had cheerfully granted that gender identity was fluid, but when asked if a person of one race could identify as another race, he dismissed the question as a silly hypothetical. Transgenderism—OK; Transracialism—not OK. All identities are equal, it seems, but some identities are more equal than others.

Unlike Mr Petankas, some are willing to bite the bullet and accept the parallel between transgenderism and transracialism. In the UK, a lecturers' union has said that people should be allowed to identify as black no matter what colour they are born. The University and College Union (UCU), in its position paper, 'UCU Position on Trans Inclusion' stated: 'The UCU has a long history of enabling members to self-identify, whether that is being black, disabled, LGBT or women.' Full marks for consistency, then, to the UCU, even if it is for consistent stupidity. The position taken by the union was criticised as 'nonsensical' by Kathleen Stock, a professor of philosophy at the University of Sussex, who wrote, 'I'm still [a] member of UCU but Christ they make it hard when [they] publish this nonsensical, anti-intellectual propaganda.'

Some final questions. Why should we not consider gender transitioning as a form of sexual 'blackface'? Why isn't transgender transitioning regarded as sexist, a matter of the patriarchal oppressor wearing 'woman face', much as the wearing of blackface is regarded as racist? And why are there no Race Recognition Acts according to which one can self-identify as a particular race? [Thanks to my colleague Tim Crowley for these speculations.]

### Equality Act, USA

The USA doesn't, as yet, have a Gender Recognition Act, but it does have an incipient Equality Act. The Equality Act was passed by the US House of Representatives in March 2019. [see U.S. Congress (2019); subsequent references by section and number] The US Senate received the Bill on 20 May 2019. The Bill may be regarded as essentially an amendment to the Civil Rights Act, and its purpose is to prohibit discrimination on the basis of the sex, sexual orientation, gender identity, pregnancy, childbirth, or a related medical condition of an individual, as

*Transgenderism and the Law (1)*   135

well as on the basis of sex-based stereotypes. [see §§2.a.9, 10 & 12] Each of these factors alone 'can serve as the basis for discrimination, and each is a form of sex discrimination.' [2.a.1] The Bill goes on to say that a given instance of discrimination may arise from several angles, so, for example, 'discrimination against a married same-sex couple could be based on the sex stereotype that marriage should only be between heterosexual couples, the sexual orientation of the two individuals in the couple, or both.' Similarly, 'discrimination against a pregnant lesbian could be based on her sex, her sexual orientation, her pregnancy, or on the basis of multiple factors.' [2.a.2] According to the Bill, LGBTQ people are commonly the subject of discriminatory acts. [2.a.3, 10 & 11] The stated purpose of the Act is to 'expand as well as clarify, confirm and create greater consistency in the protections and remedies against discrimination on the basis of all covered characteristics and to provide guidance and notice to individuals, organizations, corporations, and agencies regarding their obligations under the law.' [2.b]

While the Bill ostensibly concerns itself with the rights of women as well as with the rights of LGBTQ individuals, it doesn't seem to be particularly sensitive to the existing rights of women, specifically, the right of women to be able to have access to female-only spaces and to participate in female-only sports. Emilie Kao writes,

> How ironic that House Speaker Nancy Pelosi introduced the Equality Act during Women's History Month. The Bill's proponents insist it's meant simply to protect the rights of the LGBT community. But by embracing the ideology of "gender identity," it treats womanhood as a mutable feeling rather than an immutable fact. This, in the end, will only increase the very real dangers and disadvantages women face. Our female-only spaces—bathrooms, locker rooms and dormitories—are places where we expect to be free from the male gaze, naked male bodies and sexual assault. For the most vulnerable among us, privacy is the difference between recovery and renewed trauma. Consider the homeless women served by the Downtown Hope Center in Anchorage, Alaska. They have survived rape, domestic violence and sex trafficking. Having a space of their own is a matter of mental health and personal safety. One woman said she would prefer to sleep in the woods rather than sleep next to a man. Yet under a local gender identity ordinance, a man who identifies as a woman is suing the shelter for admittance. No one accuses him of being a sexual predator, but changing rules for admittance has consequences. After Britain passed the Gender Recognition Act, a convicted male rapist who claimed to be transgender was transferred to a women's prison where he twice committed sexual assault. Why would we want to bring this to the U.S. with a new federal law? [Kao 2019]

The Equality Act seeks to install in the US legal system a novel anthropology of sexual identity, including transgender identity, under the remit of which there appears to be little or no room for religious or free-speech exemptions.

136                           *Hidden Agender*

[see Siewers] Given the reach of Federal Law, almost every aspect of life in the US would be covered by the provisions of the new law so that those individuals and organisations that reject the new sexual anthropology would be severely constrained in their ability to exercise their freedoms of action and of speech. The new sexual anthropology would, according to Alfred Siewers, 'violate fundamental rights of religious freedom and encourage a view of physical reality as subject to human will [that] would indeed codify Orwell's terrifying satire. The Equality Act should remind us of its historical roots in anti-religious bias and in the type of disembodied gnostic idealism that, as Eric Voegelin warned, feeds a technocratic totalitarianism. We would do well to remember that such utopian projects, in which, as Orwell said, "Freedom is Slavery," did not end well.' [Siewers]

Stella Morabito takes her criticism of the Equality Act a little further, seeing it as a step towards introducing a Chinese-style 'Social Credit' system to the USA. The Chinese Social Credit system is a scoring system of rewarding compliant and punishing non-compliant citizens. Morabito believes that if the Equality Act were to become law, it would provide a basis for the introduction of a Social Credit system to the USA. The Equality Act, she writes, 'tells all Americans that they must reject the reality of sex distinctions if they are to avoid social and material punishment. It does so under the pretext of adding sexual orientation and gender identity (SOGI) as categories to be protected against discrimination. And it applies to every aspect of life, including housing, employment, transportation, education, businesses, and more.' [Morabito 2020] Jobs can be lost, promotions denied, bank accounts closed, YouTube videos removed, and financial support of 'unprogressive' causes withdrawn. With the installation of gender-coercive laws, in addition to the 'softer' forms of sanctions just described, you can also expect to experience the overt imposition of fines and prison sentences. What is required is not only a matter of refraining from certain activities and forms of speech. No, it goes beyond that to require specific performance of certain activities, including mandatory forms of speech, regardless of conscience. We have already seen the legal intimidation of bakers and florists in other contexts for attempting to give effect to their conscientious decisions, and we can expect to see ever more intrusive and minute policing of speech, thought and action. [see Casey 2019, passim] Joanna Williams draws an interesting contrast between the approach of transgenderists and earlier rights movements towards the issue of free speech. She remarks, 'Whereas the gay rights movement was about demanding more freedom from the state for people to determine their sex lives unconstrained by the law, the transgender movement demands the opposite: it calls for recognition and protection from the state in the form of intervention to regulate the behaviour of those outside of the identity group. Whereas in the past, to be radical was to

## Transgenderism and the Law (1)

demand greater freedom from the state and institutional authority, today to be radical is to demand restrictions on free expression in the name of preventing offence.' [Williams 2020, viii]

Can you really be legally required to speak in certain ways? Yes. New York City's Human Rights Law (NYCHRL) prohibits 'unlawful discrimination in public accommodations, housing and employment on the basis of gender', where gender is defined as one's 'actual or perceived sex and shall also include a person's gender identity, self-image, appearance, behavior or expression, whether or not that gender identity, self-image, appearance, behavior or expression is different from that traditionally associated with the legal sex assigned to that person at birth.' Under the NYCHRL, New York City's Commission on Human Rights requires employers and entities covered by the legislation to use people's preferred names, pronouns and titles regardless of people's sex that was assigned (their word, not mine) at birth, their anatomy, their gender, their medical history, their appearance, or the sex indicated on their forms of identification. The Commission notes that most individuals and many transgender people use female or male pronouns and titles, but that some transgender and gender non-conforming people prefer to use pronouns other than he/him/his or she/her/hers. According to the Commission, there are a number of ways in which you can go wrong, only one of which is of interest to our discussion here and that is the 'Intentional or repeated refusal to use an individual's preferred name, pronoun or title. For example, repeatedly calling a transgender woman "him" or "Mr." after she has made clear which pronouns and title she uses.'

Now, names are not really a problem. An individual may use any name he, she or it wishes and, barring certain specific circumstances, such as extreme vulgarity (calling yourself, say 'F@$% Me!' and requiring people to address you by that name), some titles (such as 'Dr' or 'Your Highness' where the person isn't a doctor or royalty), or having names consisting of 42 syllables ('Call me "supercalifragilisticexpialidocioussupercalifragilisticexpialidocioussupercalifragilisticexpialidocious"'), it's little more than a matter of elementary politeness to use a person's preferred name. Pronouns, however, are a different matter.

What limits, if any, are there to what pronouns, old or new, may be required by the NYCHRL? No principled ones, it seems, for a person may prefer whatever pronouns he/she/it/ze/zir/they wish. In some places, personal pronominal police-actions have now reached a level of insanity that makes satire almost impossible. Failure to use so-called 'gender-neutral' pronouns, such as *xu, hir, ze, nir, hiser* and so on, by which a given person desires to be referred to, can be (and has been) deemed a form of discrimination and a breach of human rights. Of course, a moment's thought will reveal the absurdity of the policy of demanding, on pain of legal sanctions, that person X be referred to by a chosen pronoun, Y. Apart from the practical problem of requiring innocent third parties to remember a possibly impossible large number of possible pronouns, thus defeating one of the purposes for which pronouns came into being in the first place, what is to prevent a pronoun warrior from demanding to be referred to as *gutface, glinky* or *gloopiness the 3rd*? Taken to its extreme, such Humpty-Dumptyish linguistic voluntarism will inevitably lead to the decline of personal pronouns altogether, and saddle those of us who wish to avoid persecution with the unenviable task of endlessly repeating name after name after name. Failure to observe the Commission's requirements can result in some stiff penalties—up to $125,000 for violations, and a mere bagatelle of $250,000 if your violation is wilful, wanton or malicious. What all this comes down to is that one can be legally forced to say what one does not want to say, to subscribe to an ideology one does not want to subscribe to, or to endorse a political message that one does not believe in, on pain of severe financial penalties

Morabito goes on to suggest some of the adverse ways in which society could be affected by the passage of the Equality Act into law. She writes,

> The Equality Act also sets up a collision course between SOGI [Sexual Orientation Gender Identity] rights and the First Amendment. It would prohibit discrimination on the basis of sexual orientation and gender identity (SOGI) while the main law it amends, the Civil Rights Act, prohibits discrimination on the basis of religion. Therefore, conflict is guaranteed. But the SOGI side wins out over freedom of religion because the Equality Act expressly states that religious beliefs *may not* be a part of freedom of expression, particularly in defense against any accusation of SOGI discrimination. The bill also specifically invalidates the Religious Freedom Restoration Act (RFRA) of 1993, which was intended to breathe new life into the First Amendment .... The Equality Act appears to explicitly promote and encourage wholesale lawsuits intended to destroy perceived enemies. The language states that nothing in it "shall be construed to limit the claims or remedies available to any individual for an unlawful practice" on the basis of sexual orientation and gender identity. This is an open invitation to put out of business anybody deemed undesirable by social engineers. And how might an "unlawful practice" be construed in the future? If a business owner or landlord is known to attend a church with traditional teachings on sex and marriage, could that in itself be construed as discrimination? The bill also encourages private surveillance and snitch culture. We already live in a highly polarized culture. If lawfare against such thought crime is encouraged, we can expect to see new depths of vindictiveness rewarded by the state and a further decline in social trust. People will feel pressure to show mandatory enthusiasm for ideas that we do not personally accept. [Morabito 2020]

*Transgenderism and the Law (1)*

All very true, no doubt, and all very depressing for those of us who value freedom of speech and tolerance. It should be noted that the decision of the US Supreme Court in *Bostock* may have rendered the Equality Act moot, since that decision appears to have achieved, by judicial fiat, the central purpose of the Act. [see below, chapter 5, § *'Bostock'*] Whether this is so, only time will tell.

# 5. Transgenderism and the Law (2)

*While individuals suffering from transgender confusion
desire a different body, the gender ideologues exploiting
the condition of those individuals desire a different cosmos*
—Jeff Shafer

*'If the law supposes that,' said Mr Bumble,
'the law is a ass—a idiot.'*
—Charles Dickens

In March 2019, Maya Forstater lost her job when she criticised UK government proposals to allow people to self-identify as the opposite sex. [Lyons 2019a] She has, it seems, become the first person to be 'not continued in her employment' for expressing what are termed 'gender critical' views on her personal Twitter account—'gender critical' meaning simply that she does not believe people can change their biological sex. Forstater may have been the first person to be fired for expressing gender-critical opinions but she's unlikely to be the last. In August 2020, Sasha White was fired by the literary agency for which she worked. The reason? She had tweeted, 'Gender non-conformity is wonderful'—so far so good—but then she went on to say, 'denying biological sex not so'—which her employers seem to have deemed was too far and not so good, Ms White. [see Murray 2020a] Ms White had also retweeted a comment on social media that said, 'TW [trans women] being vulnerable to male violence does not make you a woman.' [Showalter 2020] 'We do not,' tweeted the Tobias Literary Agency, in a display of conspicuous virtue, 'have any room for anti-Trans sentiments at TLA. Period.' [Showalter 2020]

Forstater took legal proceedings against her employer. In her statement to the employment tribunal, Ms Forstater said she believed that sex matters, and that her beliefs were based on scientific facts. 'I also believe that facts are important,' she said, 'and that ignoring them or pretending that they are not true is detrimental to an honest, just and fair society ... I have always believed that sex is a material reality, that being female or male is an immutable biological fact, and that sex matters, and I always will.'[Lyons 2019] Ms Forstater lost her case. The employment tribunal ruled that there is no legal right to question whether a transgender person is a man or a woman. The judge in the case said that what he described as Ms Forstater's 'absolutist' views were 'incompatible with human dignity and [the] fundamental rights of others', and he was of the view that she was not entitled to ignore the legal rights of a transgender person and the 'enormous pain that can be caused by misgendering a person'. Judge Tayler concluded: 'If a person has transitioned from male to female and has a Gender Recognition Certificate (GRC), that person is legally a woman. That is not something [Ms Forstater] is entitled to ignore.' [Employment Tribunals 2019b, §84]

According to Judge Tayler, Ms Forstater's position is that 'even if a trans woman has a GRC, she cannot honestly describe herself as a woman', and that belief, the Judge said, 'is not worthy of respect in a democratic society.' [Employment Tribunals 2019b, §85] Ms Forstater was less than ecstatic about the Tayler judgement, saying that she struggled with shock and disbelief at reading it, which shock and disbelief she judged would be shared by the vast majority of people. She might very well have been shocked, as the number of misspellings in this official document is truly astonishing, but one must presume her shock and disbelief was occasioned by more substantial concerns.

The well-known author J. K. Rowling was perhaps the most prominent person who came out in support of Ms Forstater. She tweeted: 'Dress however you please. Call yourself whatever you like. Sleep with any consenting adult who'll have you. Live your best life in peace and security. But force women out of their jobs for stating that sex is real?' Does it need saying that even the saintly Rowling was attacked for daring to support women and freedom of speech? She was accused of being an aggressive biological essentialist (eh?) who vocally supports transphobes and their beliefs, and among the more charming of the online comments was, 'Never thought I would say this but here we are ... F**k you, J.K.' [see Power 2020] In response to Rowling's tweet, Forstater said, 'I am grateful to JK Rowling for speaking up so carefully and compassionately about the need to protect everyone's rights, without erasing the material reality that women are female. You shouldn't have to be brave to say this, but I'm so glad that she is.' [see Swerling 2020a] While some reactions to the *Harry Potter* author's intervention from trans activists were predictably hostile, she received more than 200,000 'likes' on Twitter. By tweeting as she did, Rowling also helped draw public attention to the suppression of speech and thought encountered in public life in Britain (and elsewhere) when it comes to discussing sex and gender.

## Not worthy of respect in a democratic society

Let's look at the Tayler judgement in a little more detail. I make no apology for discussing the judgement at some length since I should be surprised if even those people who might have read a newspaper account of it, or come across a reference to the judgement on social media took the trouble to read that judgement itself and, as always, the devil is in the details.

The judgement in the Forstater case rendered by Judge Tayler is that 'The specific belief that the Claimant (Maya Forstater) holds as determined in the reasons, is not a philosophical belief protected by the Equality Act 2010.' This judgement, though stark, is perhaps not the most interesting thing about this case. We need to see something of what Mr Tayler said of Forstater's belief and the reasons adduced for that belief, and why it was not a philosophical belief protected by the Equality Act. The relevance of Ms Forstater's belief being or not being a philosophical belief will become apparent shortly.

According to Tayler, Forstater claims that she was fired ('not continued in her employment') because she expressed a 'gender critical' opinion or view. This gender critical view asserted 'that sex is immutable, whatever a person's stated gender identity or gender expression.' Ms Forstater claimed that this opinion or view is a philosophical belief and that she has been 'subject to direct discrimination' because of it or, in the alternative, that she had 'suffered indirect sex discrimination' as this opinion or view is 'more likely to be held by women than men.' [§3] Forstater said that she believed sex was a material reality that shouldn't be confused with gender or gender identity, saying, 'being female is an immutable biological fact, not a feeling or an identity.' [§5.1] She did not believe, she said, as some appear to believe, that 'everyone has an inner "gender" which may be the same as or different to their sex at birth, and that gender effectively trumps sex, so that "trans men are men" and "trans women are women".' [§5.2]

On 2 September 2018, Ms Forstater tweeted that the 'UK gov consultation on reforming the #GenderRecognitionAct—proposed to dramatically change scope of the law; from requiring medical diagnosis of gender dysphoria for change of sex on birth certificate, to using the basis of "self identification".' She went on to say that she shared the concerns of the organisation Fair Play for Women that 'radically expanding the legal definition of "women" so that it can include both males and females makes it a meaningless concept ...', and she noted that while some transgender people undergo cosmetic surgery, most retain their birth genitals. 'Everyone's equality and safety should be protected,' she said, 'but women and girls lose out on privacy, safety and fairness if males are allowed into changing rooms, dormitories, prisons, sports teams.' [§24]

## 144　　　Hidden Agender

There were other tweets from Ms Forstater that some of the staff employed by her employer alleged were 'transphobic.' Forstater denied the allegation, saying 'I have been told that it is offensive to say "transwomen are men" or that women means "adult human female". However, since these statement (*sic*) are true I will continue to say them. Yes the definition of females excludes males (but includes women who do not conform with gendered norms). Policy debates where facts are viewed as offensive are dangerous. I would of course respect anyone's self-definition of their gender identity in any social and professional context: I have no desire or intention to be rude to people.' [§30] In §39 of his judgement, Mr Tayler excerpted passages from Forstater's witness statement, including the following:

'I believe that people deserve respect, but ideas do not.' [§§1] ; 'I do not believe it is incompatible to recognise that human beings cannot change sex whilst also protecting the human rights of people who identify as transgender.' [§§2] ; 'I believe that there are only two sexes in human beings (and indeed in all mammals): male and female. This is fundamentally linked to reproductive biology. Males are people with the type of body which, if all things are working, are able to produce male gametes (sperm). Females have the type of body which, if all things are working, is able to produce female gametes (ova), and gestate a pregnancy.' [§§3] ; 'Women are adult human females. Men are adult human males.' [§§4] ; 'Some women have conditions which mean that they do not produce ova or cannot conceive or sustain a pregnancy. Similarly, some men are unable to produce viable sperm. These people are still women and men.' [§§6] ; 'I believe it is impossible to change sex or to lose your sex. Girls grow up to be women. Boys grow up to be men. No change of clothes or hairstyle, no plastic surgery, no accident or illness, no course of hormones, no force of will or social conditioning, no declaration can turn a female person into a male, or a male person into a female.' [§§7] ; 'Losing reproductive organs or hormone levels through illness or surgery does not stop someone being a woman or a man.' [§§8] ; 'A person may declare that they identify as (or even are) a member of the opposite sex (or both, or neither) and ask others to go along with this. This does not change their actual sex.' [§§9] ; 'In most social situations we treat people according to the sex they appear to be. And even when it is apparent that someone's sex is different from the gender they seek to portray through their clothing, hairstyle, voice and mannerisms, or the name, title and pronoun they ask to be referred to by, it may be polite or kind to pretend not to notice, or to go along with their wish to be referred to in a particular way. But there is no fundamental right to compel people to be polite or kind in every situation.' [§§12]

The Tayler judgement was based on the UK's Equality Act, the Gender Recognition Act and, in particular, on the case of *Grainger plc et al. v Nicholson* as it interpreted a specific passage in the Equality Act. The Equality Act lists nine protected characteristics. In addition to religion or belief, there is also age, disabil-

## Transgenderism and the Law (2)

ity, gender reassignment, marriage and civil partnership, pregnancy and maternity, race, sex, and sexual orientation. [see Equality Act, part 2, chapter 1] In respect of religion or belief, the Act states, '(1) Religion means any religion and a reference to religion includes a reference to a lack of religion; (2) Belief means any religious or philosophical belief and a reference to belief includes a reference to a lack of belief; (3) In relation to the protected characteristic of religion or belief—(a) a reference to a person who has a particular protected characteristic is a reference to a person of a particular religion or belief; (b) a reference to persons who share a protected characteristic is a reference to persons who are of the same religion or belief.' [Equality Act, part 2, chapter 1, §10]

In *Grainger*, a case hinging on whether an employee's belief in anthropogenic climate change was protected under the Equality Act, Mr Justice Burton set out five criteria against which a belief should be judged in deciding whether it should be deemed 'philosophical' within the scope of the the Equality Act. The *Grainger* criteria purport to be based on the case law of the European Court of Human Rights according to which the right of a trans person to have their acquired gender fully recognised in law was established in *Goodwin v United Kingdom*. It was as a result of that case that the UK Government introduced the Gender Recognition Act 2004 and the concept of a Gender Recognition Certificate, the effect of which, as we have seen, is that: ' .... the person's gender becomes for all purposes the acquired gender (so that, if the acquired gender is the male gender, the person's sex becomes that of a man and, if it is the female gender, the person's sex becomes that of a woman).' [S.9(1) UK Parliament, 2004] The *Grainger* criteria are:

(i) The belief must be genuinely held
(ii) It must be a belief and not ... an opinion or viewpoint based on the present state of information available
(iii) It must be a belief as to a weighty and substantial aspect of human life and behaviour
(iv) It must attain a certain level of cogency, seriousness, cohesion and importance
(v) It must be worthy of respect in a democratic society, be not incompatible with human dignity and not conflict with the fundamental rights of others [*Grainger* §24]

It should be noted that in the hierarchy of judicial tribunals, the Employment Appeal Tribunal stands pretty low on the totem pole, and there is no reason to consider that the doctrine of *stare decisis* (the requirement to follow a binding precedent) should be observed in relation to its findings, still less in relation to the reasoning it employed to reach those findings. Nonetheless, this judgement is likely to cause concern. The BBC's legal correspondent suggested that it could

146 *Hidden Agender*

have far-reaching effects, not only in employment but also in education. [Coleman 2020] For example, could workers in supermarkets who are or who profess to be ethical vegans refuse to handle meat or meat products or milk or eggs or leather goods or woollen jumpers or anything else connected with animal husbandry? This is not an idle speculation for we have a case that deals with just such a situation. Jodri Casamitjana was employed by the League Against Cruel Sports and was sacked, he claims, because he is an ethical vegan. [BBC 2020] His employers denied that his sacking was connected to his ethical veganism but was rather occasioned by what they believed to be his gross misconduct when he made disclosures about their investments in pension funds. Without ruling on the substantive issue of the legality of Mr Casamitjana's dismissal, the tribunal judge decided that ethical veganism is a philosophical belief and so was protected under the Equality Act because it met several of the tests provided by the act, including that it was worthy of respect in a democratic society, that it was not incompatible with human dignity, and did not conflict with the fundamental rights of others.

Ethical Veganism, then, *is* worthy of respect in a democratic society, but holding that men are men and women are women and neither is the other is *not* worthy of respect in a democratic society. Theodore Dalrymple remarks that 'the very idea that a tribunal should feel competent to divide beliefs into those both truly philosophical and not inimical to a democratic society ... and those that don't meet these specifications is worrying. It amounts to a virtual licensing or certification of beliefs, akin to a seal of good housekeeping that brings legal privileges. It confers on the courts both the right and the duty to decide what beliefs are compatible with democracy and what beliefs are not. This is a recipe for endless disputation, to the great advantage of lawyers, no doubt, but to the disadvantage of the peace of society.' [Dalrymple 2020] In Ms Forstater's case, there was no suggestion that her belief was a religious one, so the task of the Tribunal was to decide whether her belief was a 'philosophical belief' under the terms of the Equality Act. The Tribunal applied the *Grainger* criteria and held that while Ms Forstater's belief met the first four of them, it did not meet the fifth: her belief that trans women are not women was not worthy of respect in a democratic society, it was incompatible with human dignity, and it conflicted with the fundamental rights of others.

As it happens, Mr Tayler also had his doubts whether Ms Forstater's belief met the fourth criterion of the *Grainger* test, the test of cogency, seriousness, cohesion and importance. On this point, he wrote:

> I next considered whether the Claimant's core belief that sex is immutable lacks a level of cogency and cohesion. It is avowedly not religious or metaphysical, but is said to be scientific. Her belief is that a man is a person who, if everything is working, can produce sperm and a woman a person who, if everything is working, can produce

## Transgenderism and the Law (2)

eggs. This does not sit easily with her view that even if everything is not, in her words, "working", and may never have done so, the person can still only be male or female. The Claimant largely ignores intersex conditions and the fact that biological opinion is increasingly moving away from an absolutist approach to there being genes the presence or absence of which determine specific attributes, to understanding that it is necessary to analyse which genes are present, which are switched on, the extent to which they are switched on and the way in which they interact with other genes. However, I bear in mind that "coherence" mainly requires that the belief can be understood and that "not too much should be not [*sic*] expected". A "scientific" belief may not be based on very good science without it being so irrational that it is unable to meet the relatively modest threshold of coherence. On balance, I do not consider that the Claimant's belief fails the test of "attaining a certain level of cogency, seriousness, cohesion and importance"; even though there is significant scientific evidence that it is wrong. I also cannot ignore that the Claimant's approach (save in respect of refusing to accept that a Gender Recognition Certificate changes a person's sex for all purposes) is largely that currently adopted by the law, which still treats sex as binary as defined on a birth certificate. [Employment Tribunals 2019b, §83]

I refrain from commenting on the judge's introduction of the sublimely irrelevant stalking horse of intersex conditions which, to mix metaphors, is commonly used to muddy the waters (though there is some excuse for his doing this as Ms Forstater had made some mention of this topic), and on his inability to appreciate that the existence of deviations from a norm do not call the norm into question—the occasional three-legged dog doesn't undermine the biological fact that dogs are four-legged creatures. Mr Tayler eventually, however reluctantly and sniffily, conceded that Ms Forstater's belief met criterion (iv). Let's examine the passage containing the section of Judge Tayler's reasoning that is key to the case.

However, I consider that the Claimant's view, in its absolutist nature, is incompatible with human dignity and fundamental rights of others. She goes so far as to deny the right of a person with a Gender Recognition Certificate to be the sex to which they have transitioned. I do not accept the Claimant's contention that the Gender Recognition Act produces a mere legal fiction. It provides a right, based on the assessment of the various interrelated convention rights, for a person to transition, in certain circumstances, and thereafter to be treated for all purposes as the being of the sex to which they have transitioned. In Goodwin a fundamental aspect of the reasoning of the ECHR was that a person who has transitioned should not be forced to identify their gender assigned at birth. Such a person should be entitled to live as a person of the sex to which they have transitioned. That was recognised in the Gender Recognition Act which states that the change of sex applies for "all purposes". Therefore, if a person has transitioned from male to female and has a Gender Recognition Certificate that person is legally a woman. That is not something that the Claimant is entitled to ignore. [Employment Tribunals 2019b, §84]

148    *Hidden Agender*

Let me make it absolutely clear what Mr Tayler is saying here. Ms Forstater's belief was that even if a trans woman has a Gender Recognition Certificate, she cannot honestly describe herself as a woman, but that belief, according to Mr Tayler, is incompatible with the human rights of others that have been identified and defined by the European Court of Human Rights and put into effect through the Gender Recognition Act. He went on to say:

> Human Rights law is developing. People are becoming more understanding of trans rights. It is obvious how important being accorded their preferred pronouns and being able to describe their gender is to many trans people. Calling a trans woman a man is likely to be profoundly distressing. It may be unlawful harassment. Even paying due regard to the qualified right to freedom of expression, people cannot expect to be protected if their core belief involves violating others [*sic*] dignity and/or creating an intimidating, hostile, degrading, humiliating or offensive environment for them .... I conclude from this, and the totality of the evidence, that the Claimant is absolutist in her view of sex and it is a core component of her belief that she will refer to a person by the sex she considered appropriate even if it violates their dignity and/or creates an intimidating, hostile, degrading, humiliating or offensive environment. The approach is not worthy of respect in a democratic society. [§87; §90]

If we were to accept that the judgement of Mr Tayler correctly interpreted the line of cases and statutes from *Goodwin*, the Gender Recognition Act, the Equality Act and *Grainger*—and it is not immediately obvious that his interpretation is correct—all that this would show is how the germ of legal insanity, contracted in *Goodwin*, has now spread through the legal system. It is perhaps worth mentioning once again what the Earl of Pembroke and Montgomery said that his father said, which was that 'a Parliament could do any thing but make a man a woman, and a woman a man.' And that, my Lord Pembroke, is precisely what Parliament thinks it has done, 350 years later. 'If the law supposes that,' said Mr. Bumble in *Oliver Twist*, 'the law is a ass—a idiot.'

Ms Forstater is not the only person to run into trouble with her employers because of her inability to subscribe to the new orthodoxy. Earlier in the book, in the context of the conflation of sex and gender, I mentioned the travails of a certain Dr Mackereth. Putting this conflation to one side, let's consider the substance of this case.

Dr Mackereth worked for the NHS for over twenty five years but was told that he couldn't be employed as a disability assessor for the Department of Work and Pensions (DWP) if he refused to identify patients as being of a sex other than their biological one. [see Bird] His role in the DWP would have entailed

## Transgenderism and the Law (2)

interviewing and then writing independent reports about the health of those claiming disability benefits. 'However, when his instructor stated that reports must only refer to the patient—or "client"—by the sex that person identified themselves as, a discussion took place among the medics about the "fluid" nature of gender.' Dr Mackereth said that he believed that 'gender is defined by biology and genetics.' He said he feared many other professional people could also be dismissed simply for holding opinions about gender that are 'centuries old'. The DWP consulted lawyers and was adamant that any report or contact with clients should refer to them by their chosen sex, otherwise it 'could be considered to be harassment as defined by the 2010 Equality Act'. Dr Mackereth, who appears to believe that sex is genetic and biological and established at birth, could not conscientiously agree to this condition and so the contract between him and the DWP was terminated. He protested that the termination of his contract was a denial of free speech and even of free thought. 'Firstly,' he said, 'we are not allowed to say what we believe. Secondly, as my case shows, we are not allowed to think what we believe. Finally, we are not allowed to defend what we believe.' A DWP spokeswoman said the Equality Act makes it unlawful to discriminate directly or indirectly against a person on grounds of a 'protected characteristic', such as gender reassignment, adding, 'Dr Mackereth made it clear during his training that he would refuse to use pronouns which did not match his own view of a person's biological gender.' [see Bird 2018]

Once again, the tribunal made reference to the *Grainger* criteria [Employment Tribunals 2019a, §195 ff.] The Tribunal accepted that Dr Mackereth's beliefs in *Genesis* 1:27 ('So God created man in His *own* image; in the image of God He created him; male and female He created them.') were genuinely held, as were his lack of belief in transgenderism and conscientious objection to transgenderism. Nevertheless, the Tribunal held that 'lack of belief in transgenderism and conscientious objection to transgenderism in our judgment are incompatible with human dignity and conflict with the fundamental rights of others, specifically here, transgender individuals.' [§197] What? Did I read that correctly? Did the tribunal really judge that a *failure* to believe a proposition can be incompatible with human dignity and conflict with the fundamental rights of others? But wait, there's more! The Tribunal said, 'We accept Dr Mackereth's account that his beliefs ... are inherent to his wider faith .... In so far as those beliefs form part of his wider faith, his wider faith also does not satisfy *Grainger*.' [§231] Are we to conclude from this remarkable statement that, in not satisfying *Grainger*, Dr Mackereth's wider faith—a form of orthodox Christianity—is also unworthy of respect in a democratic society?

## Legal incoherence

You might remember that, according to the Gender Recognition Act, when a full gender certificate is issued, 'the person's gender becomes *for all purposes* the acquired gender ... so that if the acquired gender is the male gender, the person's sex become that of a man ... ' [Gender Recognition Act s. 9.1] Well, it seems that this doesn't quite happen for *all* purposes, for the Act goes on to state, 'The fact that a person's gender has become the acquired gender under this Act does not affect the status of the person as the father or mother of a child.' [Gender Recognition Act, s. 12] This latter provision, excluding the gender/sex change from affecting one's status as either father or mother, would seem to run directly counter to the bold and expansive pronouncement of s. 9.1

Freddy McConnell was born a woman but, following surgery, now lives as a man. McConnell became pregnant and gave birth to a child but, by the time of the child's birth, McConnell had legally become a man. [see YouTube 2019a] Here's the question. Is McConnell the child's father or its mother? Upon registering the child, McConnell was told that the law required those who gave birth to a child to be registered as mothers. McConnell took an action against the General Register Office on the grounds of discrimination, accusing it of breaching her/his human right to family and private life. The case was heard in the High Court and, *mirabile dictu*, McConnell lost. [UK High Court 2019; see also BBC 2019; Telegraph View 2019; Booth 2019] The High Court re-affirmed that the status of 'mother' was afforded to the person who carries and gives birth to a baby. Sir Andrew McFarlane, President of the Family Division of the High Court, said that there was a material difference between a person's gender and their status as a parent. 'It is,' he said, 'now medically and legally possible for an individual, whose gender is recognised in law as male, to become pregnant and give birth to their child.' [UK High Court 2019, §279; see also BBC 2019] Realising, as how could he not, that there is some tension in the law bearing on this issue, not least within the framework of the Gender Recognition Act itself, he remarked, 'There would seem to be a pressing need for government and Parliament to address square-on the question of the status of a trans-male who has become pregnant and given birth to a child.' [UK High Court 2019, §125] Sir Andrew noted that 'at common law a person whose egg is inseminated in her womb and who then becomes pregnant and gives birth to a child is that child's "mother", that 'the status of being a "mother" arises from the role that a person has undertaken in the biological process of conception, pregnancy and birth, and that 'being a "mother" or "father" with respect to the conception, pregnancy and birth of a child is not necessarily gender-specific, although until recent decades it invariably was so. It is now possible, and recognised by the law, for a "mother" to have an acquired

## Transgenderism and the Law (2)

gender of male, and for a "father" to have an acquired gender of female.' He went on to say that 'section 12 of the GRA is both retrospective and prospective. By virtue of that section the status of a person as the father or mother of a child is not affected by the acquisition of gender under the GRA, even where the relevant birth has taken place after the issue of a GRC.' [UK High Court 2019, §149]

McConnell appealed the High Court decision and, once again, lost. [see Swerling 2020] Having danced around the complexities raised by the proper interpretation of the GRA, and having regard to the Convention on Human Rights and the claim by McConnell that the action of the Registrar violated her/his right to privacy and family life, the Appeal Court concluded, 'The legislative scheme of the GRA required Mr McConnell to be registered as the mother of YY, rather than the father, parent or gestational parent. That requirement did not violate his or the YY's Article 8 rights. There is no incompatibility between the GRA and the Convention. In the result we dismiss these appeals.' [UK Court of Appeal §89] The ruling of the Court of Appeal means that, for the moment at least, parents, at the stage of Registration of Births, will be recognised by biology, and not by their GRA-altered birth certificates. How regressive is that!

If a man has a child, that man is the child's father; if a woman gives birth to a child, complications of surrogacy to one side, that woman is the child's mother. McConnell is legally a man and so is the child's father; McConnell gave birth to the child and so is the child's mother. Putting all that together, McConnell would appear to be both the child's father *and* the child's mother. If a woman can 'become' a man, I can see no reason why she can't be described as 'father' on a birth certificate; if she can't be described as 'father' on the birth certificate, it seems to me that the law doesn't, at least in this instance, consistently consider her to be a man. Legal coherence is normally considered a *desideratum*. So, there are two ways in which coherence might be achieved: one, allow such as McConnell to register as father or, backtrack on the nonsense emanating from *Goodwin* and reconsider undoing the damage already done by the Gender Recognition Act and its sister Acts. I'd like to think that the incoherence would be resolved by the repeal of the Gender Recognition Act but, without being unduly cynical, I suspect it will be achieved by 'reforming' (that is, distorting) the law on the registration of births. It's somewhat embarrassing to witness three distinguished judges of the Court of Appeal trying to hack their way through the statutory brambles created by the concatenation of *Goodwin*, the Gender Recognition Act, the Equality Act and *Grainger*. 'Oh, what a tangled web we weave, when first we practise to deceive' [Scott, *Marmion*]

A final point. Amidst all the legal fuss in these cases, one person seems to have been forgotten about completely and that is the actual male progenitor of

152          *Hidden Agender*

McConnell's baby or, in old-fashioned and regressive language, its father. If ever the law is changed to allow a trans man to be entered in the Register of Births as 'father', how will the actual male progenitor be described, if he is described at all—father #2? sperm donor xg734st-3? I must thank my colleague Tim Crowley for alerting me to the disposal of the male progenitor of baby McConnell down the Orwellian memory hole.

### A *Grimm* reality

You may recall from our earlier discussion that Title IX of the Education Amendments Act (1982) states, 'No person in the United States shall, on the basis of sex, be excluded from participation in, be denied the benefits of, or be subjected to discrimination under any education program or activity receiving Federal financial assistance.' One point to note immediately is that the discrimination that is prohibited is prohibited on the grounds of sex. If Title IX is interpreted in such a way that the category of sex is undermined or invalidated, then Title IX becomes effectively otiose. A second point to note is that, as I discussed earlier, Title IX doesn't explicitly ban *gender* discrimination in educational establishments in receipt of Federal funds for the very simple and obvious reason that it doesn't say anything at all about gender. What set the cat among the pigeons was a 2015 opinion contained in a letter sent to schools from the US Department of Education regarding its regulation under Title IX that permitted the separation of restrooms and locker rooms on the grounds of sex. In this letter, the Department interpreted its own regulations to mandate that establishments receiving federal funds must allow transgender students to use facilities in line with their gender identity. The meaning and intent of Title IX is key to *Grimm*, a case that exposed all this to public view.

In the 2013-14 school year, Gavin Grimm, a student at Gloucester High School, Virginia, was diagnosed with gender dysphoria. S/he obtained permission from the School's principal to use the boys' restroom in the School during the 2014-15 school year, which s/he did for almost two months. But then, following objections raised by some parents and residents in Gloucester County, a new policy was adopted by the School Board requiring that transgender students be allowed access only to single-user restrooms or to restrooms corresponding to their actual sex. That was in December 2014. Then, what has come to be known as the 'Dear Colleague' letter from the Department of Education was issued on 7 January 2015 (and in conjunction with the Department of Justice on 13 May 2016). This letter instructed schools to recognise transgender students' preferred names and pronouns, and to permit them to participate in sex-segregated activities, and to use sex-segregated facilities (including bathrooms, locker rooms, and overnight

## Transgenderism and the Law (2)

accommodations) in accordance with their gender identity. [see US Departments of Education and Justice 2016] Relying upon that letter, Grimm, via the American Civil Liberties Union [ACLU] and the ACLU of Virginia, sued the School Board for discrimination. Her/his lawyers argued that the School Board's policy was unconstitutional under the Equal Protection Clause of the Fourteenth Amendment to the Constitution and, yes, you've guessed it, under Title IX. A motion filed for a preliminary injunction that would have allowed Grimm to use the boys' restroom at the School was denied by the district court, which also granted the School Board's motion to dismiss Grimm's claim under Title IX. The decision of the district court was appealed to the US Court of Appeals for the Fourth Circuit and was duly overturned. The Court of Appeals held that the term *sex* in the Department's own regulation was ambiguous in respect of transgender students and also ruled that since the Department's interpretation of its own regulation was the result of its well-considered judgement, the district court had erred in not deferring to it. In his dissenting opinion, Judge Paul Niemeyer wrote that the Department of Education's interpretation of Title IX misconstrued its clear language and overturned 'all universally accepted protections of privacy and safety that are based on the anatomical differences between the sexes.' He added, 'This unprecedented holding overrules custom, culture and the very demands inherent in human nature for privacy and safety, which the separation of such facilities is designed to protect,' and, he continued. 'it reaches an unworkable and illogical result.' [see Grigg 2016]

The School Board then petitioned for a Writ of Certiorari (judicial review) to the Supreme Court of the USA, and the order of the Court of Appeals was stayed pending the Supreme Court's decision. The Supreme Court set an argument date in early 2017 to review the Court of Appeals' decision but, before the case could come on, the Department of Education, now under the control of the Trump Administration, rescinded the guidance contained in the Department's letter of January 2015. Since the judgement of the Court of Appeals had depended on deference to the Department's interpretation of Title IX, and since the Department had now varied its interpretation, the Supreme Court, in March of 2017, obviously considering the Court of Appeals' decision to be moot, vacated the judgement of the appellate court and sent the case back to the Court of Appeals for reconsideration. The issues to be considered included: (1) Whether courts should extend deference to an unpublished agency letter that, among other things, does not carry the force of law and was adopted in the context of the very dispute in which deference is sought; and (2) whether, with or without deference to the agency, the Department of Education's specific interpretation of Title IX and 34 C.F.R. §106.33, which provides that a funding recipient providing sex-separated

154 *Hidden Agender*

facilities must 'generally treat transgender students consistent with their gender identity,' should be given effect.

After Grimm had graduated from the School in June of 2017, s/he filed a claim with the district court contending that the School Board had violated her/his rights under the Equal Protection Clause of the Fourteenth Amendment and Title IX, and s/he sought a permanent injunction that would prohibit the Board from excluding her/him from using the boy's restroom when s/he should be on the School premises for any alumni activities. The School Board's defence, as one might expect, focused on Title IX's use of the word *sex* and what that word implied for its policies. [see Appellant Brief 2019] The School Board's legal team argued vigorously that the School Board's policy did *not* discriminate against Grimm on the basis of sex since they could be held to have discriminated against him in failing to treat him like other boys only if he *was*, in fact, a boy. However, they contended, the evidence clearly demonstrated that Grimm was not a boy, and so there was no discrimination on the grounds of sex.

> The term 'sex' refers to the biological indicators of male and female such as in sex chromosomes, gonads, sex hormones, and nonambiguous internal or external genitalia. Sex is determined or recognized at birth by external genitalia and internal reproductive organs. Grimm was born a female and remains a female to this day. Grimm was born with female genitalia and fully functioning female reproductive organs. Grimm was issued a birth certificate listing his sex as female and enrolled in high school as a girl. Grimm does not have intersex characteristics. Grimm's gender identity does not change Grimm's sex. Grimm's own expert testified that (1) choosing gender identity does not cause chromosomal changes in the body (2) a person's innate sense of belonging to a particular gender does not cause biological changes in the body. Further, it is undisputed that transgender individuals remain biologically men or biologically women. Finally, Grimm's chest-reconstruction surgery did not make him a biological and physiological male. Grimm's own expert even testified that Grimm's chest reconstruction surgery did not create any biological changes in Grimm, nor did it complete gender reassignment. Grimm remains anatomically and biologically female. (Appellant Brief 2019, 7-8)

The School Board's legal team asserted that Grimm's claim of discrimination depended on a forced interpretation of Title IX according to which sex is to be determined by gender identity. They remarked, pointedly, 'Perhaps it is a failure on Congress's part in not addressing whether transgender status is covered under Title IX, but Congress's inaction is not a license for this Court to re-write the statute to Grimm's liking.' (Appellant Brief 2019, 12-13)

Let's step back for a moment from the legal minutiae to consider the coherence of Grimm's claims. Jeff Shafer, in his outstanding analysis of this case and its

## Transgenderism and the Law (2)

related issues (of which I make extensive use) tells us that Grimm's female body 'is precisely what she wishes to erase from legal visibility, to be replaced by the mental state that she announces: a male "gender identity." If Gavin, who has a female body, has a male gender identity, it is not clear what "male" means in this context, or why her male gender identity should determine which bathroom she uses. What *is* clear is that "male" with reference to gender identity does not have (in her case, certainly) the same meaning as "male" when the school district employs it to demarcate admittance to restrooms.' [Shafer 2017] But when Grimm claims to be a boy, s/he, if that claim were to be granted would, *ipso facto*, eradicate precisely the identity s/he is claiming to have. If being a boy has no intrinsic relationship to bodily characteristics, then what exactly is Grimm's maleness supposed to denote? If it is the mind that determines what it is I really am and not the body, then how does one access the emanations of this mind? The actions of a person who claims to be trans is typically to adopt the stereotypical appearance and behaviour of the other sex that are materially manifested and are not merely mental, or, in the extreme, to acquire or to attempt to acquire a hormonally or surgically created simulacrum of the *body* of a person of the other sex. Absent such material conditions and there is no way for trans persons to manifest their gender identity. There is no objective way to determine a person's gender identity as there is to determine a person's sex.

Shafer identifies the inherently self-stultifying character of the arguments of those who would have gender identity trump sex, arguing that transgenderism, if successful, would saw off the very branch on which it sits. In words that echo many of the points I have already expressed above, he writes:

> Transgenderism—at least in its current advocacy posture—refuses to commit itself fully to slaying the categories of reality it denounces, because it needs them alive if its destabilizing demands are to be met. This makes things tricky. If transgender theory were to enjoy complete success in replacing the legal relevance of male and female bodies with reports of gender-states-of-mind, the means to reveal those states of mind would disappear. Consider: names (Gavin changed hers), wardrobe selection (she changed this, too), single-sex restroom access (which she demands in her lawsuit)—these are all dependencies of the publicly meaningful sex-binary. While aiming to replace sex with gender identity, Gavin insists on access to the male facilities that exist only because the public acknowledges the meaningfulness of bodies that she denies have meaning. Her novel theory of identity and her claim for restroom access are mutually refuting. To disqualify the legal authority of the sex binary won't leave intact its corresponding institutional expressions; these would die and disappear right along with their reason for existence. In such case, the parasitic gender identity construct would be without its host, now invisible and without a context in which its body-revolt could register. Sex-less persons would be absorbed

156 *Hidden Agender*

into the undifferentiated mass of others of infinitely variable mental states with no physical referent to serve as the *in-terms-of-which* these mental states could be deemed sensible, meaningful, or publicly identity-defining. An androgynous nirvana. And if bodies are but neutral, mute substrata in which minds reside and travel about, their mute features hardly seem cause for personal crisis, or for much concern about what we do with them. [Shafer 2017]

Bathrooms are set up to accommodate persons of distinct male and female types. If I may be permitted to be a trifle crude for a moment, it is not one's gender identity that one takes out in a men's bathroom in order to use the urinal. Furthermore, much of the debate on transgenderism makes use of an implicit gender binary when, if gender theorists are to be believed, there is a possible infinity of genders, or, at least, if not an infinity of them, a very large number of them. If bathrooms were to be provided to match gender identities, that would require either an infinite or, more realistically, an impossibly large number of them. But the issue, of course, is not one of making available a facility that could not otherwise be provided. Grimm had available to her/him both the girls' bathrooms or a single-use bathroom that s/he could use if s/he desired. The issue is, rather, forcing others to recognise one to be what one is not. Shafer, once more, makes the point with devastating clarity: 'Cross-sex bathroom access serves two roles, one for each category of participant in the transgenderism policy project. First, for the dysphoria-sufferer, bathroom access presents ... a social signaling opportunity. A female's invisible 'male' gender identity is powerfully broadcast upon her authorized use of the male restroom .... Second, for the transgender advocacy industry, cross-sex restroom access disrupts and destabilizes the otherwise still-stable public practices and institutions that reflect the sex binary that gender theory marks for ultimate annihilation.' [Shafer 2017] The provision of an infinite or impossibly large number of bathrooms being out of the question, bathrooms that are available to all and sundry without distinction is a realistic possibility. Would Grimm be happy with this? I suspect not, for in that case, a powerful and visible marker of her/his gender identity would disappear from view.

Despite the presentation of cases such as that of Grimm in terms of an emotional appeal to accommodate the desires of just one individual, the real issue is much wider that the desires of a single person. As Shafer remarks, 'Transgenderism public policy advocates are not proposing a compromise at the margins, and indeed they cannot. Their program is totalistic, as its ambition is to redefine humanity writ large. If the law governing us all says Gavin is a boy and not a girl, then "boy" and "girl" no longer mean *for anyone* what they always meant before. We've then all been redefined.' [Shafer 2017] And if boy and girl are evacuated of all meaning, then it is not possible for anyone, Grimm or anyone else, to have

*Transgenderism and the Law (2)*          157

a gender identity which is that of a boy or a girl. The successful parasite has been so successful that it has managed to devour its host.

Transgenderism, at its very root, is incoherent. Shouldn't that be a problem? 'Transgenderism,' writes Shafer, 'is supremely incoherent not only because it is irrational, but because that irrationality doesn't diminish its appeal or social standing. Its irrationality is not a defect but its principle (*sic*) feature, its point of pride and perverse strength.' He notes, as I have done, that Judge Niemeyer wrote in his dissent that, 'against transgender policy, "[V]irtually every civilization's norms on this issue stand in protest."' And that, of course, is precisely its point. 'For transgender ideology, the unanimous testimony of human civilization not only has no authority, but civilization is precisely the foe it aims to vanquish. Settled categories—of law, logic, or physical creation—are targets for subversion. [Shafer 2017]

To repeat what I said at the very beginning of this book, it is one thing to be compassionate towards someone who is genuinely experiencing a disconnect between their actual sex and the sex they perceive themselves to be, but it is another thing altogether to adopt a legal regime that is, at root, a negation of reality, as well as making impossible the very condition it is set up to alleviate. Shafer again: 'While individuals suffering from transgender confusion desire a different body, the gender ideologues exploiting the condition of those individuals desire a different cosmos. The dysphoric student, then, should be treated quite differently than her handlers. Transgenderism is not a matter for policy compromise or compatible addition to our sex discrimination laws. It is a form of total negation. And law, already besieged, cannot survive its triumph.' [Shafer 2017] In May of 2019, the US District Court of Eastern District of Virginia rejected the School Board's motion to dismiss and, later in the year, heard the motions for summary judgement. Having heard the motions, the Court acceded to Grimm's motion for summary judgement and ruled that the School Board had violated Grimm's rights under the Equal Protection Clause of the Fourteenth Amendment and Title IX. In May 2020, Grimm's case came before a three-judge panel of the US Court of Appeals for the 4th Circuit. [see Marimow 2020] The Court is reviewing the 2019 decision of U.S. District Judge Arenda L. Wright Allen who rejected the school system's claim that allowing transgender students to use bathrooms matching their gender identities caused privacy concerns for other students. She concluded, 'The perpetuation of harm to a child stemming from unconstitutional conduct cannot be allowed to stand', declaring that Grimm's rights were violated 'on the day the [School Board's] policy was first issued'. Initial indications are that the Appeal Court's judges are divided on the merits of Grimm's case. The significant question for the Court is whether federal protections prohibiting

158 *Hidden Agender*

sex discrimination in public schools would also prohibit discrimination against transgender students.

### Bostock

The Supreme Court has not directly addressed the issue, having remitted Grimm's case in 2017, but, in a case decided in June 2020 concerning the rights of gay and transgender workers, the Supreme Court, by a margin of 6 to 3, held that Title VII of the Civil Rights Act of 1964, which makes it illegal for employers to discriminate because of a person's sex, also covers discrimination because of sexual orientation or transgender status. The Court concluded: 'An employer who fires an individual merely for being gay or transgender violates Title VII of the Civil Rights Act of 1964.' [U.S. Supreme Court 2020; hereafter *Bostock*] Title VII of the Civil Rights Act of 1964 prohibits employment discrimination because of an individual's 'race, color, religion, sex, or national origin.'

This is a baffling decision, a decision that, in the words of one commentator, 'defies logic (and the dictionary)'. [Martin 2020] If an employer were to treat male homosexuals differently to female homosexuals, or *vice versa*, that would be discrimination on the grounds of sex. However, if an employer treats male and female homosexuals in exactly the same way then, whatever else might be said of it, it can scarcely be discrimination on the grounds of sex. It may well be discrimination on the grounds of sexual behaviour or sexual orientation, but discrimination on the grounds of sex *tout court*? Of course not. Similarly, if an employer were to treat trans men differently to trans women, or *vice versa*, that would clearly be discrimination on the grounds of sex. However, if an employer treats trans men and trans women in exactly the same way then, whatever else might be said of it, it can scarcely be discrimination on the grounds of sex just as such.

Mr Justice Gorsuch wrote the lead opinion in *Bostock* and was joined by five other justices: Roberts (Chief Justice), Ginsburg, Breyer, Sotomayor, and Kagan. Mr Justice Kavanaugh wrote a dissent, as did Mr Justice Alito, who was joined in his dissent by Mr Justice Thomas. In his dissenting opinion, Mr Justice Kavanaugh wrote, *inter alia*,

> Like many cases in this Court, this case boils down to one fundamental question: Who decides? Title VII of the Civil Rights Act of 1964 prohibits employment discrimination 'because of' an individual's 'race, color, religion, sex, or national origin.' The question here is whether Title VII should be expanded to prohibit employment discrimination because of sexual orientation. Under the Constitution's separation of powers, the responsibility to amend Title VII belongs to Congress and the President in the legislative process, not to this Court .... we are judges, not Members of Congress. And in Alexander Hamilton's words, federal judges exercise 'neither Force nor Will,

## Transgenderism and the Law (2)

but merely judgment.' .... Under the Constitution's separation of powers, our role as judges is to interpret and follow the law as written, regardless of whether we like the result .... Our role is not to make or amend the law. As written, Title VII does not prohibit employment discrimination because of sexual orientation .... To prohibit age discrimination and disability discrimination, this Court did not unilaterally rewrite or update the law. Rather, Congress and the President enacted new legislation, as prescribed by the Constitution's separation of powers.

It should be clear from this that Kavanaugh believes that in reaching the decision they did, the majority of the Court engaged in covert legislation. Mr Justice Alito, joined by Mr Justice Thomas, says bluntly, in his dissent, 'There is only one word for what the Court has done today: legislation. The document that the Court releases is in the form of a judicial opinion interpreting a statute, but that is deceptive. Title VII of the Civil Rights Act of 1964 prohibits employment discrimination on any of five specified grounds: "race, color, religion, sex, [and] national origin." 42 U. S. C. §2000e–2(a)(1). Neither "sexual orientation" nor "gender identity" appears on that list. For the past 45 years, bills have been introduced in Congress to add "sexual orientation" to the list, and in recent years, bills have included "gender identity" as well. But to date, none has passed both Houses.'

In reaching its decision, Mr Justice Kavanaugh believes that the Court has employed a novel and unjustified literalist principle of statutory interpretation.

Because judges interpret the law as written, not as they might wish it were written, the first 10 U. S. Courts of Appeals to consider whether Title VII prohibits sexual orientation discrimination all said no. Some 30 federal judges considered the question. All 30 judges said no, based on the text of the statute. 30 out of 30 .... But in the last few years, a new theory has emerged. To end-run the bedrock separation-of-powers principle that courts may not unilaterally rewrite statutes, the plaintiffs here (and, recently, two Courts of Appeals) have advanced a novel and creative argument. They contend that discrimination "because of sexual orientation" and discrimination "because of sex" are actually not separate categories of discrimination after all. Instead, the theory goes, discrimination because of sexual orientation always qualifies as discrimination because of sex: When a gay man is fired because he is gay, he is fired because he is attracted to men, even though a similarly situated woman would not be fired just because she is attracted to men. According to this theory, it follows that the man has been fired, at least as a literal matter, because of his sex.

If the Court takes this literalist approach to statutory interpretation, as it clearly does, then discrimination based on sexual orientation will qualify as sex discrimination. In fact, Kavanaugh remarks sardonically, it would seem to have already done so since 1964, though nobody realised this until now. 'Under this literalist

160 *Hidden Agender*

approach, sexual orientation discrimination automatically qualifies as sex discrimination, and Title VII's prohibition against sex discrimination therefore also prohibits sexual orientation discrimination—and actually has done so since 1964, unbeknownst to everyone.' Mr Justice Alito makes a similar point in his dissent:

> Many will applaud today's decision because they agree on policy grounds with the Court's updating of Title VII. But the question in these cases is not whether discrimination because of sexual orientation or gender identity *should be* outlawed. The question is *whether Congress did that in 1964*. It indisputably did not. The answers to those questions must be no, unless discrimination because of sexual orientation or gender identity inherently constitutes discrimination because of sex. The Court attempts to prove that point, and it argues, not merely that the terms of Title VII *can* be interpreted that way but that they *cannot reasonably be interpreted any other way*. According to the Court, the text is unambiguous ...The arrogance of this argument is breathtaking. As I will show, there is not a shred of evidence that any Member of Congress interpreted the statutory text that way when Title VII was enacted ... But the Court apparently thinks that this was because the Members were not "smart enough to realize" what its language means .... The Court seemingly has the same opinion about our colleagues on the Courts of Appeals, because until 2017, every single Court of Appeals to consider the question interpreted Title VII's prohibition against sex discrimination to mean discrimination on the basis of biological sex ... And for good measure, the Court's conclusion that Title VII unambiguously reaches discrimination on the basis of sexual orientation and gender identity necessarily means that the EEOC [Equal Employment Opportunity Commission] failed to see the obvious for the first 48 years after Title VII became law. Day in and day out, the Commission enforced Title VII but did not grasp what discrimination "because of ... sex" unambiguously means.

As he reached the end of his dissent, Mr Justice Kavanaugh noted, on a tone of regret, that 'many Americans will not buy the novel interpretation unearthed and advanced by the Court today. Many will no doubt believe that the Court has unilaterally rewritten American vocabulary and American law—a "statutory amendment courtesy of unelected judges." ... Some will surmise that the Court succumbed to "the natural desire that beguiles judges along with other human beings into imposing their own views of goodness, truth, and justice upon others."'

Given that the Supreme Court's decision in *Bostock* effectively redefines the term *sex* in the 1964 Civil Rights Act to include sexual orientation and transgender status, it is not unlikely that the Court will, if it ever comes to review *Grimm*, also find that that the prohibition of discrimination on grounds of sex in Title IX of the 1972 Federal Education Amendments prohibits discrimination based upon sexual orientation, gender, gender identity and transgender status—unless,

## Transgenderism and the Law (2)

of course, the members of the Court were to find some significant difference between *Bostock* and *Grimm*, and it is difficult to imagine what such a significant difference might be. If the Court's decision in *Bostock* does in fact have the consequence of expansively re-interpreting the term *sex* in Title IX, then the Supreme Court would seem to have pre-empted the passage of the Equality Act into law, at least in part. The Supreme Court has not (yet) reviewed *Grimm* but, given its decision in *Bostock*, it seems likely that if it were to do so, it would lean in the direction of finding for Grimm. What the *Bostock* decision means in practice we shall have to wait and see, but the omens are not good for those who believe that the expansion of the term *sex* in US Statutes to include gender, gender identity, sexual orientation and transgender status is seriously misguided, both as a matter of judicial activism and of public policy.

As things turned out, we didn't have to wait very long to see what the practical implications of *Bostock* might be. The final sentence in the previous paragraph was written immediately after the *Bostock* decision in June 2020. Scarcely two months later, in August 2020, the US Court of Appeals for the Eleventh Circuit in a 2 to 1 split decision upheld the ruling of a lower court that a School Board in Florida was wrong to deny a trans male access to the boys' restroom in the school. Significantly, Judge Beverley Martin cited *Bostock* as having held that 'workplace discrimination against transgender people is contrary to law.' [US Court of Appeal 2020, 45 (hereafter *Adams*); see also Ring 2020, Pandey 2020 and Farrington 2020]

The Chief Judge of the Court of Appeals, William Pryor, rejected the majority decision in a scathing dissent. (*Adams*, 46-74) He denied that *Bostock* supported the majority's findings, writing, 'To be sure,' he noted, '*Bostock* clarified that "discrimination based on homosexuality or transgender status necessarily entails discrimination based on sex" in the context of employment discrimination under Title VII .... But this appeal concerns the converse question: whether discrimination on the basis of sex necessarily entails discrimination based on transgender status. Of course, a policy can classify on the basis of sex without also classifying on the basis of transgender status .... Indeed, *Bostock* expressly disclaimed reaching any conclusion on the permissibility of sex-separated bathrooms and locker rooms.' (*Adams*, 57) Judge Pryor also firmly rejected the majority's acceptance of the claim that the St John's School Board's bathroom policy violated Title IX, noting the qualification embodied in that Title to the effect that it does not prohibit qualifying educational institutions from maintaining separate living facilities for the different sexes and, indeed, stating specifically that institutions 'may provide separate toilet, locker room, and shower facilities on the basis of sex, but such facilities provided for students of one sex shall be comparable to such facilities provided for students of the other sex.' [*Adams*, 65-6] His dissent concluded: 'The majority misunderstands the policy at issue, ignores decades of precedent, dismisses any sex-specific interest in bathroom privacy, and flouts foundational principles of statutory interpretation. In the process, it issues a holding with radical consequences for sex-separated bathrooms .... there is nothing unlawful, under either the Constitution or federal law, about a policy that separates bathrooms for schoolchildren on the basis of sex.' (*Adams* 73-4)

The legal battle continues.

# 6. A Struggle against Reality

*Any extension of sexual opportunity*
*must always be the immediate cause of a cultural decline*
—J. D. Unwin

*Unless we gratify our sex desire, the race is lost;*
*unless we restrain it, we destroy ourselves.*
—G. B. Shaw

Thus far I have discussed transgender ideology more or less in isolation. But to understand it outside its current cultural immediacy, it must be situated in its social context, and that context is provided by the sexual revolution that has dominated Western society for the last sixty years. While I remain, as always, resolutely libertarian in my approach to social and political matters, this chapter extends the discussion beyond the minimal requirements of libertarianism to reflect my socially conservative leanings. You may find this chapter, or parts of it, to be persuasive; on the other hand, you may find little in it that speaks to your experience. Whether or which, nothing I say here, whether persuasive or unpersuasive, affects the cogency of the principal arguments I have developed against the transgenderist ideology in chapters 1 to 5.

### The sexual revolution

History has given us many revolutions: some political—such as the French, the German, the American and the Russian; some technological—such as the Agricultural and the Industrial. The latest revolution to make our lives interesting is the sexual revolution that burst upon us in the second half of the twentieth century, whose social and cultural consequences we are still working out with fear and trembling. It is impossible to underestimate the importance of this seismic development, whose social, economic and political consequences rank in significance with the political and technological revolutions I've just mentioned. Revolutions are forms of substantial social and political change; whether they are changes for the better or for the worse depends to a large extent on the perspective one takes on human flourishing.

164         *Hidden Agender*

The sexual revolution that began in the 1960s—or perhaps even earlier, if Pitirim Sorokin is to be believed—and which continues today, is in many ways an assault on the very nature of what it is to be human, and an attempt, as in previous millenarian apocalyptic revolutions, to reshape human beings from the ground up. It is intrinsically connected with—indeed, it was in large part made possible by—the changes in human fertility and reproduction facilitated by the invention of the contraceptive pill. Sexual differences, distinct familial roles, work practices, the intrinsic connection between marriage and children and family, and the idea that marriage is the foundational unit of human society—all these ideas are taken to be arbitrary, contingent, and, as often than not, bigoted. 'The so-called "sexual revolution" of the 1960s,' writes Catherine Hakim, 'was made possible by the contraceptive revolution. For the first time in history, the pill and other modern forms of reliable contraception controlled by women gave women easier access to recreational sex without fear of pregnancy.' [Hakim 2015, 8] Chemical contraception, then, together with the widespread acceptance of effectively unrestricted (in its earlier stages, at least) abortion, constitutes an experiment in radical social re-engineering whose personal, social, sexual, demographic and political implications are difficult to foresee. These revolutions also irrevocably altered the relationship between the sexes— in precisely what ways, and whether for good or for ill, only time will tell.

Transgenderism is but the latest manifestation of the sexual revolution. 'The transgender mania,' Jane Robbins writes,

> naturally results from the relentless march of the sexual revolution. The denial of human nature began with the birth-control pill's decoupling of sex from reproduction. That led to the separation of sex from marriage, which dissolved restraints on non-marital sexual activity and non-marital childbearing. A family of mother and father was no longer considered necessary for creating children, which meant there was nothing special about the maleness and femaleness of romantic partners. Enter *Obergefell*, which by discovering homosexual marriage as a constitutional right obliterated even physical, biological distinctions between the sexes. And if there is no meaningful distinction, a human being should not be confined to one sex but rather should be inherently capable of moving between the sexes or stopping somewhere in the middle. [Robbins 2019]

Why now? Why is the revolutionary impulse, unleashed in the 1960s, now rampaging through our social norms like the broom of the sorcerer's apprentice, hardly controllable even by those who purportedly have their hands on the broom handle. For an answer to this question, we need to step back and take a broader view of cultural and social change.

## A Struggle Against Reality

Rod Dreher, in his *The Benedict Option*, describes the sexual revolution as a form of modern repaganisation, and identifies it as *the* major solvent of cultural norms. As does Robbins, he too notes that easy divorce stretches the bond of matrimony to the breaking point but, significantly, it doesn't deny sexual complementarity. Gay marriage, however, does. He goes on to say, 'transgenderism doesn't merely bend but breaks the biological and metaphysical reality of male and female. Everything in this debate ... turns on how we answer the question: Is the natural world and its limits a given, or are we free to do with it whatever we desire?' [Dreher 2017, 201] He concludes, 'Gay marriage and gender ideology dignify the final triumph of the Sexual Revolution and the dethroning of Christianity because they deny Christian anthropology at its core and shatter the authority of the Bible. Rightly ordered sexuality is not at the core of Christianity, but as Rieff says, it's so near to the center that to lose the Bible's clear teaching on this matter is to risk losing the fundamental integrity of the faith.' [Dreher 2017, 203-4]

But perhaps people like Robbins and Dreher are just hopeless old fuddy duddy reactionaries. After all, if there is one truth that surely still stands firm amidst the general atmosphere of scepticism and cynicism of the 2020s, it is surely that the sexual revolution of the 20th century was a Good Thing. 'Ah yes, the 60s', we say nostalgically, 'those were the days when it was bliss to be alive, but to be young was very heaven.' Out with guilt and shame and hypocrisy—in with frank enjoyment of sex as often and with as many people as possible. As a result, as is plainly evident, relations between the sexes are now universally mutually satisfying and all is happiness, sweetness and light. Theodore Dalrymple writes, 'The sexual revolutionaries' ideas about the relations between men and women—entailing ever greater sexual liberty, ever less mastery of the appetite—were so absurd and utopian that it is hard to understand how anyone could have taken them seriously.' [Dalrymple 2005, 242] Dalrymple wrote these words almost 20 years ago and one may be surprised—but then, why should one be?—to find that these ideas are still taken seriously.

Or perhaps not. One of the consequences of the sexual revolution of the 1960s and the years following was the apparent empowerment of women, liberating them to engage in sex anytime and with anyone. Happiness all around, then? Female empowerment, it would seem, has led many young women on university campuses to have casual sexual encounters that they don't particularly want to have, hooking up, to use Tom Wolfe's term, sex with no strings attached, no relationship, just plain unadorned sex. It might be fun for women to act like this—then again, it might not—but it hardly seems like empowerment. I would be prepared to maintain that given the typical difference in sexual dynamics between males and females, a difference futilely denied by feminists, hooking up with men she

166    *Hidden Agender*

barely knows is a sure and certain recipe for loss of power for a woman. Without realising it, raunch feminism has walked young women into the ideal situation for young feckless men to take advantage of them in an environment where there is no dating, no courtship, just a few drinks and Robert is your father's brother. It is little wonder that in this swamp of casual sex, there is increasingly bitterness and disappointment and, in a significant number of cases, accusations of rape, when what probably happened is that two people engaged in a drunken or drugged sexual encounter with few or no social constraints, no expectations and, as it used to be thought, no consequences. Writing almost thirty years ago, Roger Kimball noted,

> The demand for excessive freedom is a curious thing. Beginning in wholesale rebellion against restraint, it soon sets about erecting its own restraints—often harsher and more irrational than those it intended to replace. What was meant to shatter the bonds of convention and establish liberty ends up forging a new set of tyrannous conventions, all the more noxious for being imposed in the name of freedom. The latest access of sexual liberation is a case in point. Born in the 1960s, the movement for sexual liberation has followed a predictable trajectory. It started in naïve abandon— chanting "Down with monogamy, emotional commitment," etc.—and proceeded quickly through shock, disillusionment, bitterness, and rage. Herbert Marcuse, Norman O. Brown, and a thousand lesser gurus foretold the sensual paradise awaiting those who were bold enough to dispense with the repressive trappings of bourgeois morality. [Kimball 1993]

But it seems that all may not be well in our latter-day Garden of Eden. The removal of all sexual restrictions does not seem to have brought us joy unalloyed. As usual, the problem in the Garden of Eden is with the snakes. There were biological kickbacks—sexually transmitted ailments of various kinds—and psychological kickbacks as well. Sex without strings seemed like a good idea until it was realised that the strings were perhaps a not insignificant part of what made sexual relationships satisfying in the first place. But, like an idiot driver who, upon realising that he is going in the wrong direction, drives even faster to get where he doesn't want to go instead of admitting his mistake and turning around, our free-love zealots, instead of conceding that the old rules that surrounded sex had developed for a reason (no, that reason *wasn't* the subjugation of women), felt the need to invent new rules that would restore some order to chaos. Rules we will have, one way or another. Will we have rules that have developed over time and have been stress-tested by experience, rules that we assimilate as part of the process of moral and social maturation; or will we have quasi-mechanical rules that are incapable of being implemented, for example, the bizarre and scarcely coherent notion of

## A Struggle Against Reality

affirmative consent? The revolutionary rejection of time-tested, experientially grounded and culturally assimilated rules has provided the soil in which the sex harassment industry has grown and flourished. Kimball again: 'The restrictiveness and intrusiveness of the sexual-harassment industry have led some to describe it as a "new puritanism." In fact, it is a new marriage of radicalism and intolerance. In this sense, it represents the underside of the movement for sexual liberation: sharing crucial goals and assumptions but differing over questions of implementation and method. Far from signaling a return to traditional sexual scruples (as some commentators have suggested), the sexual-harassment industry is really a kind of guerrilla arm of feminism.' [Kimball 1993]

'Evidence of sexual chaos is everywhere,' Dalrymple writes. 'Not a day passes without several of my patients providing ample testimony of it.' He tells of a woman who tried to commit suicide when her not-yet-sixteen year old daughter moved out of the woman's home with her 8-month baby to go and live with her boyfriend. This boyfriend is not to be confused with the boyfriend who fathered the child, fathered it biologically, at least. That charmer beat up his teenage paramour when he discovered she was pregnant. But back to the would-be suicidal mother. Why is *she* so upset? Well, it seems that she has spent a considerable amount of money on her grandchild and objects to its removal from her home. She didn't, it seems, find anything problematic with the behaviour of her daughter in having sex while a teenager and giving birth to a child for which she was unable to provide. As Dalrymple puts it, 'She had not considered the sexual conduct of her daughter, or that of either of the two men, to be in any way reprehensible. If the father of her grandchild had not turned violent, it would never have crossed her mind that he had done anything wrong in having sex with her daughter; and indeed, having done nothing to discourage the liaison, she in effect encouraged him. And her daughter had behaved only as she would have expected any girl of her age to behave. [Dalrymple 2005, 236]

But, it might be objected, 'twas ever thus—such things have always happened. Since historical records have been kept, and presumably long before that, young men and women have, ahem, had sexual relations, often producing evidence of this in the form of babies. Well, yes, that is so but, as Dalrymple remarks, ' ... this is the first time in history that there has been mass denial that sexual relations are a proper subject of moral reflection or need to be governed by moral restrictions. The result of this denial, not surprisingly, has been soaring divorce rates and mass illegitimacy, among other phenomena. The sexual revolution has been above all a change in moral sensibility, in the direction of a thorough coarsening of feeling, thought, and behavior.' [Dalrymple 2005, 236] More evidence of this, if more evidence were needed, can be seen from the contemporary phenomenon of the precocious sexualisation of the very young, with girls as young as six sending sexually explicit messages from their phones. [Toogood, 2020] Once you make sex and sexual satisfaction the only, or, at least, the only important, issue in male/female relations; once you separate sex from reproduction (contraception for all and abortion as a backup or substitute) and separate reproduction from sex (homosexual couples, for example, can have babies by means of surrogacy, and women, finding no man willing to be a father to the children they want to have, are DIYing motherhood by means of IVF); once you remove the obligation on those who bring other human beings into existence to provide for their care, feeding and education, why should you be surprised at the inevitable results?

Dalrymple is unflattering in his depiction of the character of the earliest sexual revolutionaries, writing, 'The revolution has its intellectual progenitors, as shallow, personally twisted, and dishonest a parade of people as one could ever wish to encounter. They were all utopians, lacking understanding of the realities of human nature; they all thought that sexual relations could be brought to the pitch of perfection either by divesting them of moral significance altogether or by reversing the moral judgment that traditionally attached to them; all believed that human unhappiness was solely the product of laws, customs, and taboos.' [Dalrymple 2005, 239] As is the custom with revolutionaries when the revolution fails to produce the promised paradise, this failure, our revolutionaries are disposed to tell us, results from the insufficient loosening of restrictions and a too tender-hearted approach to the violation of taboos. We simply didn't go far enough. What we needed was more and ever more license, less and less control. Unbelievable as it may seem, as late as the 1990s when the sexual revolution had been in progress for well over thirty years, John Honey, whom we have already encountered as the inventor of the new, shiny term 'gender', was able to assert, seemingly without a blush, that we were still living in an anti-sexual society!

Some revolutions start from the bottom up, instigated by the peasantry against their rulers. The global sexual revolution, including its latest manifestation transgenderism, starts at the top with the social, media and political elites, and it is a struggle waged by those enlightened ones, the *illuminati*, against the stubborn resistance of those recalcitrant elements in society that continue to resist their blandishments and their promises of a new dawn in which our morals, our manners, our customs, our traditions, are all to be changed to allow a glorious new system of complete freedom to prevail. without a blush, that we were still living in an anti-sexual taboo-ridden society!

'The core of this global revolution,' writes Gabrielle Kuby, in her masterly treatment of the subject, 'is the dismantling of sexual norms. The lifting of moral limitations on sexuality would appear to increase people's freedoms, but it creates

## A Struggle Against Reality

169

rootless individuals, leads to the dissolution of the supporting social structure, and creates social chaos.' [Kuby 2015, 12] In the case of the sexual revolution, the benighted peasantry need to be inspired and guided by the enlightened few, those who know, those who have seen the light, those who are truly virtuous. Their goal is so luminously clear, so transparently good, that those who oppose it must be acting from malice and bad faith, must be, to use the smear of choice, fascists, and so need not expect the courtesy of rational engagement. The idea of reason is, after all, not only an instrument of the patriarchy, but is also merely a tool of conservative reactionaries. The defenders of reason and the present social order must be defeated by intimidation or violence, not engaged by argument, and the order they defend must be destroyed, not reformed.

To make all these changes possible, and to ensure that they are not overturned by counter-revolutionary forces, our language must be changed and, when necessary, purged. Education, in many contexts already a form of indoctrination, must be redesigned to support the new normative environment. Under no circumstances can reality be allowed to intrude and to affect how we think. The new social reality and its normative environment must be rigorously enforced and policed. Speech, action and even thought, if possible, must be controlled. Repression must be internalised by those who are to be repressed so that the need for crude overt repression becomes unnecessary. Older forms of totalitarianism relied on brute force for their implementation. Today's totalitarianism is technocratic and bureaucratic and has a smiley face. The most effective form of coercion is one in which those being coerced have internalised the dynamics of coercion and so no longer are even aware that they are being coerced. The mob required to enforce the new orthodoxies by extra-legal means is available at a moment's notice. They no longer need to have their torches ready at the door, waiting to be lit. All you need now is a Twitter account, and a Hitchcock-like *Birds* attack is ready to be unleashed from the digital thunderdome upon you if, like J. K. Rowling, you dare to be ever-so-slightly heterodox by woke standards of heterodoxy. The polite apolitical tyranny of our liberal media platforms is an enemy of freedom, just as much as political tyranny is.

Our brave new world is no country for old or even for young female heretics. In July 2020, Bari Weiss, an opinion editor at the *New York Times* resigned from her job, claiming that she had been smeared, demeaned and harassed in her work by those who disagreed with her, and who had no fear that their behaviour would be checked. 'Intellectual curiosity is now a liability at The Times,' she wrote, 'Instead, a new consensus has emerged in the press, but perhaps especially at this paper: that truth isn't a process of collective discovery, but an orthodoxy already known to an enlightened few whose job is it to inform everyone else.' [Bauder 2020; see

Moore 2020] What is under attack is not merely our right to free speech, our right to the presumption of innocence and to a fair trial, but the very notion of truth itself. Without truth there can be no freedom, or at best a freedom that is of no real significance. The task of the *illuminati* is made significantly easier because most people haven't yet realised that a radical revolution is in progress and so are not in any position to contest it.

Not just society, but reality itself, is the enemy. The radical feminist's problem, for example, isn't with this or that legal anomaly or injustice supposed to affect women adversely, but with nature itself. Shulamith Firestone, for example, in her best Aldous Huxley manner, thought that pregnancy was barbaric. For her, the object (one object at least) of the feminist revolution was the creation of the possibility of reproducing human beings technologically. None of that icky sex and pregnancy nonsense! Of course, that most repressive of institutions, the family, with its sexual exclusivity and its distinctively different roles for mother and father, must also go the way of the dinosaur. Sexual roles of all kinds, indeed, the very idea that there are or even could be different roles for men and for women, must be eliminated. To that end, lesbianism is not just a deviant form of sexuality, but also a political statement of the non-necessity of men. In the New Dawn, the sexes (or genders) must themselves disappear, and in their place will arise the new androgynous human being in all its asexual glory. As I have tried to demonstrate throughout this book, the Firestonian rejection of human, specifically female, nature is channelled and amplified by the transgender activists' wider rejection of the binary sexual constraints.

It is a familiar trope that the old have always believed that the world is going to hell in a handbasket. In one of his *Odes*, Horace opined, 'The age of our sires was worse than our grandsires. We, their sons, are more worthless than they; so in our turn we shall give the world a progeny yet more corrupt.' A letter from an eighteenth-century Frenchman complained, 'Where has the manly vigour and athletic appearance of our forefathers flown to? Can these be their legitimate heirs? Surely, no; a race of effeminate, self-admiring, emaciated fribbles can never have descended in a direct line from the heroes of Potiers and Agincourt ... ' Anthony Ashley Cooper, afterward the Earl of Shaftsbury, warned the House of Commons of 'a fearful multitude of untutored savages ...[boys] with dogs at their heels and other evidence of dissolute habits ... [girls who] drive coal-carts, ride astride upon horses, drink, swear, fight, smoke, whistle, and care for nobody ... the morals of children are tenfold worse than formerly.' And if that isn't sufficient to establish the constant degeneration of each age in comparison to those that have preceded it, we have the unrebuttable evidence of the *At Last the 1948 Show*'s 'Four Yorkshiremen' sketch, in which a group of middle-aged, champagne-drinking buddies compete

A Struggle Against Reality                                               171

to tell the wildest and most extreme stories of poverty and deprivation, capped with this gem from Eric Idle: 'Right. I had to get up in't morning at ten o'clock at night, half an hour before I went to bed, drink a cup of sulphuric acid, work twenty-nine hours a day down't mill, and pay mill owner for permission to come to work, and when we got home, our Dad and our mother would kill us, and dance about on our graves singing "Hallelujah".' Michael Palin adds, 'But you try and tell young people today that ... and they won't believe ya.' [YouTube 1967] A trope the increasing degeneracy of succeeding generations may be, but it may also be true, just as being paranoid doesn't mean that people *aren't* out to get you! The question now is not so much whether we in the West live in a sick society—that much can hardly be doubted—the question is whether its illness is terminal. As Brendan O'Neill remarked, 'A society that cannot say even to a man convicted of rape, "You are not a woman", is a society that has truly lost the moral plot. It is a society that has left the realm of reason and objectivity for the unbalanced, unpredictable and plain dangerous terrain of post-modernism, in which what an individual feels counts for more than what others know to be true. It is time we asserted our right to opt out of trans people's fantasies.' [O'Neill, 2017]

The depth and extent of the changes wrought by the sexual revolution can hardly be overstated. In the space of fifty or sixty years, abortion has gone from being either illegal or exceptional to being in effect a relatively routine backup form of contraception. Divorce no longer has any social stigma attached to it and is generally available in 'no-fault' form, that is, on demand by one or other of the parties. The concept of illegitimacy, even the use of that term, is *streng verboten*, and in its place we have the brave new world of single-motherhood, stigma-free and state-supported. Homosexual conduct has moved from being vilified and illegal, to being tolerated, to being valorised, with the state offering its support to the new normative environment in its recognition of so-called gay marriage. All these changes, and others, stem from our increasing ability to separate sex and reproduction. Sex without reproduction has been commonplace for almost sixty years; reproduction without sex is already with us and is set to become increasingly common. The biological constraints that informed human sexual morality from our very beginnings are no longer operative.

**Absolute freedom**
The goal of the sexual revolution is freedom, a freedom so absolute that it is intended to liberate us not only from our political and social shackles, but, as can be seen from the goal of radical feminists and transgender activists, to liberate us from the constraints of reality itself. It may seem strange to find a libertarian such as I am making what seems to be a derogatory remark about freedom. But

freedom is *not* the highest of all social goods; still less is it the only one. It is a *fundamental* good, a requirement of there being anything that can count as moral action in the first place. Who doesn't like freedom? Who, other things being equal, wants to be constrained, to be limited? But the notion that freedom is some substantive good in itself is absurd. 'Freedom in itself is nonsensical,' writes D. G. Garan. 'A lone savage having all the freedom he wishes has no feeling of freedom. The meaning as well as the motivational force of freedom derives only from its opposite, restriction.' [Garan 1963, 250]

It is undeniable that much of what we are is simply given to us and is not a matter of our choice. The family we belong to, the nation we conceive of as ours, the language we speak, the way we speak it, indeed, many of our ideas—all these are important, perhaps constitutive, parts of what we are, parts of our very identity if you will, and yet *not* a matter of choice. It is also the case that our existence as sexual beings, as male or female, is something that is given to us, not chosen by us, and a constitutive aspect of what we are.

It might be objected that in giving the sexual revolution the prominence and the character that that I have done, I am guilty of exaggeration. 'Cultures,' you may say, 'have always changed. Values have always changed. There is nothing particularly unusual in what has taken place in the West over the last fifty or so years.' This objection is not without some force. I am happy to accept that not all social changes in the last half century have necessarily been for the worse. However, to support my general argument, I'm going to place it in a larger historical context, and to enable me to do so, I shall make use of the work of Pitirim Sorokin, the pre-eminent 20th century theorist of social change. In 1937, Sorokin, the Russian-American sociologist, published three volumes of his *Social and Cultural Dynamics*; the fourth volume came out in 1941. In this monumental work, Sorokin attempts to provide a large-scale explanation of cultural and social change. Unlike the comparable works of Arnold Toynbee (*A Study of History*) and Oscar Spengler (*The Decline of the West*), Sorokin's work is notable for the extent and depth of the empirical and statistical research he undertakes in respect of almost every aspect of culture—philosophy, economics, literature, art and history—in order to provide support for his conclusions. In what follows, I give a brief account of Sorokin's analysis of social and cultural change, of necessity omitting almost all the evidence he adduces to support his claims. For those interested in a Sorokinesque overview of where we stood at the end of the 20th century, an excellent treatment is to be had in Glyn-Jones's 1996 book, *Holding Up a Mirror*.

A major symptom of civilisational decline is the emergence of the phenomenon of sexual efflorescence. It would be difficult to deny that Western society is

## A Struggle Against Reality

sex-obsessed, and obsessed with the most bizarre and exotic forms of sex at that. 'Seen as an ingredient in the long march of the cultural revolution of the 1960s, the sudden efflorescence of a phenomenon that belongs in the pages of Krafft-Ebing is just the latest item on the agenda to "disestablish" traditional manners and morals.' [Anon 2016] Sorokin's work relies substantially on J. D. Unwin's massively extensive study, *Sex and Culture*, that showed, by means of an analysis of 80 tribal societies and six of the better known world-wide civilisations, that the greater the sexual restrictions in a society, the higher its cultural level. According to Unwin, all instances of cultural collapse are linked with an outbreak of sexual efflorescence, that sexual efflorescence itself being both a product of, and a producer of, cultural collapse.

Based on his research, Sorokin distinguished two basic types or patterns of culture. It should be noted that these are pure types that are never instantiated perfectly consistently in any phase of human history by any culture. Type 1 culture Sorokin called the **Sensate** culture. It could also be called Materialist culture, since its dominating principle is that only the material world is real—there is no other. This principle is the foundation of society, of politics, of art and of economics. The people who live in such a culture are practically unable to think in any terms other than materialistic or sensory ones. Insofar as such cultures possess religion, it is religion in an emaciated and degraded form, denuded of any real idea of the transcendent and commonly found as an anti-rational fideism. Intellectual interest focuses on science and technology, to the virtual exclusion of any interest in spirituality. Such a culture is not without its values but those values are solidly this-worldly—wealth and health, repute, power, and the pleasure of sensuality in all its forms. The Sensate culture's ethics, law and politics tend to be, at root, matters of convention and ultimately utilitarian, not absolute and unchanging, but rather relative and changeable at need. Art tends to be at the service of such a culture's sensualism, and is correspondingly sensual sometimes even decadent or transgressive.

Type 2 culture Sorokin termed **Ideational**. This could also be called the spiritual culture since what is most truly real is not matter in any of its forms, or any aspect or even the totality of this world, but rather a transcendent, spiritual reality that is beyond the capacity of the senses to attain. The everyday world of matter is not necessarily unreal or illusory (though some forms of this kind of culture hold this position) but is, at most, an appearance of a reality that lies behind or beyond it. In such cultures, religion, at its best, is an effort, individual and communal, to access the ultimate reality, sometimes by means of revelation, sometimes by forms of mysticism. Asceticism is pursued by at least some in this culture. In ethics, there is a tendency to manifest a rigid and absolute moralism. The interests of

174          *Hidden Agender*

intellectuals in such a culture are directed towards metaphysics and theology, with technology and science taking second place. Wealth and comfort are de-valued and economic activity is constrained by religious and spiritual regulations. Art is at the service of religion and spirituality.

As I mentioned, these two cultures are pure types, and Sorokin is not committed to holding that there ever have been cultures that were purely one or the other, just as individual human beings are rarely purely one or the other. Many cultures, while being primarily Sensate or Ideational, nonetheless contain elements of the other. A third type of culture, a dynamic mixture of Sensate and Ideational, is what Sorokin calls the **Idealist** culture (perhaps not the best term to choose, given the possibility of confusing *ideational* with *idealistic*). This mixed type of culture may also, and less confusingly, be called the **Integral** culture. In such a culture, the elements of the sensate and the ideational are held in an harmonious balance. What is real is not only spiritual or material but both, related and interpenetrated in various ways. This interpenetration of the sensate and the ideational affects all aspect of the culture, its economics, its art, its ethics, its politics. Theology and metaphysics are pursued, but not at the cost of ignoring science and technology. Art, too, deals with things both spiritual and sensory.

Now, Sorokin's thesis is that the two basic types of culture tend to alternate regularly over longer or shorter historical periods, with mixed types intervening. At the cusp of transitional periods, society experiences crises of various kinds, even wars and revolutions. According to Sorokin, the Greek Dark Age was primarily Sensate and ran from 1200 to 900 BC. After this came the Ideational phase of Archaic Greece, from 900 to 440 BC. The Classical Greek period, from 550 to 320 BC was, for Sorokin, an Integral culture, in which the best of the Sensate and the Ideational were balanced and found religious, philosophical, political and ethical expression. In the West, he sketches a picture of a primarily Sensate Hellenistic-Roman period from 320 BC to AD 400, followed by a brief transitional period, itself followed by the Ideational culture of the so-called Middle Ages, from AD 600 to AD 1200. After this came the Integral culture of the High Middle Ages through to the early Renaissance, from AD 1200 to AD 1500. Then began the current Sensate culture, at the end phase of which we are now living. In his own individual, even idiosyncratic work, the psychologist D. G. Garan expressed his agreement with Sorokin's thesis: 'Europeans started on their higher economic and industrial development about 500 years ago, at the time of the highest Medieval spirituality and other-worldliness. Spirituality is the restrictive way of life, therefore best for all progress. But the paradox of economic progress through restriction is not understood and everybody attributes material progress to direct materialistic drives.' [Garan 1975, 358]

# A Struggle Against Reality

The change from one type of culture to another emanates primarily from factors and forces within a culture rather than from without. They are, to use the jargon, endogenous rather than exogenous. Cultures contain the seeds of change within themselves, though external events—invasions, population shifts—can speed up or retard the process of change. As we now approach the end of our current Sensate culture, we are, according to Sorokin, due soon to make a transition to a new Ideational, or, if we're lucky, an Integral cultural era. This transition won't be painless, not least because we can expect to have to endure social and economic crises precipitated by the inability of the social and political institutions of the current culture to adapt to the changes without resistance. It is likely that the absurdities of the present situation will become ever more apparent, leading to an escalation in existential crises until eventually a social collapse becomes inevitable.

> *The organism of the Western society and culture seems to be undergoing one of the deepest and most significant crises of its life. We are seemingly between two epochs: the dying Sensate culture of our magnificent yesterday, and the coming Ideational or Idealistic culture of the creative tomorrow. We are living, thinking, acting at the end of a brilliant six-hundred-year-long Sensate day. The oblique rays of the sun still illumine the glory of the passing epoch. But the light is fading, and in the deepening shadows it becomes more and more difficult to see clearly and to orient ourselves safely in the confusions of the twilight. The night of the transitory period begins to loom before us and the coming generations—perhaps with their nightmares, frightening shadows, and heart-rending horrors. Beyond it, however, the dawn of a new great Ideational or Idealistic culture is probably waiting to greet the men of the future.* [Sorokin 1937; italics in original]

Those of us who have to live through a transitory period will experience it as a time of trouble, with, as Sorokin notes, its nightmares, frightening shadows, and heart-rending horrors. How long will this transitory period last? Who can tell? How disruptive will it be? Again, who can tell? I find it interesting that despite the rigour of his explanatory schema, Sorokin hedges his bets with that significant word *probably* in the last sentence of the quotation.

Within the larger context of his architectonic schema of social change, Sorokin produced a book in the 1950s that must have seemed to many at the time to be the product of a thinker with a too-fertile imagination or perhaps of someone in the throes of an incipient intellectual decline. In his *The American Sex Revolution*, Sorokin argued that American culture had become obsessed with sex, and that this was having severely deleterious effects on all aspects of its culture and social *mores*. He wrote:

> While the Ideational values tend to restrain unlawful sex activities, the Sensate values aim to disinhibit and approve them. At their present disintegrating stage

# Hidden Agender

the Sensate values tend to approve potentially an unrestrained sex freedom, and recommend the fullest possible satisfaction of sex love in all its forms. This basic change in psychosocial factors has manifested itself in the revaluation of the previous standards by modern American (and Western) men and women. The sex drive is now declared to be the most vital mainspring of human behavior. In the name of science, its fullest satisfaction is urged as a necessary condition of man's health and happiness. Sex inhibitions are viewed as the main source of frustrations, mental and physical illness and criminality. Sexual chastity is ridiculed as a prudish superstition. Nuptial loyalty is stigmatized as an antiquated hypocrisy .... Sexual profligacy and prowess are proudly glamorized. *Homo sapiens* is replaced by *homo sexualis* packed with genital, anal, oral and cutaneous libidos. The traditional 'child of God' created in God's image is turned into a sexual apparatus powered by sex instinct, pre-occupied with sex matters, aspiring for, and dreaming and thinking mainly of, sex relations. Sexualization of human beings has about reached its saturation point .... If the mind, behavior, and values of contemporary men and women have been notably sexualized, similar sexualization of our entire culture and of every social institution must be expected. And if this is so, then the depth and extent of the current sex revolution must be incomparably more than a mere change in the personality and conduct of our contemporaries. [Sorokin 1956, 17-18]

It should be noted that these words were written in 1956, not in 2016! There is little of what Sorokin says in this book that could not be rehearsed today, this time seeming less obviously out of step with the *zeitgeist*. As befits the work of a sociologist, Sorokin's book is replete with data and statistics, but the main points can be grasped without any need for an expertise in numeracy. He points to phenomena with which we have since become only too well acquainted: an explosion of erotic content in films, TV, books, plays, magazines, songs, increased (and now no-fault) divorce, a declining birth-rate, below replacement level in most Western countries, plummeting education standards, pre-and post-marital sex, promiscuity (now called polyandry), and so on. On this point, D. G. Garan is once more in substantial agreement with Sorokin. 'If permitted to be enjoyed unrestrictedly, the sexual function would become the whole fulfillment of life, as it biologically is meant to be, and the only genuine enjoyment. Human culture, as well as biological conditions among higher animals, has advanced side by side with restrictions on sexual satisfactions. Family life among animals and men is nurtured by continuous, never fully satisfied sexual needs. All cultural norms, religions, and morals invariably aim at the restriction of sexual enjoyment.' [Garan 1963, 197-98]

Drawing on the work of J. D. Unwin, Sorokin sees a causal connection between the rise of a society's obsession with sex and a decline in its creative energy in all areas, artistic, religious and economic. 'The regime that permits chronically

*A Struggle Against Reality* 177

excessive, illicit, and disorderly sex activities contributes to the decline of cultural creativity.' [Sorokin 1956, 107] He continues, ' ... there is no example of a community which has retained its high position on the cultural scale after less rigorous sexual customs have replaced more restricting ones .... When the ruling group and the society as a whole relax their code, within three generations there is usually a cultural decline, as was the case in the later stages of the Babylonian, the Persian, the Macedonian, the Mongol, the Greek, and the Roman civilizations, as well as at the end of the Old and the Middle Kingdoms and of the New Empire, and during the Ptolemaic period, in Egypt.' [Sorokin 1956, 110-11] A generation is a span of years somewhere between twenty and forty so that three generations could be as little as sixty and as much as one hundred and twenty years. If we take our starting point as 1950, then we might expect the cultural decline predicted by Sorokin to occur somewhere between 2010 and 2070.

Whatever about cultural and economic deleterious effects, surely one might expect that a society in the grip of an obsession with sex would at least have no problem sustaining its population, in fact, we might expect it to have a problem with over-population. On the contrary, however, such a society usually demonstrates a systematic decline in population growth, often below replacement level. It is a mistake to confuse an obsessive interest in sex with a like obsession with children. The last thing a sex obsessive desires is to be burdened with the responsibility for the education and maintenance of children. Far from facilitating his obsession, the need to provide and care for children would have the opposite effect. So, enter contraception, abortion, infanticide and self-induced sterility. Some wit once remarked that 'family planning' meant no planning and no family. The destructive effect on society is, unsurprisingly, mirrored by a like destructive effect on the life of the individual. Just as gluttony has a devastating effect on the physical structure of the human body, so too, sex gluttony has physical and psychical destructive effects. Sorokin writes, ' ... the total fund of energy of the human organism is limited: the more of it that is spent in one kind of activity, the less that remains for others. Each sexual act involves an expenditure of vital physiological forces. When this becomes too frequent, the organism as a whole begins to wither, and the profligate goes into physical decline ...' [Sorokin 1956, 58] Sorokin, as a good sociologist, supports his assertions with empirical evidence. In addition to the negative physical effects, there are also negative psychical effects. Sorokin writes,

> [T]he inner world and the actions of the libertine are a chaos. Lust dominates his thinking and feeling, and controls his overt behavior. Because his is an organism in a state of biological disequilibrium, he cannot control its processes for his own well-being, nor can he resist the innumerable external forces incessantly bombarding

178                                    *Hidden Agender*

it .... His personality is underdeveloped. His ego is shot through and through by innumerable tensions and conflicts: of his biological drives, one against the other, especially the preponderant sex drives against other urges; of the fragments of values and motivations with each other and with the biological drives .... His conflicting emotions and passions are continuously excited. He is a house divided against himself, whose various parts are at incessant war with one another.' [Sorokin 1956, 63-4]

I have adverted to the work of D. G. Garan in support of some of Sorokin's claims. Garan provides a psychological counterpart to the work of Sorokin (and Unwin) that is worthy of consideration in its own right. For Garan, the human brain is primarily an instrument of restriction. 'The role of the forebrain, the newest addition to it, for instance, is negative more than anything else. Remove it partly or isolate it by lobotomy, and man feels only relief or an upsurge of energy, without an apparent loss of capacities. The later effects, however, are a reduction of adjustment toward the more primitive levels of the animal.' [Garan 1963, 34] The psychological restrictions imposed on man by his brain are the psychological equivalent of the economic process of capital formation. Most new businesses fail not because of lack of good ideas, or because of lack of energy on the part of the entrepreneur, but because of insufficiency of capital. Capital is the burst of initial energy that is needed to see the new business through the fraught period of infancy. Capital is the source of an increase in wealth and it is formed by saving, by restriction, by a willingness to delay gratification. Similarly, moral wealth is formed by the accumulation of moral capital in the form of rules, traditions and taboos. The dissipation of capital is an economic disaster but it feels good as long as the money lasts, as does the dissipation of moral capital, while it lasts. So too, the manifold systems of psychological release, usually, but not always, facilitated by drugs, feels good while it lasts. As someone once pointed out, the reason why people take drugs is that it makes them feel good! If they could continue to do so without the inevitable negative psychological (and often physiological) consequences, they would be happy to continue doing so for ever. Morality plays a role in society equivalent to the restrictions psychologically imposed on us by the brain. 'Moral rules always mean unpleasant restrictions. There have been no morals yet which were pleasant to follow, especially for those not conditioned to them. Religious dogmas and practices are even more onerous. All cultural education means hard work applied to every individual during long formative years; and cultural tradition takes thousands of years to build.' [Garan 1963, 261] A civilised existence, then, requires both freedom *and* order. Just as a sound economy requires capital that can be produced only by saving, by delayed gratification, so too, cultural capital is similarly produced by delayed gratification. Freedom without order is like a sudden release of energy, a pointless and destructive explosion;

## A Struggle Against Reality

order without freedom is a lifeless corpse. Freedom and order together produce a living, vital society. 'The imposition of restrictions is what cultural tradition and conditioning strive for.' [Garan 1963, 61-2] We do not produce and maintain our systems of social and moral restrictions, our manners and our morals, primarily by some process of detached reason. As D. G. Garan notes, our 'cultural, educational, moral and religious systems are restrictive. Restriction of enjoyment of the natural drives, especially of sexual pleasures, has been the main purpose of all cultural traditions. Sexual satisfactions are the source of feelings of the highest beauty, and of the richest psychological releases. But they are under the strictest taboos in all cultures.' [Garan 1963, 8] These systems arise naturally in the context of social relations. Such judgements as they embody are the kind of pre-reflective judgement that Edmund Burke calls prejudice.

Manners as prejudices allow us to act swiftly and surely and rightly without the need for agonised reflection and reasoning. At the root of manners is the notion of restraint, of limitation, of delayed gratification, and its product is a kind of social capital, just as the product of monetary delayed gratification and restraint is economic capital. When manners decline as the result of cultural decay, then the law (or rather legislation) rushes in to fill the resultant vacuum. Matters that in a culturally rich society are dealt with by informal sanctions—for example, what is called date-rape or hate speech—now have to be overtly regulated by laws, with consequent intrusion upon our liberty. But the law is a blunt and crude instrument, and such micro-regulation is both ineffective and also stifling. Man does not live by legislation alone. A society replete with minute and detailed legislation is a society whose stock of social capital has declined. This, I suggest, is a correct description of much of contemporary Western society. Whether this society can recover is a matter for conjecture. Some societies have done so in the past, but others have not, and have perished. Order, as well as freedom, is needed for human flourishing. You can have it, or a simulacrum of it, by micro-managing legislation, or you can have it by what Burke calls manners. Burke contrasts this form of ordered liberty with mere licence, the freedom to do whatever one wants to do without regard to circumstances. Will you have ordered liberty, or will you have licence? You cannot have both. Which shall it be? The choice is yours. I know what I would choose.

'Men act to improve their situations by removing felt dissatisfactions,' writes D. G. Garan. 'In order for us to act, something about our current situation must be apprehended as being capable of improvement and we act to bring that improvement about ... there can be no value or satisfaction without need .... In simple words, a person must first want painfully a thing in order to derive joy from it. No other thing can do. A person simply cannot have any positive emotions or values than those for which he has accumulated needs. But accumulation of needs is painful, and that is the whole problem.' [Garan 1963, 47] Whether we actually achieve an improvement is, of course, another matter. A man came across his friend banging his head against a wall and asked him why he was doing this. 'Because,' replied his friend, 'it feels so good when I stop.' A being perfectly satisfied in every way wouldn't act—it's a moot point whether he *could* act, at least in the way in which man does. Just as in economics, equilibrium is ever tended towards but never reached, because of the constantly changing, kaleidoscopic nature of the world, so too, in our human lives, complete satisfaction is never attained but is, at best, intended. Our ever-changing physiological conditions force us to act to preserve homeostasis. But we are also psychologically unstable and, if St Augustine is to be believed, spiritually unstable too. 'You have made us for yourself, O Lord,' he wrote, 'and our hearts know no rest until they rest in Thee.' We can live hand to mouth, as our remote ancestors did, or we can try in a more ordered and long-term way to improve our situations—the way we do this economically is by the creation of economic, social and moral capital. I have remarked already, but it is perhaps worth repeating, that I believe that a civilised existence requires both freedom *and* order; that just as a sound economy requires capital that is produced by saving and by delayed gratification, so too, cultural capital is similarly produced by delayed gratification:

Capital, then, plays a role in culture, just as it does in economics and it is no more miraculously produced in one area than in the other. Both forms of capital require saving, restriction, limitation, delayed gratification, perhaps initially induced by our family and our upbringing, and supported and endorsed by our society, but later personally appropriated and self-imposed. As David Mamet remarks, 'the essential mechanism of societal preservation is not inspiration, but restraint.' [Mamet, 171] The libertarian may (and I believe should) agree with Augusto Del Noce when he notes that the subjugation of man's sensuous and appetitive faculties is a primary function of reason which, as subjugator, acts repressively. The subjugation of the lower by the higher is necessary to produce properly functioning individuals and properly functioning societies. [see Del Noce, 141] A libertarian will want such subjugation to emerge organically from within the individual and his society, especially by means of education in the family, and not merely to be imposed on either from outside.

### The shadow of that hyddeous strength ...
Transgenderist ideology is predicated on a bizarre voluntaristic and nihilistic metaphysics, and upon an equally bizarre magical theory of causality. The metaphysics amounts to holding the position that nothing is anything in particular

## A Struggle Against Reality

except what I will it to be, and the magic consists in believing that tinkering with language can effect changes in reality. In the case of transgenderism, these two positions may actually be incoherent, for in order for someone to be a woman or a man, there must *be* something that a woman or a man is; if not, you cannot possibly be one or the other. But why should that incoherence bother anyone who is a functional voluntarist or nihilist? They may not be able to out-White Queen the White Queen—'Why, sometimes I've believed as many as six impossible things before breakfast'—but they can give her a run for her money.

A renowned philosopher, who shall be nameless, once remarked that 'Empiricism is a bundle of blunders, and its history is their successive clarification'. Much the same might be said, *mutatis mutandis*, of transgenderist ideology. [see Tinker 2018] In the long-run, it must fail, and its failure must become undeniably evident. Its patent denial of reality, the dubious value of transgender therapies with their physiological 'side-effects' and their failure to address underlying psychological problems, the absurdity of the explosion in the number of possible genders that has produced a minefield in social etiquette and, not least, a rapidly-escalating victim war between transgender activists and radical feminists all point towards its imminent implosion. Descartes's famous epigram, which ran: *'Cogito, ergo sum'*—'I think, therefore I am', has been transmogrified into the transgender activists' statement of faith, *'Quodcumque cogito sum, sum'*—'Whatever I think I am, I am.' If this principle prevails for sex and gender, how can its extension to other areas, such as age, or race, or disability or whatever, be resisted? If the transgenderist impulse is not resisted, the whole fabric of reality begins to unwind. Transgenderist ideology, then, must fail in the long run, but the long run may be very long and very painful indeed.

What can one do in the short run? One can, and one should, speak truth to error, politely but firmly, but one must be prepared to be reviled for so doing and, if one has a public profile, one must also be prepared to see attempts made to have one 'cancelled', that is, socially ostracised, removed from social media platforms, and fired from one's job. [see Walden 2020a] There is no shortcut to the restoration of a liberal and tolerant social environment, although the de-propagandisation of education would be a very present help in time of trouble. However, a start could be made by the repealing of the Gender Recognition Acts, root and branch, and by the deletion of all mention of gender and gender identity from equality legislation. I recommend that one doesn't hold one's breath while waiting for this eminently desirable state of affairs to be realised unless one wants to depart this vale of tears in short order.

# References

I have included web references where I thought it might otherwise be difficult to access the material I mention; otherwise, I have omitted them. All links were live at the time of writing.

ACLU. (2019) *Grimm v. Gloucester County School Board.* Available at https://www.aclu.org/cases/grimm-v-gloucester-county-school-board (27 November)

Adkins, Deanna. (no date) 'Expert Declaration of Deanna Adkins, M.D.,' in the case of *Carcaño et al. v. McCrory et al.* United States District Court for the Middle District of North Carolina, case no. 1:16-cv-00236-TDS-JEP. Available at https://www.aclu.org/sites/default/files/field_document/AdkinsDecl.pdf

American Psychiatric Association. (2013) *Diagnostic and Statistical Manual of Mental Disorders, 5th ed.* Washington, DC: American Psychiatric Publishing.

Anderson, Ryan T. (2018a) *When Harry Became Sally: Responding to the Transgender Moment.* New York: Encounter Books.

Anderson, Ryan T. (2018b) 'The Philosophical Contradictions of the Transgender Worldview.' *Public Discourse.* (1 February)

Anderson, Ryan T. (2018c) 'A New York Times Writer's Reckless Hit Piece on My Transgender Book.' *The Heritage Foundation.* (28 February)

Anderson, Ryan T. and Robert George. (2019) 'Physical Interventions on the Bodies of Children to "Affirm" their "Gender Identity" Violate Sound Medical Ethics and Should be Prohibited.' *Public Discourse.* (8 December)

Anon. (2007) *The Yogyakarta Principles: Principles on the Application of International Human Rights Law in Relation to Sexual Orientation and Gender Identity.*

Anon. (2010) *An Activist's Guide to the Yogyakarta Principles.*

Anon. (2016) 'Sex & Power: On the Obama administration's lavatory overreach.' *The New Criterion*, vol. 34, no. 10. (June)

Anon. (2017) *The Yogyakarta Principles plus 10: Additional Principles and State Obligations on the Application of International Human Rights Law in*

184 *Hidden Agender*

*Relation to Sexual Orientation, Gender Identity, Gender Expression and Sex Characteristics to Complement the Yogyakarta Principles.*

Appellant Brief. (2019) 'Appellant Brief in the case of Grimm vs Gloucester County School Board.' Available at https://www.aclu.org/sites/default/files/field_document/19_brief_of_appellant_gloucester_county_sch._board.pdf

Aristotle. (1986) *De Anima*, trans. Hugh Lawson-Tancred. London: Penguin.

Associated Press. (2019) 'Virginia teacher sues after being fired for refusing to call trans student "he".' *The Guardian*. (1 October)

Associated Press. (2020) 'US judge blocks law banning trans athletes from women's sports.' *The Guardian*. (18 August)

Banger, Marnie. (2019) 'Bill passed allowing transgender Victorians to change their sex on birth certificates without surgery.' *New.com.au.* (28 August)

Barber, Nigel. (2018) 'The Gender Reassignment Controversy.' *Psychology Today*. (16 March)

Barnes, Robert and Ann E. Marimow. (2019) 'Trump nominess could play pivotal role as Supreme Court decides on protections for gay, transgender workers.' *The Washington Post*. (9 October)

Barnstone, Willis & Marvin Meyer (eds.) (2003) *The Gnostic Bible*. Boston: Shambhala.

Baskerville, Stephen. (2017) *The New Politics of Sex: The Sexual Revolution, Civil Liberties, and the Growth of Governmental Power*. Kettering, Ohio: Angelico Press.

Bauder, David. (2020) 'New York Times opinion editor resigns, saying she was harassed for her ideas.' *Chicago Tribune*. (15 July)

Bawer, Bruce. (2019) 'A Transgender Hero Breaks Ranks.' *PJ Media*. (13 February)

BBC News. (2019) '"Seahorse" transgender man loses challenge to be named father.' *BBC News*. (25 September)

BBC News. (2020) 'Ethical Veganism is Philosophical Belief, Tribunal Rules.' *BBC News*. (3 January)

Pandey, Manish. (2020) 'US trans rights: The teen who sued his school, and won, over bathroom use.' *BBC News*. (23 August)

Bell, Cadance. (2020) 'I forgot how to cry as a man. HRT gave me a range of emotions I never thought possible.' *The Guardian*. (19 July)

Bird, Steve. (2018) 'Government drops doctor who says gender given at birth.' *The Daily Telegraph*. (8 July)

Birke, Lynda. (2001) 'In Pursuit of Difference: Scientific Studies of Women and Men,' in Lederman and Bartsch (eds), 309-22.

## References

Blackall, Molly. (2020) 'Twitter closes Graham Linehan account after trans comment.' *The Guardian*. (27 June)

Bleier, Ruth. *Science and Gender. A Critique of Biology and its Theories on Women*. Oxford: Pergamon Press, 1984. [The Athene Series]

Bodkin, Henry. (2017) 'Sex-change men "will soon be able to have babies".' *The Daily Telegraph*. (4 November)

Bogardus, Tomas. (2019) 'Some Internal Problems with Revisionary Gender Concepts.' *Philosophia*. Available at https://doi.org/10.1007/s11406-019-00107-2 (31 July)

Bogardus, Tomas. (2020) 'Evaluating Arguments for the Sex/Gender Distinction.' *Philosophia*. Available at https://doi.org/10.1007/s11406-019-00157-6 (27 January)

Booth, Robert. (20190 'Transgender man loses court battle to be registered as father.' *The Guardian*. (25 September)

Boylan, Jennifer Finney. (2018) 'Trump Cannot Define Away My Existence.' *The New York Times*. (22 October)

Breggin, Peter. (1993) *Toxic Psychiatry: Drugs and Electroconvulsive Therapy—The Truth and the Better Alternative*. London: HarperCollins.

British Medical Association. (2016) *A Guide to Effective Communication: Inclusive Language in the Workplace*.' Available at https://www.west-info.eu/politically-correct-language-about-pregnancy-going-overboard/bma-guide-to-effective-communication-2016/

Brooks, Libby. (2018) 'Scotland to embed LGBTI teaching across curriculum.' *The Guardian*. (9 November)

Brown, Gregory. (2015) 'Conservatives and Transgenderism: A Response to Jennifer Gruenke.' *Public Discourse*. (30 July)

Brown, Mark. (2020) 'Paul McCartney calls for meat to no longer be mandatory in England's school meals.' *The Guardian*. (22 June)

Brown, Oliver. (2018) 'Transgender weightlifter under strain: Laurel Hubbard's exit may be blessing in disguise as eligibility debate rages.' *The Daily Telegraph*. (9 April)

Budziszewski, J. (2011) *What We Can't Not Know: A Guide*. San Francisco: Ignatius Press. [Originally published in 2003 by Spence Publishing Company, Dallas]

Bulman, May. (2018) 'Anthony Ekundayo Lennon: White theatre director who described himself as "African born again" given a job meant for people of colour.' *Independent*. (4 November)

BUMC (Boston University Medical Center). (2015) 'Transgender: Evidence on the biological nature of gender identity.' *Science Daily*. (13 February)

186                              *Hidden Agender*

Burke, Monica. (2018) 'This Teacher Was Fired for "Misgendering" a Student. Who Could Be Next?' *The Heritage Foundation*. (11 December)

Butler, Dawn. (2020) 'Babies are born without sex says Labour shadow cabinet member.' YouTube. Available at https://www.youtube.com/watch?v= nniqQSQrlYM (17 February)

Butler, Judith. (2004) *Undoing Gender*. London: Routledge.

Butler, Judith. (2006/1990) *Gender Trouble*. London: Routledge.

Carey, Nessa. (2012) *The Epigenetics Revolution*. London: Icon Books.

Carr, Howie. (2018) 'Jim Lyons out-PCs the Democrats.' *Boston Herald*. (5 August)

Casey, Gerard. (2019) *ZAP: Free Speech and Tolerance in the Light of the Zero Aggression Principle*. Exeter: Societas.

Casey, Gerard. (2020) *After #MeToo: Feminism, Patriarchy, Toxic Masculinity and Sundry Cultural Delights*. Exeter: Societas.

Castricum, Simona. (2019) 'Our gender is not for others to decide. A bill for trans people to self-identify is a good start.' *The Guardian*. (20 June)

Charen, Mona. (2018) *Sex Matters: How Modern Feminism Lost Touch with Science, Love, and Common Sense*. New York: Crown Forum.

Chipkin, Logan. (2019) 'Memes, Genes, and Sex Differences—An Interview with Dr. Steve Stewart-Williams.' *Quillette*. (14 May)

Cohen, Leonard. (2009) *The Lyrics of Leonard Cohen*. London: Omnibus Press.

Cohen, Leonard. (2009a) 'Closing Time,' in Cohen 2009, 32-4.

Cohen, Stanley. (2011) *Folk Devils and Moral Panics*. London: Routledge.

Coleman-Phillips, Ceri. (2019) 'Transgender rugby player playing with "a smile on my face".' *BBC News*. (22 August)

Coleman, Clive. (2020) 'Analysis: Far-reaching Effects.' *BBC News*. Available at https://www.bbc.com/news/uk-50981359 (3 January)

Collin, Lindsay et al. (2016) 'Prevalence of Transgender Depends on the "Case" Definition: A Systematic Review.' *The Journal of Sexual Medicine*, vol. 13, no. 4, 613-26.

Congregation for Catholic Education. (2019) *'Male and Female He Created Them': Towards a Path of Dialogue on the Question of Gender Theory in Education*. Vatican City.

Converse, Adrien. (no date) 'The big list of gender identities (+ vocab to know).' Available at https://deconforming.com/gender-identities/

Cook, Teddy. (2019) 'Trans people just want to live fulfilling lives. Our mere existence shouldn't threaten you.' *The Guardian*. (15 August)

Courtney, Lorraine. (2015) 'Challenging Gender Conventions is a Sign of

Progress.' *The Irish Independent.* (15 September)

Crews, Frederick. (2002) *Postmodern Pooh*. London: Profile Books.

Crowther, Anne. (2019) 'Hot seeds, cold wombs: How human beings have thought about sex throughout history.' *Times Literary Supplement.* (29 August)

Daisley, Stephen. (2020) 'Network Rail's cowardly JK Rowling decision.' *The Spectator.* (30 July)

Dalrymple, Theodore. (2000) 'All Sex, All the Time,' in Dalrymple 2005, 234-50.

Dalrymple, Theodore. (2001) 'The Dystopian Imagination,' in Dalrymple 2005, 103-15.

Dalrymple, Theodore. (2004) 'The Frivolity of Evil,' in Dalrymple 2005, 1-16.

Dalrymple, Theodore. (2005) *Our Culture, What's Left of It: The Mandarins and the Masses*. Chicago: Ivan R. Dee.

Dalrymple, Theodore. (2019) 'A Matter of Truth: On Ricky Gervais, J. K. Rowling, and Speaking Frankly.' *City Journal.* (29 December)

Dalrymple, Theodore. (2020) 'Recipe for Chaos: A Disruptive "Ethical Vegan" launches a Religious-Discrimination Debate in England.' *City Journal.* (21 January)

Dalrymple, Theodore. (2020a) 'An Orgy of Self-Righteous Sentimentality.' *Law & Liberty.* (26 June)

Davies-Arai, Stephanie and Susan Matthews. (2019) 'Queering the curriculum: creating gendered subjectivity in resources for schools,' in Moore and Brunskell-Evans.

Davies, James. (2014) *Cracked: Why Psychiatry is Doing More Harm than Good*. London: IconBooks.

Del Noce, Augusto. (2014) *The Crisis of Modernity*, ed. and trans. Carlo Lancellotti. Montreal & Kingston: McGill-Queen's University Press.

Dentons. (2019) *Only Adults? Good Practices in Legal Gender Recognition for Youth.* (November) Available at https://www.iglyo.com/wp-content/uploads/2019/11/IGLYO_v3-1.pdf

Desanctis, Alexandra. (2019) 'On Abortion, One 2020 Democrat Hit the Gas Pedal.' *National Review.* (27 June)

Dineen, Tana. (1999) *Manufacturing Victims*. London: Little, Brown Book Group.

Dirks, Paul. (2020) 'Transition as Treatment: The Best Studies Show the Worst Outcomes.' *Public Discourse.* (16 February)

Ditum, Sarah. (2020) 'The hounding of JK Rowling shows a society that has forgotten how to think.' *The Daily Telegraph.* (11 June)

Dolgin, Robyn. (2020) 'More and more "transgender" people regret surgery, want to return to a normal life.' *Life Site News*. (14 January)

Donnelly, Laura. (2018) 'Primary school pupils should be taught what it means to be LGBT, Royal College of Paediatricians says.' *The Daily Telegraph*. (12 November)

Dorman, Sam. (2020) 'J. K. Rowling slammed for defending concept of biological sex: "It isn't hate to speak the truth".' *Fox News*. (7 June)

Doward, Jamie. (2018) 'NHS told: give trans patients equal access to fertility service.' *The Guardian*. (4 August)

Dreher, Rod. (2017) *The Benedict Option: A Strategy for Christians in a Post-Christian Nation*. New York: Sentinel.

EIGE (2020) 'What is gender mainstreaming.' European Institute for Gender Equality. Available at https://eige.europa.eu/gender-mainstreaming/what-is-gender-mainstreaming

Elias, Norbert. (2000) *The Civilizing Process: Sociogenetic and Psychogenetic Investigations*, rev. ed., trans. Edmund Jephcott. Oxford: Blackwell. [Originally published as Über den Prozess der Zivilisation as two separate volumes by Haus zum Falken, Basel.]

Employment Appeal Tribunal. (2009) *Grainger PLC et al. v Mr T. Nicholson*. Appeal No. UKEAT/0219/09/ZT.

Employment Tribunals. (2019a) *Dr David Mackereth v The Department for Work and Pensions & Advanced Personnel Management Group (UK) Ltd.* Case number: 1304602/2018.

Employment Tribunals. (2019b) *Forstater vs CGD Europe et al*. Case number: 2200909/2019.

European Court of Human Rights. (2002) *Case of Christine Goodwin v. The United Kingdom*. Available at http://hudoc.echr.coe.int/eng?i=001-60596

Farrington, Brendan. (2020) 'Federal appeals court rules for transgender student in bathroom case.' *The Washington Times*. (10 August)

Fausto-Sterling, Anne. (2018) 'Why Sex Is Not Binary.' *The New York Times*. (25 October)

Fee, Elizabeth. 'Women's Nature and Scientific Objectivity,' in Lowe and Hubbard, 9-27.

Feser, Edward. (2005) *Philosophy of Mind*. Oxford: Oneworld.

Feuer, Lewis S. (2010/1975) *Ideology and the Ideologists*. London: Transaction Publishers. [Originally published in 1975 by Basil Blackwell.]

Fine, Cordelia. (2010) *Delusions of Gender: The Real Science Behind Sex Differences*. London: Icon.

Fink, Jenni. (2019) 'LGBTQ Group Drops Martina Navratilova for Saying

## References

Women Competitions With Transgender Women are "Unfair." *Newsweek*. (20 February)

Flood, Alison. (2020) 'JK Rowling returns human rights award to group that denounces her trans views.' *The Daily Telegraph*. (28 August)

Forster, E. M. (2011/1909) *The Machine Stops*. London: Penguin Classics.

Fowler, Henry Watson. (1994) *The King's English*. Ware, Hertfordshire: Wordsworth Editions.

Francis, Babette and John Ballantyne. (2018) 'Where Angels Fear to Tread: The Fraud of Transgenderism.' *Public Discourse*. (14 November)

Francis, Richard C. (2011) *Epigenetics: How Environment Shapes Our Genes*. New York: W. W. Norton & Company.

Frankl, Viktor. (1964/1946) *Man's Search for Meaning: An Introduction to Logotherapy*. London: Hodder and Stoughton.

Franks, Angela. (2019) 'Andrea Long Chu Says You Are a Female, and He's Only Partly Wrong.' *Public Discourse*. (10 December)

Freiburger, Calvin. (2018) 'LGBT activists: Soviet camps were "compassionate" means of "re-education." Send bigots there.' *LifeSite News*. (12 September)

Fukuyama, Francis. (2018) *Identity: Contemporary Identity Politics and the Struggle for Recognition*. London: Profile Books.

Garan, D. G. (1963) *The Paradox of Pleasure and Relativity: The Psychological Causal Law*. New York: Philosophical Library.

Garan, D. G. (1975) *The Key to the Sciences of Man: The "Impossible" Relativity of Value Reactions*. New York: Philosophical Library.

Gbadamosi, Nosmot. (2018) 'Jesus treated women as equals, says author Chimamanda Adichie.' *CNN African Voices*. (28 September).

George, Robert P. (2016) 'Gnostic Liberalism.' *First Things*. (December)

Gittos, Luke. (2018) 'The male rapist in a women's prison.' *Spiked*. (15 October).

Glavin, Terry. (2015) 'Rachel Dolezal is nothing new in a culture littered with racial pretenders.' *National Post*. (18 June)

GLEN. (2016) 'Being LGBT in School.' Available at https://www.education. ie/en/Publications/Education-Reports/Being-LGBT-in-School.pdf

Glyn-Jones, Anne. (1996) *Holding Up a Mirror: How Civilizations Decline*. Exeter: Imprint Academic. [First published by Century Random House]

Goldberg, Steven. (1977) *The Inevitability of Patriarchy*. London: Temple Smith.

Goldman, Bruce. (2017) 'Two Minds.' *Stanford Medicine*. Available at https:// neuroscience.stanford.edu/news/two-minds

Goldsbrough, Susannah. (2020) 'Cancel culture: what is it, and how did it begin?' *The Daily Telegraph*. (30 July)

Gov.uk. (2019) 'Relationships education, relationship and sex education (RSE) and health education: FAQs.' Available at https://www.gov.uk/government/news/relationships-education-relationships-and-sex-education-rse-and-health-education-faqs

Government Equalities Office. (2018) *LGBT Action Plan: Improving the Lives of Lesbian, Gay, Bisexual and Transgender People.* Available at https://assets.publishing.service.gov.uk/government/uploads/system/uploads/attachment_data/file/721367/GEO-LGBT-Action-Plan.pdf

Grady, Denise. (2018) 'Anatomy Does Not Determine Gender, Experts Say.' *The New York Times*. (18 October)

Gray, John. (2016) *The Soul of the Marionette*. London: Penguin. [Allen Lane, 2015]

Green, David. (2006) *We're Nearly All Victims Now!* London: Civitas.

Green, Erica et al. (2018) '"Transgender" Could be Defined out of Existence under Trump Administration.' *The New York Times*. (21 October)

Greene, Chad Felix. (2017) 'Transgender Suicides: What to Do About Them.' Available at https://www.thepublicdiscourse.com/2017/07/19769/ (27 July)

Greer, Germaine. (1985) *Sex and Destiny: The Politics of Human Fertility*. Picador: London.

Grigg, William Norman.' (2016) 'Gavin Grimm's Totalitarian Fairy Tale.' *Pro Libertate*. Available at http://freedominourtime.blogspot.com/2016/04/gavin-grimms-totalitarian-fairy-tale.html

Grosz, Elizabeth A. (1989) *Sexual Subversions*. Sydney: Allen & Unwin.

Gruenke, Jennifer. (2015) 'Rethinking the Conservative Approach to Transgenderism.' *Public Discourse*. (29 July)

Guyton, Morgan. (2017) 'Why is NT Wright Calling Transgender People Gnostics?' *United Methodist Insight*. (8 August)

Hakim, Catherine. (2015) *Supply and Desire: Sexuality and the Sex Industry in the 21st Century*. London: IEA. [IEA Discussion Paper No. 61]

Halliday, Josh. (2018) 'Graham Linehan given police warning after complaint by transgender activist.' *The Guardian*. (7 October)

Harris, Tamara Winfrey. (2015) 'Black like who? Rachel Dolezal's harmful masquerade.' *The New York Times*. (16 June)

Harris, Tom. (2020) 'Coronavirus has not wiped out wokeness, but at least kept it at bay.' *The Daily Telegraph*. (23 April)

Hay, Katharine. (2020) 'JK Rowling's hand prints in Edinburgh vandalised with red paint amid trans rights row.' *Edinburgh Evening News*. (12 July)

Hayek, F. A. (1982), *Law, Legislation and Liberty*. London: Routledge.

Hayton, Debbie. (2019) 'Trans activists are making life harder for trans people.' *The Spectator*. (14 December)

Hayton, Debbie. (2020) 'The silencing of Graham Linehan.' *The Spectator*. (29 June)

Heinrichs, Terrence. (2018) 'Report from Canada—Some Women Have Balls.' *Daily Caller*. Available at https://dailycaller.com/2018/10/23/opinion-report-from-canada/

Hellen, Nicholas. (2017) 'The female NHS nurse I asked for came with stubble.' *The Times*. (31 December)

Helmore, Ed. (2020) 'Anti-Trump British journalist quits New York Magazine in "woke" row.' *The Observer*. (18 July)

Hempel, Jessi. (2016) 'My Brother's Pregnancy and the Making of a New American Family.' *Time*. (12 September)

Heuchan, Claire. (2017) 'If feminist Linda Bellos is seen as a risk, progressive politics has lost its way.' *The Guardian*. (6 October)

Heyer, Walt. (2011) *Paper Genders: Pulling the Mask Off the Transgender Phenomenon*. Make Waves Publishing.

Heyer, Walt. (2017a) 'Bravo to the Truth: What's Wrong with Transgender Ideology.' *Public Discourse*. (27 April)

Heyer, Walt. (2017b) 'The Transgender Matrix: It's Time to Choose the Red Pill.' *Public Discourse*. (10 October)

Heyer, Walt. (2019) 'Diagnosis of Gender Dysphoria—Too General and Too Much Harm.' *Public Discourse*. (7 August)

Heyes, Cressida J. (2009) 'Changing race, changing sex: The ethics of self-transformation,' in *You've changed: Sex reassignment and personal identity*, ed. Laurie Shrage. New York: Oxford University Press.

Hodges, Mark and John Jalsevac. (2015) 'Feminist icon: Transgender "women" like Bruce Jenner aren't women. They're delusional.' *LifeSite News*. (27 October)

Holt, Alison. (2020) 'NHS gender clinic "should have challenged me more" over transition.' *BBC News*. (1 March)

Hopwood, Nick et al. (eds) (2018) *Reproduction: Antiquity to the Present Day*. Cambridge: Cambridge University Press.

Hornstein, Gail A. (2009) *Agnes's Jacket: A Psychiatrist's Search for the Meanings of Madness*. New York: Rodale.

Horton, Helena. (2018) 'Cancer research removes the word "women" from smear campaign amid transgender concerns.' *The Daily Telegraph*. (15 June)

House of the Oireachtas. (2018) Prohibition of Conversion Therapies Bill 2018. Available at https://data.oireachtas.ie/ie/oireachtas/bill/2018/39/eng/initiated/b3918s.pdf

Humphery, Kim. (2020) 'Trans rights have been pitted against feminism but we're not enemies.' *The Guardian*. (7 July)

Hutchinson, Robert J. (2019) 'Brittania Rules the Christian Faith "Not Worthy of Respect".' *Crisis Magazine*. (8 October)

Huxley, Aldous. (1998/1932) *Brave New World*. New York: Perennial Classics.

Iantiffi, Alex and Meg-John Barker. (2018) *How to Understand your Gender: A Practical Guide for Exploring Who You Are*. London: Jessica Kingsley Publishers.

IGLYO et al. (2019) 'Only Adults? Good Practices in Legal Gender Recognition for Youth: A Report on the Current State of Laws and NGO Advocacy in Eight Countries in Europe, with a Focus on Rights of Young People.' Available at https://www.iglyo.com/wp-content/uploads/2019/11/IGLYO_v3-1.pdf (November)

Ingle, Sean. (2020) 'Trans women face potential women's rugby ban over safety concerns.' *The Guardian*. (19 July)

Irish Statute Book. (2015) Gender Recognition Act. Available at http://www.irishstatutebook.ie/eli/2015/act/25/enacted/en/html?q=Gender+Recognition

Jeffreys, Sheila. (2012) 'Let us be free to debate transgenderism without being accused of "hate speech".' *The Guardian*. (29 May)

Jeffreys, Sheila. (2014) *Gender Hurts*. London: Routledge.

Johnson, Simon. (2019) 'Scots to be allowed to change legal gender in six months with no medical treatment.' *The Daily Telegraph*. (17 December)

Johnson, Simon. (2020) 'Mother of dead transgender girl to launch legal bid to preserve her sperm so she can have grandchild.' *The Daily Telegraph*. (24 August)

Jones, Amy. (2020a) 'Liz Truss to scrap "self-identification" plans in the next few days.' *The Daily Telegraph*. (13 July)

Jones, Amy. (2020b) 'Gender Recognition Act: Will the Government give the green light to self-identification.' *The Daily Telegraph*. (24 July 2020)

Jones, Andrea. (2019) 'Males Don't Belong in Women's Sports—Even If They Don't Always Win.' The Heritage Foundation. (27 November)

Jones, Andrea. (2020) 'Compelled Speech Is Hitting Close to Home.' The Heritage Foundation. (4 February)

Jones, Peter. (1992) *The Gnostic Empire Strikes Back*. Phillipsburg, New Jersey: P & R Publishing.

# References

193

Joyce, Helen. (2018) 'The New Patriarchy: How Trans Radicalism Hurts Women, Children—and Trans People Themselves.' *Quillette*. (4 December)

Joyce, Helen. (2020) 'Speaking Up for Female Eunuchs.' *Standpoint*. (30 January)

Kao, Emilie and Nicholas Marr. (2019) 'Newly Proposed Transgender Policies Could Harm Elderly and the Young.' The Heritage Foundation. (2 July)

Kao, Emilie. (2019) 'Equality Act Would Create Inequality for Women.' The Heritage Foundation. (27 March)

Kaveney, Roz. (2012) 'Radical feminists are acting like a cult.' *The Guardian*. (25 May)

Kearns, Madeleine. (2019) 'This Week at the U.N: Feminists Concern about Transgenderism is "Misplaced".' *National Review*. (7 February)

Kearns, Madeleine. (2019a) 'Rachel McKinnon Is a Cheat and a Bully.' *National Review*. (October 29)

Kennedy, Kerry. (2020) 'A Statement from Kerry Kennedy.' *Robert F. Kennedy Human Rights News*. Available at https://rfkhumanrights.org/news/a-statement-from-kerry-kennedy-president-of-robert-f-kennedy-human-rights (3 August)

Kennedy, Maev. (2017) 'Jenni Murray: trans women shouldn't call themselves "real women".' *The Guardian*. (5 March)

Kersten, Katherine. (2016) 'Transgender Conformity,' in *First Things*. (December).

Kimball, Roger. (1993) 'Sex in the twilight zone: Catharine MacKinnon's crusade.' *The New Criterion*, vol. 38, no. 10 (June)

King, Karen L. (2003) *What is Gnosticism?* Cambridge, Massachusetts: Belnap Press (Harvard University Press).

Kirkup, James. (2019) 'The document that reveals the remarkable tactics of trans lobbyists.' *The Spectator*. (2 December)

Kirkup, James. (2019a) 'Jo Swinson has finally made the BBC do its job on trans rights.' *The Spectator*. (9 December)

Kirkup, James. (2020) 'The NHS has quietly changed its trans guidance to reflect reality.' *The Spectator*. (4 June)

Kirkup, James. (2020a) 'What explains the rising number of children with gender issues?' *The Spectator*. (14 August)

Knapton, Sarah. (2017) 'Two British men become first to give birth after putting gender surgery on hold.' *The Daily Telegraph*. (9 July)

Knapton, Sarah. (2018) 'NHS must offer transgender men egg storage so they can be parents, says British Fertility Society guidance.' *The Daily Telegraph*. (4 January)

Knoedler, J. R and N. M. Shah. (2018) 'Molecular mechanisms underlying sexual differentiation of the nervous system.' *Current Opinion in Neurobiology*. vol. 53, 192-7.

Knox, Liam. (2019) 'Media's "detransition" narrative is fueling misconceptions, trans advocates say.' *NBC News*. (19 December)

Kuby, Gabrielle. (2015/2012) *The Global Sexual Revolution: Destruction of Freedom in the Name of Freedom,* trans. James Patrick Kirchner. Kettering, Ohio: Lifesite. [First published as *Die globale sexuelle Revolution: Zestörung der Freiheit im Namen der Freiheit*, Fe-Medienverlags Gmbh, 2012.]

Kumar, Anugrah. (2017) 'Catholic Hospital Sued for Refusing to Remove Transgender Man's Uterus.' *The Christian Post*. (7 January)

Labour Campaign for Trans Rights. (2020) 'Founding Statement' & 'Pledges.' Available at https://docs.google.com/forms/d/e/1FAIpQLSd_wPyenUicSJgKv1YTknZ47gDGU4b_389zYbqH10TGSTRrpg/viewform

Lamnisos, Athena. (2020) 'It's not woke to say that "people" get cervical cancer.' *The Daily Telegraph*. (10 August)

Lasch, Christopher. (1979/1991) *The Culture of Narcissism: American Life in an Age of Diminishing Expectations*. New York: W. W. Norton & Company.

Lasch, Christopher. (1995/1996) *The Revolt of the Elites and the Betrayal of Democracy*. New York: W. W. Norton & Company.

Leader. (2017) 'Teenage girl boards with boys, as schools grapple with rise of "gender-fluidity".' *The Daily Telegraph*. (1 October)

Leader. (2018) 'Very fishy: China rules rainbow trout can be sold as salmon.' *The Guardian*. (14 August)

Lederman, Muriel and Ingrid Bartsch. (eds) (2001) *The Gender and Science Reader*. London: Routledge.

Lester, C. N. *Trans Like Me: A Journey for All of Us*. London: Virago.

Liddle, Rod. (2018) 'Women come last in Labour's deranged victim hierarchy.' *The Spectator*. (27 January)

Liddle, Rod. (2018a) 'I am black—get over it.' *The Spectator*. (10 November)

Lowe, Marian and Ruth Hubbard (eds). *Women's Nature: Rationalizations of Inequality*. Oxford: Pergamon Press, 1985. (The Athene Series)

Lyons, Izzy. (2019a) '"Bar of offence" is too low when discussing transgender policy proposals, tribunal hears.' *The Daily Telegraph*. (15 November)

Lyons, Izzy. (2019a2) 'Transgender people who agree with using terms "men" and "women" too afraid to speak out, tribunal hears.' *The Daily Telegraph*. (18 November)

Lyons, Izzy. (2019b) 'Test case rules against May Forstater, tax expert sacked over transgender tweet.' *The Daily Telegraph*. (18 December)

## References

Lyons, Izzy. (2019c) 'Transgender woman accused of "hate speech" after wearing t-shirt stating that she is still biologically male.' *The Daily Telegraph.* (22 December)

Lyons, Izzy. (2020) 'Psychotherapists avoid questioning children who want to be transgender as they fear conversion therapy accusations.' *The Daily Telegraph.* (1 August)

Machan, Tibor. (1984) 'Libertarianism: The Principle of Liberty,' in G. W. Carey (ed.) (1984) *Freedom and Virtue: the Conservative/Libertarian debate.* Lanham, Maryland: University Press of America, 35-58.

Mainwaring, Doug. (2019) 'Ex-transgender starts "detransitioning" advocacy group: "I felt I had to do something".' *Lifesite News.* (7 October)

Mamet, David. (2012) *The Secret Knowledge: On the Dismantling of American Culture.* New York: Sentinel.

Marimow, Ann E. (2020) 'Transgender student Gavin Grimm's battle over bathroom access returns to court.' *The Washington Post.* (26 May)

Marsh, David. (2013) *For Who the Bell Tolls: The Essential and Entertaining Guide to Grammar.* London: Guardian Books.

Marshall, Francesca. (2018) 'Quakers caught in Terf war with Oxford University protesters after hosting "transphobic" feminist meeting.' *The Daily Telegraph.* (26 April)

Martin, Jenny Beth. (2020) 'Supreme Court makes "sex," "sexual orientation" and "gender identity" interchangeable.' *The Washington Times.* (23 June)

Mastrangelo, Alana. (2019) 'Scholar makes "moral case" for allowing legal age change based on emotions.' *Breitbart.* (20 March)

Mather, Victor. (2019) 'Woman Beats Man at Darts Championship for the First Time.' *The New York Times.* (18 December)

Mayer, Lawrence S. and Paul R. McHugh. (2016) 'Sexuality and Gender: Findings from the Biological, Psychological, and Social Sciences.' *The New Atlantis.* (Fall)

McCarthy, Margaret Harper. (2019) 'Overruling the Visible: The Emperor's New Gender.' *Public Discourse.* (6 October)

McConnell, Fred. (2015) 'Bruce Jenner: he or she, using a person's preferred pronouns is about respect.' *The Guardian.* (29 April)

McHugh, Paul. (2014) 'Transgender Surgery isn't the Solution.' *Wall Street Journal.* (13 May).

McManus, Leigh. (2019) 'Oxford-educated rapper "smashes female weight-lifting records while identifying as a woman" in row over transgender athletes.' *Mail Online.* (3 March)

McWhorter, John. (2003) *The Power of Babel: A Natural History of Language.* London: Arrow.

McWhorter, John. (2018) 'How Anti Racism Hurts Black People.' *YouTube.* (3 December) Available at https://www.youtube.com/watch?v=mT2rlJe9cu-U&t=15s

McWhorter, John. (2018a) 'The Virtue Signalers Won't Change the World.' *The Atlantic.* (23 December)

Meenan, John Paul. (2017) 'The New Totalitarian Laws of Canada.' *Crisis.* (13 July)

Megarry, Robert. (1973) *A Second Miscellany-at-Law: A Further Diversion for Lawyers and Others.* London: Stevens & Sons Limited.

Mele, Christopher. (2016) 'Oregon Court Allows a Person to Choose Neither Sex.' *The New York Times.* (13 June)

Melnick, R. Shep. (2019) 'Regulating Identity.' *Law & Liberty.* (30 January)

Moody, Oliver. (2018) 'Science pinpoints DNA behind gender identity.' *The Sunday Times.* (19 March)

Moore, Charles. (2020) '"Liberal" media platforms have been seized by cowardice and militant wokery.' *The Daily Telegraph.* (17 July)

Moore, Michele and Heather Brunskell-Evans. (eds) *Inventing Transgender Children and Young People.* Newcastle Upon Tyne: Cambridge Scholars Publishing.

Moore, Suzanne. (2020) 'Who decided that letting posh young actors police my womanhood was progress?' *The Daily Telegraph.* (11 June)

Morabito, Stella. (2020) 'Democrats' "Equality" Act Would Be A Big Nudge Towards A U.S. Social Credit System.' *The Federalist.* (28 January)

Moran, Caitlin. (2011) *How to be a Woman.* London: Ebury Press.

Morefield, Scott. (2019) 'Lesbian Activist Defends "Biological Reality" After Being Booted From Baltimore LGBTQ Commission.' *Daily Caller.* (12 February)

Morgan, Eleanor. (2020) 'The way trans people's rights are discussed is causing them fear and pain.' *The Guardian.* (9 July)

Morgan, Tom. (2020a) 'Safety risks in sport could lead to reforms of transgender rules in Britain.' *The Daily Telegraph.* (20 July)

Moyer, Justin Wm. (2015) 'There is no such thing as "transracial": Why Caitlyn Jenner and Rachel Dolezal are nothing alike.' *National Post.* (17 June)

Mulready, Molly. (2018) 'My trans child needs to be himself—I understand that now.' *The Guardian.* (11 June)

Murray, Douglas. (2020) 'J K Rowling holds the answer to ending cancel culture.' *The Daily Telegraph.* (25 July)

# References 197

Murray, Douglas. (2020a) 'Trans people are real—but so is biology.' *The Times*. (27 August)

Murray, Jenni. (2017) 'Be trans, be proud—but don't call yourself a "real woman".' *The Times*. (5 March)

Myers, Alex. (2018) 'Trump wants to deny my trans identity and erase years of progress.' *The Guardian*. (24 October)

NAHT & Stonewall. (2017) 'Guidance for school leaders on supporting trans staff.' Available at https://troyjenkinson.files.wordpress.com/2019/08/naht_transstaff_guide.pdf

NBC News. (2020) 'In landmark case, Supreme Court rules LGBTQ workers are protected from job discrimination.' *NBC News*. (15 June)

NHS. (no date) 'Treatment: Gender Dysphoria.' Available at https://www.nhs.uk/conditions/gender-dysphoria/treatment/

NHS. (2019) 'Information for trans and non-binary people.' Available at https://assets.publishing.service.gov.uk/government/uploads/system/uploads/attachment_data/file/834656/Screening_for_trans_and_non-binary_people_Sept_2019.pdf

Nieli, Russell. (2006) 'Critic of the Sensate Culture: Rediscovering the Genius of Pitirim Sorokin.' *The Political Science Reviewer*, vol. 35, 264-379. Online version available at https://isi.org/modern-age/critic-of-the-sensate-culture-rediscovering-the-genius-of-pitirim-sorokin/

O'Hagan, Ellie Mae. (2018) 'This troll is playing the media with a trans-baiting age-change ploy.' *The Guardian*. (13 November)

O'Neil, Tyler. (2019) 'First Trans Person to Obtain Legal "Non-Binary" Sex Status Changes Back to Birth Sex in Blow to LGBT Movement.' *PJ Media*. (31 December)

O'Neill, Brendan. (2017) 'The Orwellian Nightmare of Transgender Politics.' *Spiked*. (5 July)

O'Neill, Brendan. (2018) 'A manifesto for heresy.' *Spiked*. (10 May)

O'Neill, Brendan. (2019) 'It isn't TERFs who are bigoted—it's their persecutors.' *Spiked*. (28 January)

O'Neill, Brendan. (2020) 'Dawn Butler's Transgender Madness.' *The Spectator*. (18 February)

Oakley, Ann. (1972) *Sex, Gender and Society*. London: Taylor & Francis Ltd.

Orwell, George. (1954/1949) *Nineteen Eighty-Four*. London: Penguin.

Owen, G. (2018) 'BBC chief stunned as secret staff sex survey reveals 417 of the corporation's workers are transgender.' *Mail Online*. (1 July)

Paglia, Camille. (2017) *Free Women Free Men: Sex * Gender * Feminism*. New York: Pantheon Books.

Palmer, Frank. (1971) *Grammar*. London: Penguin.

Palmer, Frank. (1975) 'Language and Languages,' in Whitney F. Bolton (ed.) (1975) *The English Language*. London: Sphere Books, 12-37.

Pang, Ken C. et al. (2020) 'Association of Media Coverage of Transgender and Gender Diverse Issues With Rates of Referral of Transgender Children and Adolescents to Specialist Gender Clinics in the UK and Australia.' *Journal of the American Medical Association*. (28 July) Available at https://jamanetwork.com/journals/jamanetworkopen/fullarticle/2768726?resultClick=1

Parnell, Thain. (2017) 'Transition is no casual matter, and we need to talk about those who regret it.' *Feminist Current*. (5 August)

Pasha-Robinson, Lucy. (2017) 'Rachel-Dolezal: White woman who identifies as black calls for "racial fluidity" to be accepted.' *Independent*. (27 March)

Penman, Jim. (2015) *Biohistory*. Newcastle upon Tyne: Cambridge Scholars Publishing.

Popper, Karl and John Eccles. (1983) *The Self and its Brain: An Argument for Interactionism*. London: Routledge & Kegan Paul.

Power, Ed. (2020) 'JK Rowling, ruiner of childhoods: why "woke" Harry Potter fans have turned on their idol.' *The Daily Telegraph*. (28 May)

Purves, Libby. (2017) 'The sisterhood is crazy to bar its door to trans women.' *The Times*. (8 March)

Quinn, Ben. (2020) '"White Lives Matter" plane organiser says police have offered protection.' *The Guardian*. (24 June)

Regnerus, Mark. (2019) 'New Data Show "Gender-Affirming" Surgery Doesn't Really Improve Mental Health. So Why Are the Study's Authors Saying It Does?' *Public Discourse*. (13 November)

Reilly, Katie. (2019) 'Woman Wins Mixed-Gender Worlds Darts Championship Match For the First Time Ever.' *Time*. (18 December)

Riley, Elizabeth. (2016) 'The participation of trans athletes in sport—a transformation in approach?' *Bird & Bird*. (February)

Ring, Trudy. (2020) 'Courts Deliver Two Victories for Trans Americans.' *The Advocate*. (7 August)

Robbins, Jane. (2019) 'The Cracks in the Edifice of Transgender Totalitarianism.' *Public Discourse*. (13 July)

Robles, Monique. (2019) 'Understanding Gender Dysphoria and Its Treatment in Children and Adolescents.' *Public Discourse*. (22 April)

Rorty, Richard. (1993) 'Human Rights, Rationality, and Sentimentality,' in *On Human Rights: The Oxford Amnesty Lectures*, eds Stephen Shute and Susan Hurley (New York: Basic Books)

Rothbard, Murray N. (1984) 'Frank S. Meyer: The Fusionist as Libertarian

## References

Manqué,' in G. W. Carey (ed.) *Freedom and Virtue: the Conservative/Libertarian debate*. Lanham, Maryland: University Press of America. 91-111.

Rudgard, Olivia. (2017) 'Transgender people can end up "badly damaged" says Lord Robert Winston.' *The Daily Telegraph*. (1 November)

Ruse, Austin. (2019) 'Lesbian feminists join conservative think-tank to protect kids from transgenderism.' *LifeSite News*. (4 February)

Sax, Leonard. (2002) 'How common is intersex?: A Response to Anne Fausto-Sterling.' *The Journal of Sex Research,* vol. 39. No. 3, 174-78.

Scalia, Antonin. *J.E.B. v. Alabama ex rel. T. B.* Available at https://supreme.justia.com/cases/federal/us/511/127/

Serena, Katie. (2017) 'Doctor on Transgender Women giving Birth: "You Could Do It tomorrow".' *ATI*. (6 November)

Shafer, Jeff. (2017) 'Supreme Incoherence: Transgender Ideology and the End of Law.' *First Things*. (28 March)

Showalter, Brandon. (2020) 'Woman fired from literary agency for tweeting that trans-identified males aren't women.' *The Christian Post*. (27 August)

Sidwell, Marc. (2020) 'The Long March—A Quiet Revolution to Destroy Western Civilisation.' YouTube. Available at https://www.youtube.com/watch?v=jIJxVEOdcn0

Sidwell, Marc. (2020a) *The Long March: How the Left won the Culture War and what to do about it*. London: The New Culture Forum.

Siegel, Nina. (2018) 'In This Exhibition, You Walk through Excrement.' *The New York Times*. (7 July)

Siewers, Alfred Kentigern. (2019) 'The Orwellian Dangers of the "Equality Act".' *Public Discourse*. (24 April)

Singh, Anita et al. (2020) 'JK Rowling fans row: fans urged to stop buying Harry Potter books.' *The Daily Telegraph*. (11 June)

Singh, Anita. (2020a) 'Authors quit JK Rowling's literary agency in row over trans rights.' *The Daily Telegraph*. (22 June)

Skalko, John. (2017) 'Why There Are Only Two Sexes.' *Public Discourse*. (5 June)

Smith, Andrew Phillip. (2008) *The Gnostics: History Tradition, Scriptures, Influence*. London: Watkins Publishing.

Soh, Debra. (2020) *The End of Gender: Debunking the Myths about Sex and Identity in Our Society*. New York: Threshold Editions.

Sorokin, Pitirim A. (1925). *The Sociology of Revolution*. Philadelphia: J. B. Lippincott Co. [Reprinted in 1967 by H. Fertig, New York.]

Sorokin, Pitirim A. (1928/1958) *Contemporary Sociological Theories*. New York: Harper and Row.

Sorokin, Pitirim A. (1937) *Social and Cultural Dynamics, vols I-III.* New York: American Book Company.

Sorokin, Pitirim A. (1941) *Social and Cultural Dynamics, vol. IV.* New York: American Book Company.

Sorokin, Pitirim A. (1942) *The Crisis of Our Age*: *The Social and Cultural Outlook.* Boston: E.P. Dutton.

Sorokin, Pitirim A. (1948) *The Reconstruction of Humanity.* Boston: Beacon Press.

Sorokin, Pitirim A. (1950) *Social Philosophies of an Age of Crisis.* Boston: Beacon Press.

Sorokin, Pitirim A. (1954) *The Ways and Power of Love: Types, Factors, and Techniques of Moral Transformation.* Boston: Beacon Press, 1954.

Sorokin, Pitirim A. (1956) *The American Sex Revolution.* Boston: Porter Sargent.

Sorokin, Pitirim A. (1956a) *Fads and Foibles in Modern Sociology and Related Sciences.* Chicago: Henry Regnery.

Sorokin, Pitirim A. (1957/1985) *Social and Cultural Dynamics,* rev. and abridged in one volume by the author. New Brunswick: Transaction Books.

Sorokin, Pitirim A. (1966) *Sociological Theories of Today.* New York: Harper and Row.

Southworth, Phoebe. (2020) 'Government's decision to ban parents from withdrawing children from "relationship education" lessons faces judicial review.' *The Daily Telegraph.* (18 July)

Sowell, Thomas. (1987) *A Conflict of Visions: Ideological Origins of Political Struggles.* New York: William Morrow.

Sowell, Thomas. (2011) *Economic Facts and Fallacies*, 2nd ed. New York: Basic Books.

Sowell, Thomas. (2108) *Discrimination and Disparities.* New York: Basic Books.

Stanford, Peter. (2020) 'The bonfire of JK Rowling and the day her starlets turned on her.' *The Daily Telegraph.* (11 June)

Stanley, Tim. (2020) 'The man who refused to be cancelled.' *The Daily Telegraph.* (18 July)

Stirner, Max. (2005/1844) *The Ego and His Own: The Case of the Individual Against Authority*, trans. Steven T Byington, ed. James J. Martin. Mineola, New York: Dover Publications, Inc.

Stock, Kathleen. (2020) 'Sticks, Stones and Lawsuits.' *Standpoint.* (30 January)

Stonestreet, John & Shane Morris. (2020) 'What is a Woman? Two Marches, Contradictory Catechisms.' *Breakpoint.* (10 February)

## References

Stonewall. (2018) *Creating an LGBT-Inclusive Curriculum: A Guide for Secondary Schools*. Available at https://www.stonewall.org.uk/system/files/inclusive_curriculum_guide.pdf

Sutherland, Keith. (2020) 'The Trans Taliban and the long tail of 1970s social philosophy.' Private communication to author.

Swerling, Gabriella. (2020) 'Transgender father loses Court of Appeal case after fighting against being called "mother" on birth certificate.' *The Daily Telegraph*. (29 April)

Swerling, Gabriella. (2020a) 'I'm not anti-trans, says JK Rowling after "periods" row.' *The Daily Telegraph*. (8 June)

Swerling, Gabriella. (2020d) 'Changing gender should not be made easier, nearly half of Britons polled believe.' *The Daily Telegraph*. (16 July)

Swinburne, Richard. (1986) *The Evolution of Soul*. Oxford: Clarendon Press.

Swinburne, Richard. (2019) *Are We Bodies or Souls?* Oxford: Oxford University Press.

Szasz, Thomas. (1974) *The Myth of Mental Illness: Foundations of a Theory of Personal Conduct*, rev. ed. New York: Harper & Row, Publishers.

Szasz, Thomas. (1988) *The Myth of Psychotherapy: Mental Healing as Religion, Rhetoric, and Repression*. Syracuse, New York: Syracuse University Press. [Originally published by Anchor Press/Doubleday, 1978]

Szasz, Thomas. (1996) *The Meaning of Mind: Language, Mortality, and Neuroscience*. Westport, Connecticut: Praeger.

Szasz, Thomas. (1997) *Insanity: The Idea and its Consequences*. Syracuse, New York: Syracuse University Press. [Originally published by John Wiley & Sons, Inc. in 1987]

Szasz. Thomas (1990) *The Untamed Tongue: A Dissenting Dictionary*. La Salle, Illinois: Open Court.

Tannehill, Brynn. (2017) 'Debunking the New Atlantis Article On Sexuality and Gender.' *Huffpost*. (24 March)

Tatchell, Peter. (2018) 'Pride has changed the world for LGBT+ people. Long may it continue.' *The Guardian*. (6 July)

Taylor, J. K., D. C. Lewis, and D. P. Haider-Markel. (2018) *The Remarkable Rise of Transgender Rights*. Ann Arbor: University of Michigan Press.

Telegraph View. (2019) 'The High Court is right to rule against motherless birth certificates.' *The Daily Telegraph*. (26 September)

TENI. (2020) 'Gender Recognition.' Available at https://www.teni.ie/gender-recognition/

Thomas, Diana. (2020) 'Trust me, JK Rowling is spouting dangerous nonsense about trans people.' *The Daily Telegraph*. (11 June)

Thomas, Diana. (2020a) 'My transgender diary: "Women have a huge privilege compared to transwomen".' *The Daily Telegraph*. (25 June)

Thomas, Diana. (2020b) 'My transgender diary: "There's still one part of my anatomy that's very male. I dislike it more every day".' *The Daily Telegraph*. (9 July)

Thomson, Alice. (2016) 'Let's halt the tyranny of the gender brigade.' *The Times*. (22 June)

Timothy, Nick. (2020) 'Our fearful leaders are failing to stand up to the radical woke minority.' *The Daily Telegraph*. (12 July)

Tinker, Melvin. (2018) *That Hideous Strength: How the West was Lost*. Welwyn Garden City: EP Books.

Tollefsen, Christopher O. (2015a) 'Sex Identity.' *Public Discourse*. (13 July) [Part 1 of 2]

Tollefsen, Christopher O. (2015b) 'Gender Identity.' *Public Discourse*. (14 July) [Part 2 of 2]

Tominey, Camilla. (2019) 'Two thirds of British public think it is cheating for women born male to compete in women's sport, says poll.' *The Daily Telegraph*. (10 March)

Tominey, Camilla. (2020) '"Niche" transgender ideology "corrosive" to society, says report.' *The Daily Telegraph*. (1 July)

Toogood, Laura. (2020) 'Girls as young as 6 have been sexting in lockdown - where are we going wrong?' *The Daily Telegraph*. (26 June)

Transgender Trend. (no date) Site with multiple contributions available at https://www.transgendertrend.com/

Trinko, Katrian. (2019) '"I Perfectly Understand Why This Kills People": Former Transgender Jamie Shupe Details How Process Affected Him.' *The Daily Signal*. (15 March)

Trueman, Carl R. (2018) 'The New Gulags.' *First Things*. (27 September)

Turner, Camilla. (2017) 'School told to give transgender pupils a cake to celebrate their transition.' *The Daily Telegraph*. (13 April)

Turner, Camilla. (2017a) 'Primary schools should use books that feature transgender parents, Government-backed guidance says.' *The Daily Telegraph*. (13 December)

Turner, Camilla. (2018) 'Teacher accused of "misgendering" child was told by police that she committed a hate crime.' *The Daily Telegraph*. (23 February)

Turner, Camilla. (2019) 'Revealed: The academics who need panic alarms or face death threats for their "radical" views.' *The Daily Telegraph*. (8 October)

Turner, Camilla. (2020) 'Oxford College Investigates after Female Lecturer is "No Platformed" at Feminist Summit.' *The Daily Telegraph*. (3 March)

## References

Turner, Camilla. (2020b) 'Cambridge defends academic who said "white lives don't matter".' *The Daily Telegraph*. (25 June)

Turner, Janice. (2016) 'The trans lobby peddles a pink and blue world.' *The Times*. (14 May)

Turner, Janice. (2019) 'Jo Swinson chose wokeness over women's rights.' *The Times*. (7 December)

Tuvel, Rebecca. (2017) 'In Defense of transracialism.' *Hypatia*, vol. 32, no. 2, 263-78.

U.S. Congress. (2019) *Equality Act*. Available at https://www.congress.gov/bill/116th-congress/house-bill/5/text/eh

U.S. Court of Appeal. (2020) *Adams v. School Board of St. Johns County, Florida*. Available at http://media.ca11.uscourts.gov/opinions/pub/files/201813592.pdf

U.S . Departments of Justice and Education (2016) 'Letter.' Available at https://www2.ed.gov/about/offices/list/ocr/letters/colleague-201605-title-ix-transgender.pdf

U.S. Senate. (2019) *Equality Act*. Available at https://www.congress.gov/116/bills/hr5/BILLS-116hr5rfs.pdf

U.S. Supreme Court. (2020) *Bostock v. Clayton County*. 590 U.S. ___ (2020). Available at https://supreme.justia.com/cases/federal/us/590/17-1618/

Uglow, Tea. (2018) 'We understand the solar system, so why do people still struggle with gender?' *The Guardian*. (8 March)

UK Court of Appeal. (2020) R(*McConnell and YY*) vs *The Registrar General for England and Wales et al*. [2020] EWCA Civ 559. Available at https://www.judiciary.uk/wp-content/uploads/2020/04/McConnell-and-YY-judgment-Final.pdf

UK Government. (2018) 'Reform of the Gender Recognition Act.' Available at https://www.gov.uk/government/consultations/reform-of-the-gender-recognition-act-2004

UK Government. (2019) *Relationships Education, Relationship and Sex Education (RSE) and Health Education*. Available at https://assets.publishing.service.gov.uk/government/uploads/system/uploads/attachment_data/file/805781/Relationships_Education__Relationships_and_Sex_Education__RSE__and_Health_Education.pdf

UK High Court. (2019) *R(TT) v The Registrar General for England and Wales et al*. [2019] EWHC 2384 (Fam) Available at https://www.judiciary.uk/wp-content/uploads/2019/09/TT-and-YY-APPROVED-Substantive-Judgment-McF-25.9.19.pdf

UK Parliament. (2004) *Gender Recognition Act*. Available at https://www.

legislation.gov.uk/ukpga/2004/7/contents

UK Parliament. (2010) *Equality Act*. Available at http://www.legislation.gov.uk/ukpga/2010/15/contents

Unger, Peter. (2006) *All the Power in the World*. Oxford: Oxford University Press.

Unwin, Joseph Daniel. (1934) *Sex and Culture*. Oxford: Oxford University Press.

Urquhart, Evan. (2018) 'How Republicans Laid the Groundwork for Trump's Assault on Transgender Existence.' *Slate*. (21 October)

Van Maren, Jonathon. (2019) 'This Transgender Mass Delusion Will End When Enough People Simply Refuse to Play Along.' *Life Site*. (12 February)

Van Maren, Jonathon. (2019a) 'Prominent gay atheist: Transgenderism is a "lie". Agreeing to it demoralizes you.' *LifeSiteNews*. (30 May 2019)

Van Mol, Andre. (2018) 'Transgenderism: A State-Sponsored Religion?' *Public Discourse*. (24 January)

Various. (2017) 'Theresa May vows to "streamline" process for changing gender as she says "being trans is not an illness".' *The Daily Telegraph*. (19 October)

Various. (2020) 'Transgender Women could be allowed to enter Female-only Competitions as Sporting Bodies Draw up New Guidelines.' *The Daily Telegraph*. (8 March)

Various. (2020a) 'Workers can't be fired for being gay or transgender, Supreme Court says in landmark ruling.' *The Daily Telegraph*. (15 June)

Vigo, Julian. (2018) 'Capitulating to Bullies: Brown University and the Transgender Lobby vs. Science.' *Public Discourse*. (7 October)

Vigo, Julian. (2018a) 'The Degenderettes: The Transgender Hate Group Taking Aim at Women.' *Public Discourse*. (3 June)

Vincent, John. (1996/1995) *An Intelligent Person's Guide to History*. London: Duckworth.

Voegelin, Eric. (1967) 'On Debate and Existence.' *Intercollegiate Review III*, 143-152.

Wade, Nicholas. (2014) *A Troublesome Inheritance: Genes, Race and Human History*. New York: The Penguin Press.

Walden, Celia. (2020) 'For all those thinking they are doing the right thing today, the next generation will find it wrong.' *The Daily Telegraph*. (15 June)

Walden, Celia. (2020a) 'The "woke" have won—it's too late for our unis if academics need to hide their views.' *The Daily Telegraph*. (2 August)

Walker, Andrew T. (2017) 'What's in a Name? Why Christians Should Be Wary of the Word "Transgender".' *Public Discourse*. (30 May)

## References

Walsh, Joani. (2019) 'Meet the "detransitioners": the women who became men —and now want to go back.' *The Daily Telegraph*. (16 November)

Ward, Keith. (2010) *More than Matter: What Humans Really Are*. Oxford: Lion.

Ward, Victoria. (2019) 'Police response to "transphobic" stickers branded "extraordinary".' *The Daily Telegraph*. (14 October)

Ward, Victoria. (2020) 'Action Aid is embroiled in trans row after declaring there is "no such thing" as biological sex.' *The Daily Telegraph*. (17 July)

Washington Post. (2020) *Police Shootings Database*. Available at https://www.youtube.com/watch?v=jIJxVEOdcn0

Waterson, Jim. (2020) 'Authors quit JK Rowling agency over transgender rights.' *The Guardian*. (22 June)

Weinberg, Justin. (2017) 'Philosopher's Article On Transracialism Sparks Controversy.' *Daily Nous*. (1 May)

West, Patrick. (2017) 'Genderfluidity is the Latest Fashion Craze.' *Spiked*. (26 October)

White, Jim. (2020) 'Women are taking men on at their own game ... and beating them: Increase in awareness and funding has allowed female athletes to close the gap in sports like snooker, horseracing and darts.' *The Daily Telegraph*. (25 May)

Whitehouse, Helen. (2019) 'Transgender man gives birth to non-binary partner's baby with female sperm donor.' *The Mirror*. (28 December)

Williams, Joanna. (2019) 'The High Court's transgender ruling spells a rare victory for sanity.' *The Daily Telegraph*. (25 September).

Williams, Joanna. (2020) *The Corrosive Impact of Transgender Ideology*. London: Civitas. Available at http://www.civitas.org.uk/content/files/2454-A-The-Corrosive-Impact-of-TI-ppi-110-WEB.pdf

Williams, Nicola. (2019a) 'Women's rights hanging by a thread with changes to transgender law.' *Sky News*. (10 April)

Williams, Zoe. (2020) 'Feminist Solidarity Empowers Everyone. The Movement must be Trans-inclusive.' *The Guardian*. (10 March)

Willis, Raquel. (2017) 'A Trans woman's Response to Chimamanda Ngozi Adichie.' *Channel 4 News*. (11 March)

Wittgenstein, Ludwig. (1969) *On Certainty*. (Über Gewissheit; trans. Denis Paul & G. E. M. Anscombe; ed. G. E. M. Anscombe and G. H von Wright. Oxford: Blackwell.

Wood, Peter. (2003) *Diversity: The Invention of a Concept*. San Francisco: Encounter Books.

Woods, Judith. (2020) 'Selina Todd, the Academic the Trans Lobby is

Desperate to Silence.' *The Daily Telegraph*. (6 March)

Wright, Colin. (2019a) 'Evolution denialism is back. This time it's coming from the left.' *Genetic Literacy Project*. (24 January)

Wright, Mike. (2019b) 'Whites can be black if they wish, says lecturers' union.' *The Daily Telegraph*. (18 November)

Wright, N. T. (2017) 'Letter.' *The Times*. (3 August)

Yan, Sophie and Yiyin Zhong. (2020) 'Chinese court rules in favour of transgender woman over wrongful termination in landmark decision.' *The Daily Telegraph*. (11 July)

Yenor, Scott. (2017) 'The Rolling Revolution in Sex and Gender: A History.' *Public Discourse*. (31 July)

Yorke, et al. (2017) 'Women-only Cambridge college to allow students who simply "identify as female" for first time.' *The Daily Telegraph*. (3 October)

Yorke, Harry. (2017) 'BBC issues Dame Jenni Murray with warning over her transgender comments.' *The Daily Telegraph*. (6 March)

Young, Katherine K. and Paul Nathanson. (2010) *Sanctifying Misandry: Goddess Ideology and the Fall of Man*. Montreal: McGill-Queen's University Press.

YouTube. (1959) *I'm All Right Jack*: 'Fred Kite and the Works Committee'. Available at https://www.youtube.com/watch?v=3a9OAvqyjn0

YouTube. (1967) *At Last the 1948 Show*: 'The Four Yorkshiremen Sketch.' Available at https://www.youtube.com/watch?v=VKHFZBUTA4k

YouTube. (1975) *Monty Python and the Holy Grail*: 'The Black Knight – 'Tis But a Scratch.' Available at https://www.youtube.com/watch?v=ZmInkxb-vlCs

YouTube. (1979/2007) *Monty Python's Life of Brian*: 'PFJ Union Meeting.' Available at https://www.youtube.com/watch?v=hUBAx8jbYNs

YouTube. (2015) 'Germaine Greer: Transgender women are "not women".' Available at https://www.youtube.com/watch?v=7B8Q6D4a6TM

YouTube. (2018) 'Transformation Street | ITV.' Available at https://www.youtube.com/watch?v=cTvQW9jNI18

YouTube. (2019) 'Castro Calls for "Reproductive Justice" in Abortion Debate.' Available at https://www.youtube.com/watch?v=EIoLBlJF_Pw

YouTube. (2019a) 'Seahorse: "If all men got pregnant, it'd be taken more seriously".' Available at https://www. youtube.com/watch?v=bu6fQIZN3c0

YouTube. (2020) 'Thomas Sowell/Black Wisdom Matters – Good Intentions of the Welfare State.' Available at https://www.youtube.com/watch?v=-1s2Ishme9P0